TELEVISION TIMELINE

A Chronological Narrative

PETER FOX

Blue Ocean Publishing

Television Timeline

Published by Blue Ocean Publishing
St John's Innovation Centre
Cowley Road
Cambridge CB4 0WS
United Kingdom

www.blueoceanpublishing.biz

Text design and layout by Spitfire Design, Upminster.

A catalogue record for this book is available from the British Library.

ISBN 978-1-907527-15-9

First published in the United Kingdom in 2013 by Blue Ocean Publishing.

Cover image shows children watching Andy Pandy (1952).

Peter Fox spent 30 years in local government, retiring at Chief Officer level in 1995. He led on a number of projects in social housing, including the development of the early CCTV systems. Upon early retirement, he became a housing consultant and led on a number of local government computer projects before working as a housing consultant for Sky Television over seven years. Since then, he has focused his energies as a self-employed general housing consultant for a number of clients and as an author and a photographer.

To John

best wishes

Peter

12/4/13

Television Timeline

"If you let a television set through your front door, life can never be the same again" (Daily Mirror, 1950)

What is television?

Television (TV) is a telecommunication medium for transmitting and receiving moving images that can be monochrome (black-and-white) or colour, with or without accompanying sound. The term has a mixed Latin and Greek origin, meaning 'far sight': Greek tele (τῆλε), far, and Latin visio, sight (from video, vis- to see, or to view).

Television has inarguably become the most powerful home medium in history (along with the internet in the 20th century), bringing the outside world into our private space. With the BBC at its core, the UK has produced some of the world's best television and has exported programmes and films worldwide. Television has been available from the late 1920s, but at that time to only a limited few who had receivers. Nowadays the television set is a common communications receiver in homes, businesses and institutions. It is seen as a source of entertainment and news. Some see it as an intrusion to social life and having an adverse effect on the institution of the family.

World Growth

For most of its life television was broadcast via the radio wave spectrum (VHF – very high frequency, followed by UHF – ultra high frequency) on designated channels in the 54-890 megahertz frequency band. Until 2010 such broadcasting was generally recorded and transmitted as an analogue radio signal. As time went by the public and commercial broadcasters have been progressively introducing improved methods of delivering television – digital streaming from land transmitters to wide band UHF TV home aerials, microwave signals from satellites in space to home dishes (instead of aerials), signals delivered along telephone wires connected to receiver boxes with television sets, and digital signals over the air through 3G (3rd generation) / 4G (4th generation) wi-fi (wireless fidelity) broadband networks to mobile 'phones and tablets. Underground cable routes have also been developed – analogue cable at first and later (digital) fibre optical cable to quicken speeds for digital cable telephony, internet connectivity and digital intelligent television.

This book takes the reader through the long journey of the creation of television as we know it today and explains the complexities in a simple and straightforward way. The book is written as a chronological narrative as opposed to just many chapters of script. It is also highly illustrated to present the information graphically.

So why is television so interesting?

Television today has become the acceptable 'window on the world'. So much of it is now taken for granted. For many of us the 'box in the corner' has always been there – to entertain and to inform.

It will be seen that the creation of television was fraught with difficulties and seemingly had impossible barriers to overcome. The book tries to overlay the political perspective of how the Liberal, Labour and Conservative UK governments have influenced the direction and the development of television, for example, introducing legislation, regulation, policy and licensing.

This political perspective even covers how monarchical change affected the will to invent – such as the opinions of monarchs with their respective Prime Ministers. It will be seen that Governments took charge of the development of broadcasting. They wanted control over social cohesion, political debate and the preservation of culture and the economy. Politicians in the 40s and 50s became suspicious of the potential power of television and they feared that their political influence might weaken. Governments world over became very nationalistic and territorial about radio and television not wishing influence from abroad. Hence, for example, the hatred of pirate radio stations in the 1960s – Radio Luxembourg, Radio Caroline etc., by the then UK Government.

Other key events in history are included to give a real time perspective to the television timeline. It will also be seen from this book that the future of television is both exciting and innovative with the convergence of the internet, television itself and the personal computer. The digital revolution is now upon us all.

So who invented television?

This is always the first question. Television is not one invention. It comprises numerous components. It is very difficult to name one person as the inventor of television because different pioneering scientists and  inventors, at different times, all over the world have invented or discovered different components that together made television work. The evolution of television can be traced back through the following crucial milestones:

- Work of Faraday in the field of induction electricity up to and beyond 1833.

- Discovery of the photoconductivity properties of 'selenium' by Smith in 1873.

- Invention of sound recording technology by Edison in 1877.

- Discovery of the image scanning disc by Nipkow in 1884.

- Development of the cathode ray tube (CRT) by Braun in 1897 and by A A Campbell-Swinton and Boris Rosing in 1907.

- Demonstration by Baird of a mechanical televised moving image in 1926.

- The BBC's decision to select the Marconi electronic television system for regular broadcasting in the 1930s over its existing wireless network.

First to demonstrate television?

The first person to demonstrate a system of television in the laboratory was Francis Jenkins the USA inventor on 13 June 1925. Jenkins never achieved broadcast of content. American Philo Farnsworth also invented an early television system, which he conceived of while plowing his father's Idaho (USA) potato field at the age of 14. He filed for a patent which he called the Image Dissector. On 7 September, 1925 he managed to transmit the first American image on television in San Francisco, but this was not broadcast to an audience.

The most accurate date which can be attributed to the invention of television, is put by this author as 30 October 1925 when John Logie Baird demonstrated a working version of his mechanical television system. He had previously demonstrated a crude device in the laboratory earlier in 1924, and he transmitted within the laboratory an image of 'Stookey Bill' in 1925 on his Televisor. By 1929, Baird had achieved broadcast of television over the BBC radio network from the Crystal Palace transmitter, in London.

Baird's Progress

When Baird started his work many of the components had already been invented. His genius was to put the parts together to achieve a crude live picture transmitted across the laboratory. Here is a summary of Baird's progress:

- **1888** John Logie Baird born. He was a Scottish engineer (from Helensburgh, Dunbartonshire). When he was twelve he built his own home telephone system. Baird was forced to resign from his position as an electrical engineer through persistent ill health.

- **1922** In retirement, he moved to Hastings, West Sussex. Under these circumstances, he used his time to research ways of transmitting pictures.

- **1923** This year, he started his work on building his 'televisor' system in Hastings.

- **1924** In February this year, John Logie Baird had entered the shop of Hasting radio dealer Victor Mill and asked for assistance, saying "I've fitted up a set of apparatus for transmitting pictures and I can't get it to go." Mills accompanied Baird back to his laboratory/apartment and waved his hand in front of the neon when Baird shouted "It's here, it's here."

- **1925** On 25 March, Baird gave the first public demonstration of televised silhouette images in motion, at Selfridge's Department Store in London. Also, this year saw Baird improving his mechanical system to transmit his image of the dilapidated ventriloquist's dummy 'Stookey Bill' with real detail. Baird achieved this on 30 October 1925 at 22 Frith Street, Soho, London W1. This is the date that most historians record as the date television was invented (but not broadcast).

- **1926** Thirty Members of the Royal Institution and other visitors went to the laboratory in an upper room at 22 Frith Street, Soho, London W1 on 26 January. They saw a demonstration of apparatus invented by Baird. They were shown a transmitting machine, consisting of a large wooden revolving disc containing lenses, behind which was a revolving shutter and a light sensitive cell.

- **1929** The BBC became involved in television development from this year. The first experimental British television broadcast (September) was made by Baird Television's electromechanical system over the BBC radio transmitter – just 30 lines of resolution. Baird named his world's first television 'station' 2TV, but this brand name was not recognized or used by the BBC.

- **1930** Baird provided a limited amount of programming five days a week broadcast, after the BBC radio broadcasts closed each night. It was 14 March when the experimental sound and vision transmissions of Baird's 30-line television system began from the Brookmans Park transmitter on radio frequency 261.3m to 356.3m.

- **1931** Baird this year transmitted, for the BBC, live coverage of the Derby from Epsom. However, the picture was so poor that the viewer could not discern one horse or jockey from another.

- **1936** The Postmaster General, now controlling the broadcast of television in the UK through legislation, decided with the BBC that the EMI electronic and the Baird electro-mechanic television systems would be compared in over-air tests. The crude Baird mechanical system was used one week and the basic EMI-Marconi electrical system the next.

- **1937** The British government, on advice from a special advisory committee, decided that Marconi-EMI's 405-line electronic system gave the superior picture, and the Baird 240-line system was dropped.

- **1940** Baird now adopted the electronic version of television. The World's First Baird so-called 'High Definition' colour television system was demonstrated. It was never broadcast and remained experimental.

- 1944 Baird gave the world's first demonstration of a fully electronic colour television display with his improved 600-line colour system using triple interlacing, using six scans to build each picture. This was not adopted by any broadcaster.

- **1946** This year saw the death of Baird on 14 June in Bexhill-on-Sea, Sussex, England. He wasaged 57.

This author takes the view that the first person to achieve demonstration and then to broadcast television content is the inventor of television. Second place goes to Karl Braun (1897) and Vladimir Zworykin (1921) for the invention of the cathode ray tube (CRT) which became the television screen for many years until the emergence of plasma, LCD and LED screens in the 20th century.

The work of Baird is reproduced again in this book in much greater detail, under each chronological date – along with the concurrent work of others. In this way, you will see who did what and when.

What came before television?

It is impossible to talk about television without mentioning what came before – electricity, telegraphy, telephony and radio – so this is covered in the book before the focus turns to the early experiments of sending pictures over the air.

Legislative framework

Over the last 100 years or so, many pieces of legislation have regulated, controlled and governed the development of radio and television in the United Kingdom:

1　The Telegraphy Act 1869

2　Wireless Telegraphy Act 1904

3　Wireless Telegraphy Act 1906

4　Wireless Telegraphy Act 1949

5　The Television Act 1954

6 The Television Act 1958

7 The Television Act 1963

8 The Television Act 1964

9 Wireless Telegraphy Act 1967

10 The Marine, etc., Broadcasting (Offences) Act 1967

11 Sound Broadcasting Act 1972

12 The Independent Broadcasting Authority Act 1973

13 Independent Broadcasting Authority Act 1974

14 Independent Broadcasting Act 1978

15 Independent Broadcasting Act 1979

16 Broadcasting Act 1981

17 Cable and Broadcasting Act 1984

18 Telecommunications Act 1984

19 Broadcasting Act 1990

20 Broadcasting Act 1996

21 Wireless Telegraphy Act 1998

22 Communications Act 2003

23 Wireless Telegraphy Act 2006

The significance of each statute (and the associated politics) is touched upon as this chronology unfolds through the decades.

The timeline

The chronology is the main section of this book and by its nature is very long indeed. Some of the key dates for radio and television firsts are set out below as an executive summary of the television timeline:

- **1475** First automated mass media – in the form of print being introduced to the UK.

- **1600** The first discovery of electricity.

- **1752** First research into the practical use of electricity by Benjamin Franklin.

- **1831** The first truly democratic government in the United Kingdom.

- **1839** Print technology first supplemented with photography.

- **1844** Morse transmits the first intelligible message in Morse code.

- **1862** First still image transmitted by Casselli.

- **1864** Englishman James Maxwell first talks about his theory of electro-magnetic waves.

- **1879** Thomas Edison invents the first commercially practical incandescent electric lamp.

- **1881** The first electrical power transformer developed by Lucien Gaulard demonstrated.

- **1890** First use of the word 'television' at the World Fair, Paris.

- **1895** Birth of first cinematography equipment.

- **1891** Edison invented and patented the first motion picture camera.

- **1899** The Edison phonograph was the first device to record sound – voice and music.

- **1904** The first British law to regulate wireless telecommunications – giving The Post Office control of radio telegraphy.

- **1906** First radio broadcast ever achieved in the USA.

- **1907** The first electronic component – Lee De Forest made the diode into an amplifier by adding a third electrode, and electronics had begun.

- **1922** First General Manager appointed by the BBC – John Reith. First live radio broadcast.

- **1923** Baird achieves first laboratory transmission of a moving picture. First BBC radio broadcast of the weather forecast. Radio Times first published on 28 September – carrying only details of BBC radio programmes and costing 2d.

- **1925** Francis Jenkins in America was able to demonstrate, on 13 June, the transmission of the silhouette image of a toy windmill in motion from a naval radio station to his laboratory in Washington. John Logie Baird's first demonstration of a working version of his television system (the 'televisor') – transmitting an image of 'Stookey Bill' on 30 October.

- **1926** John Logie Baird gives the first public (20 people from the Royal Society) demonstration of his mechanical television system.

- **1927** First USA television image transmitted by wire by Farnsworth to one source. First USA politician to appear on a Closed Circuit Television transmission – Herbert Hoover. This year John Logie Baird invented the world's first video recording system, 'Phonovision' – by modulating the output signal of his TV camera down to the audio range.

- **1928** Kurt Stille formed the Echophone Company in Germany with Karl Bauer and contracted with Ferdinand Schuchard to invent magnetic recording tape.

- **1929** First BBC/Baird television wireless broadcast of a single programme to the London audience.

- **1931** First live outside broadcast by BBC/Baird from Epsom horse racing course.

- **1934** German, Joseph Begun built the world's first sound tape recorder used for broadcasting. For the first time television listings appears in the Radio Times on 5 January.

- **1936** Baird and EMI-Marconi agree with the BBC to form the first television station anywhere in the world to broadcast daily and varied content to a 15,000 London television audience. The Baird mechanical system was used one week and the EMI-Marconi electrical system the next. The service went on the air at 3.00pm on Monday 2 November.

- **1937** The BBC makes its first choice of the television system to be used into the future. The BBC chose the EMI-Marconi electronic system of 405 lines transmission over Baird's 240-line electro-mechanical system.

- **1938** The first cable television introduced to the United Kingdom when towns such as Bristol used wires to carry television signals to homes that couldn't receive transmissions off air.

- **1939** In the USA, Roosevelt became the first President to appear on television at the New York's World Fair – 100 New York homes form the audience.

- **1940** Baird demonstrated first colour television picture in laboratory conditions.

- **1947** First Party Political broadcasts in the UK.

- **1950** Margaret Thatcher fights (and loses) her first general election in Dartford, Kent as the youngest UK candidate. The first television remote control introduced this year – the 'Lazy Bones' – connected by a long wire cable.

- **1951** This year, American Charles Ginsburg led the research team at the Ampex Corporation in developing the first practical videotape recorder (VTR). This year saw the first VTR capturing live images from television cameras by converting the information into electrical impulses and saving the information onto magnetic tape.

- **1952** The official launch of BBC television in Scotland on 14 March.

- **1953** First TV audience of 27m for a BBC outside broadcast – the Coronation of Queen Elizabeth II. The television listings in the BBC Radio Times were moved, for the first time, from the back of the magazine and integrated day-by-day with radio.

- **1954** First colour television broadcasts in the USA. First Act of Parliament in the UK for the development of commercial television (and the creation of the ITA).

- **1955** Launch of the first commercial television channels in the UK. ITN News formed to become the first independent news service supplying the new regional ITV broadcasters with news content. First colour television broadcast in USA. First British daily BBC news TV programme with the reader on screen. "Here is an illustrated summary of the news," announced Richard Baker on the first night of the BBC television news.

- **1956** Robert Adler invents the first practical TV infra-red remote control. Ampex introduces the first practical videotape system of broadcast quality. World's first broadcast via videotape – American network CBS airing of the Douglas Edward and the News programme on 30 November from New York. CBS Television City was received on the West Coast. Hollywood replayed the broadcast three hours later.

- **1958** The integrated circuit can be credited as being invented by both Jack Kilby of Texas Instruments and Robert Noyce of Fairchild Semiconductor working independently of each other. Kilby recorded his initial ideas concerning the integrated circuit in July and successfully demonstrated the first working integrated circuit in September. First stereo records appears.

- **1959** First transatlantic television broadcast through telephone wires to bring home pictures of Queen Elizabeth and President Eisenhower opening the St Lawrence Seaway.

- **1960** First episode of Coronation Street aired on 9 December.

- **1962** First transatlantic television transmission by Telstar orbital satellite.

- **1964** First audience of 73m in the USA with the Beatles on the CBS Ed Sullivan Show, broadcast in monochrome (but filmed in colour).

- **1965** Launch of Intelsat I Early Bird, the first commercial geostationary communication satellite marking the true beginning of satellite television.

- **1967** First regular colour transmission on BBC2. First 400m live global television satellite link to 26 countries for the Beatles Our World concert.

- **1969** First live television pictures broadcast from the moon. First live colour transmissions in the UK. Next stage was in the development of the first inexpensive VCR system this year by Sony.

- **1974** BBC ceefax and ITV oracle teletext launched this year.

- **1975** Betamax VCR (video cassette recording) machine format introduced

- **1976** VHS VCRs go on sale for the first time. First PC invented by Apple.

- **1977** First PC goes on sale – made by Radio Shack/Commodore.

- **1978** The London Borough of Hammersmith & Fulham instals the first UK CCTV entryphone system to a social housing block of flats on the Charecroft Estate, in Shepherds Bush, West London.

- **1982** First 4th channel in UK – launch of Channel 4.

- **1983** First time on British television for breakfast television – launch of BBC Breakfast Time and on ITV with TV-AM. The Eutelsat satellite service started its first operations this year with the launch of its first satellite

- **1984** First TV cable company to be licensed by the new cable broadcast Act – Swindon Cable. First 2 inch handheld monochrome television set on the UK market – Sony Watchman.

- **1985** Europe's first private satellite operator Société Européenne des Satellites (SES ASTRA) is formed with the Luxembourg State becoming a major shareholder.

- **1988** On 11 December, the Société Européenne des Satellites (SES ASTRA) successfully launches and positions its first satellite for analogue and digital television services.

- **1989** First analogue television pay-tv satellite service in the UK – launch of Sky TV – referred to as multi-channel television. Parliament broadcast by terrestrial broadcasters for the first time.

- **1990** First launch of a second television satellite service in the UK – British Satellite Broadcasting (BSB) which broadcast in digital rather than analogue. First merger of UK satellite providers with Sky and BSB becoming BSkyB.

- **1991** The cable television companies were first granted the right by government to offer telephony alongside their television services.

- **1994** The first of many mergers in ITV took place with Granada buying LWT.

- **1995** The first plasma television screen on the UK market.

- **1996** The WBA Bruno vs Tyson world heavyweight title fight was the first nationwide domestic pay-per-view event in the UK.

- **1997** Sky Box Office launched first pay-per-view television movies. First DVD player on the UK market.

- **1998** The British ONdigital television service became the first terrestrial digital pay-tv service in the world. First Sky digital satellite television service launched in the UK.

- **2001** The Tivo DVR first on the UK market.

- **2004** Sky+ becomes the first DVR/satellite tuner combined – which allows viewers to record digital channels at the touch of a button.

- **2005** First Sky+HD box on the UK market – allowing 720p and 1080i lines on HD-ready television screens. First announcement by the UK government to switch-off all analogue television broadcast. Tessa Jowell, the then Secretary of State for Culture, Media and Sport in her keynote address to the Royal Television Society set out the Governments intention to switch off analogue transmission over a period leading to 2012.

- **2006** Sky launches the UK's first nationwide HD TV service. DVR first appears in the market.

- **2008** The first launch of the BBC/ITV consortium into its own satellite television service with Freesat on 6 May.

- **2009** First integrated internet television joining the home wireless network along with PCs and Laptop.

- **2010** Television first equipped with internet broadband connectivity and telephone software – allowing free calls from the television set to other similar users – and those on videophone or PC with similar software. 3D television first demonstrated at CES (consumer electronics show), in Las Vegas, USA. Sky becomes the first broadcaster in the world to air a 3D television programme – football on 31 January.

Format wars

Over the years of sound and television development there have been a number of format wars. A format war describes competition between mutually incompatible proprietary formats, typically for television broadcast, data storage devices and recording formats for electronic media. It is often characterized by political and financial influence on content publishers by the developers of the technologies. Developing companies may be characterized as engaging in a format war if they actively oppose or avoid interoperable open industry technical standards in favor of their own. The format wars:

1877   Sound recording media: cylinder records vs disk records.

1881   Electricity: AC vs DC for general use.

1920   78 rpm gramophone records: lateral vs vertical 'hill-and-dale' / groove cutting.

1936   TV broadcast: Baird's mechanical TV system vs EMI-Marconi electrical system.

1948   Vinyl records: Columbia Records' 12-inch (30 cm) Long Play (LP) 33☐ rpm microgroove record vs RCA Victor's 7-inch (17.5 cm) 45 rpm Extended Play (EP).

1970   Quadraphonic sound encoding methods: CD-4 vs SQ vs QS-Matrix vs 8-track

1976   Videotape machines: JVC VHS vs Sony Betamax vs Philips Video 2000.

1977   Personal computers: Apple Mac vs IBM.

1982   Portable music: Vinyl record vs Compact Cassette.

1984   Radio broadcast: AM stereo vs FM.

1985   Camcorder analogue videotape tape: Hi8 vs S-VHS-C.

1987   Digital videotape: Sony's Digital Audio Tape (DAT) vs
Philips' Digital Tape (DT) vs Digital Audio Cassette (DAC)
vs Sony's MiniDisc.

2000   Wireless data transfer: Bluetooth vs WiFi.

2001   Recordable DVD formats: DVD+R vs DVD-R vs DVD-
RAM.

2002   Non-recordable video disc formats: Capacitance
Electronic Disc (CED) vs LaserDisc (LD) vs VHD (Video
High-Density).

2003   Digital television delivery platforms: satellite vs terrestrial
vs cable vs internet vs telephone.

2006   High-definition optical disc format war: Blu-ray Disc vs
HD DVD.

2008   Television screens: Plasma vs LCD vs LED (all replacing
CRTs).

The monarchy and its influence in invention

In the United Kingdom, the role of the Monarch changed over
the years affecting the control and influence of government
legislation in radio and television development. The changing role
has significance to the timeline of the invention of television. As
time changed different 'Houses' of the Monarchs and a period as
a republic ruled the United Kingdom:

The Stuarts 1603–1649

The Republic of England 1649–1660

The Stuarts 1660–1714

The Hanoverians 1714–1901

The Sax-Coburg-Gothas 1901–1910

The House of Windsor 1910 to date

The chronology of the history of television

First awareness of electricity

1250 BC Long before any knowledge of electricity existed, people were aware of shocks from electric fish. Ancient Egyptian texts referred to these fish as the 'Thunderer of the Nile', and described them as the 'protectors' of all other fish. The future technology of television would be based on electrical variable resistance, photosensitivity to electrical impulse and fluorescence – so the discovery of electricity was fundamental in the later development of television.

600 BC Thales of Miletus (Θαλῆς ὁ Μιλήσιος) was a Greek philosopher from Asia Minor.

He made a series of observations on static electricity from which he believed that friction rendered amber magnetic, in contrast to minerals such as magnetite, which needed no rubbing. Thales was incorrect in believing the attraction was due to a magnetic effect, but later science would prove a link between magnetism and electricity due to a magnetic effect.

Depth perception

280 AD The Greek mathematician Euclid of Alexandria was the first to recognize that depth perception is obtained when each eye simultaneously receives one of two dissimilar images of the same object. This was the start of thinking in 3D imagery to mimic human eyesight – which eventually led to 3D television screens in the 21st century.

15th Century

1475 First mass media introduced to the UK – printing on paper for the distribution of news. The cultural impact of the printed word was immense.

16th Century

1584 Leonardo da Vinci studied the perception of depth and, unlike most of his contemporaries, produced paintings and sketches that showed a clear understanding of shading, texture and viewpoint projection.

17th Century

1600 Giovanni Battista della Porta produced the first artificial 3-D drawing based on Euclid's notions on how 3D perception by humans works. Electricity remained little more than an intellectual curiosity for millennia until this year when the English physician William Gilbert made a careful study of electricity and magnetism, distinguishing the lodestone effect from static electricity produced by rubbing amber. He coined the new Latin word electricus ('of amber' or 'like amber', from ήλεκτρον *elektron*, the Greek word for 'amber') to refer to the property of attracting small objects after being rubbed. As a result, Gilbert is called the father of modern electricity. This year, Otto von Guericke invented a crude machine for producing static electricity. It was a ball of sulfur, rotated by a crank with one hand and rubbed with the other. Successors, such as Francis Hauksbee, made improvements that provided experimenters with a ready source of static electricity.

1603 James I (who reigned 1603–1625) became the English monarch. He is Queen Elizabeth II's 9th Great Grandfather.

1611 Kepler's Dioptrice – The general principles of stereoscopy, that is showing 3 dimensions on a 2-dimensional surface was first published which included a detailed description of the projection theory of human stereo vision.

1625 Charles I (who reigned 1625–1649) became the English monarch.

1646 The first use of the words 'electric' and 'electricity' in print this year.

1649 The 'Interregnum' with Oliver Cromwell as head of the Republic of England (1649–1660). Cromwell's convincing military successes at Drogheda in Ireland (1649), Dunbar in Scotland (1650) and Worcester in England (1651) forced Charles I's son, Charles, into foreign exile despite being accepted as  king in Scotland. From 1649 to 1660, England was therefore a republic during a period known as the Interregnum (between reigns). A series of political experiments followed; the country's rulers tried to redefine and establish a workable constitution without a monarchy. Throughout the Interregnum, Cromwell's relationship with Parliament was a troubled one, with tensions over the nature of the constitution and the issue of supremacy, control of the armed forces and debate over religious toleration. There was little interest in invention.

1660 Charles II (who reigned 1660–1685) became the English monarch.

1685 James II (who reigned 1685–1688) became the English monarch.

1689 William III was now the English monarch (reigning until 1702).

18th Century

1702 Queen Anne (who reigned 1702–1714) became the English monarch.

1707 The Union of the Crowns. After the Act of Union the king or queen became thereafter the monarch of Great Britain (Scotland and England).

1714 George I (who reigned until 1727) became monarch of the United Kingdom.

Work to develop electricity

1745 Progress quickened in the development of electricity after the Leyden jar was invented in this year by Pieter van Musschenbroek. The Leyden jar stored static electricity which could be discharged all at once.

1747 William Watson discharged a Leyden jar through a circuit, and comprehension of the current and circuit started a new field of experimentation. Henry Cavendish measured the conductivity of different materials (he compared the simultaneous shocks he received by discharging Leyden jars through the materials), and Charles A Coulomb expressed mathematically the attraction of electrified bodies, and this started the quantitative study of electricity.

1752 Benjamin Franklin conducted extensive research into electricity, selling his possessions to fund his work. In June, he is reputed to have attached a metal key to the bottom of a dampened kite string and flown the kite in a storm-threatened sky. A succession of sparks jumping from the key to the back of the hand showed that lightning was indeed electrical.

The start of telegraphy

1753 Charles Marshall from Scotland sent an article to 'The Scots Magazine', explaining the process of telegraphy through an electrical medium. This was the first recorded mention of the use of a telegraph-type machine. He had written a detailed account of a telegraph line which was conceived in his research. The idea was to designate a wire for each of the letters of the alphabet, which would connect two locations. At the receiving side, bits of paper were held at the wire endings. On transmitting a charge through the wire from the sending station to the receiving side, the papers were attracted to the wire ends. The letter corresponding to the wire through which the charge was transferred was located and thus, the message was decoded at the receiving end.

Different types of electricity

1791 Luigi Alvani published his discovery of bioelectricity, demonstrating that electricity was the medium by which nerve cells passed signals to the muscles. Nine years later, Alessandro Volta's battery was made from alternating layers of zinc and copper, providing scientists with a more reliable source of electrical energy than the electrostatic machines previously used. The recognition of electromagnetism, the unity of electric and magnetic phenomena, is due to Hans Christian Orsted and Andre-Marie; Michael Faraday who invented the electric motor and George Ohm who mathematically analysed the electrical circuit. These names are now enshrined in the definition of electricity:

Volt = the value of the 'voltage' across a conductor when a current of one ampere dissipates one watt of power in the conductor, for example, most electrical devices now operate with 220 or 240 volts of electricity.

Ampere = the 'ampere' is the measure of the amount of electrical charge passing a point per unit of time. Around 6.242 × 1018 electrons passing a given point each second constitutes one ampere, for example, the typical 'fuse' in today's electrical appliances is 5 or 13 amps.

Ohm = is the unit of electrical impedance (resistance).

Resistors, as found in all pre-microprocessor electrical equipment.

1760 George III (who reigned 1760 –1820) became monarch of the United Kingdom.

The last absolute Monarch

1783 King George III (the last absolute sovereign) asked William Pitt to form a government, and at the age of 24, Pitt became Prime Minister, (without an election). The opposition leader was Charles Fox. The King had gone through a period of ill-health which became known as the 'madness of King George'. This period of uncertainty heightened the debate on the conflicting roles of the Monarch and Parliament.

1785 1 January saw the first publication of The Times newspaper. The Times was a daily national newspaper published in the UK – it was first known as The Daily Universal Register and was published by John Walter. Born in London in 1739, Walter started as a coal merchant in 1755 and later joined as an underwriter at Lloyds, but in 1785 he lost a great deal of money after an increase in insurance claims as a result of a hurricane in Jamaica. Walter decided to look for a new form of business. While an underwriter he became aware of a new method of typesetting called logography. The inventor, Henry Johnson, claimed that this new method of typesetting was faster and more accurate because it allowed more than one letter to be set at a time. John Walter purchased Johnson's patent and decided to start a printing company. He came to the conclusion that he had to find a good way of publicizing his logography system. Eventually he came up with the idea of producing a daily advertising sheet. The first edition of the Daily Universal Register was published on 1 January 1785. The Daily Universal Register was in competition with eight other daily newspapers in London, and like the other newspapers, it included parliamentary reports, foreign news and advertisements. John Walter made it clear in the first edition of the Daily Universal Register that he was primarily concerned with advertising revenue: "The Register, in its politics, will be of no party. Due attention should be paid to the interests of trade, which are so greatly promoted by advertisements". After a couple of years, John Walter had discovered that logography was not going to have the impact on the printing industry that he had initially thought when he started the Daily Universal Register. However, he was now convinced he could make a profit from newspapers, especially when he was able to negotiate a secret deal where he was paid £300 a year to publish stories favourable to the government.

1786 A new interest in electrical current began with the invention of the battery. In this year, Italian physician Luigi Galvani had noticed that a discharge of static electricity made a frog's leg jerk.

Joule's law

Consequent experimentation produced what was a simple electron cell using the fluids of the leg as an electrolyte and the muscle as a circuit and indicator. Galvani thought the leg supplied electricity, but Alessandro Volta thought otherwise, and he built the voltaic pile, an early type of battery, as proof. Continuous current from batteries smoothed the way for the discovery of G S Ohm's law, relating current, voltage (electromotive force), and resistance (see above), and of J P Joule's law of electrical heating. Ohm's law and the rules discovered later by G R Kirchhoff regarding the sum of the currents and the sum of the voltages in a circuit are the basic means of making circuit calculations.

19th Century

1801 In the UK, there were 1.9m homes.

1802 Various scientists proposed that electricity and magnetism, both capable of causing attraction and repulsion of objects, were linked. This year, Gian Domenico Romagnosi suggested the relationship between electric current and magnetism, but his reports went unnoticed.

1813 The birth of the inventor of Morse code, Samuel Morse in Charlestown, Massachusetts, USA. In England, Michael Faraday became one of the most influential scientists in the field of electricity. He spent his professional career in the laboratory of the Royal Institution in London where in this year he got his start as an assistant to Sir Humphry Davy.

1819 This year, in the field of electricity, Hans Christian Ørsted discovered that a magnetic field surrounds a current-carrying wire. D F Arago invented the electromagnet, and Michael Faraday had devised a crude form of electric motor. Practical application of a motor had to wait 10 years, however, until Faraday (and earlier, independently, Joseph Henry) invented the electric generator with which to power the motor. A year after Faraday's laboratory approximation of the generator, Hippolyte Pixii constructed a hand-driven model. From then on engineers took over from the scientists, and a slow development followed with the first power stations being built some 50 years later.

Electromagnetism

1820 This year, Danish physicist and chemist, Hans Christian Ørsted demonstrated his widely known experiment on man-made electric current and magnetism. He demonstrated that a wire carrying a current could deflect a magnetized compass needle. Ørsted's experiments discovered the relationship between electricity and magnetism in a very simple experiment. Ørsted's work influenced André-Marie Ampère to produce a theory of electromagnetism. During its early development and long after wide use of the technology, disputes persisted as to who

could claim sole credit for this obvious boon to mankind. Closely related, radio was developed along with two other key inventions, the telegraph and the telephone.

Frenchman André-Marie Ampère's fame mainly rests on his establishing the relations between electricity and magnetism, and in developing the science of electromagnetism, or, as he called it, electrodynamics. On 11 September, this year he heard of Ørsted's discovery that a magnetic needle is acted on by a voltaic current. Only a week later, on 18 September, Ampère presented a paper to the University of Lyon academy containing a far more complete exposition of this and kindred phenomena. On the same day, Ampère also demonstrated before the Academy that parallel wires carrying currents attract or repel each other, depending on whether currents are in the same (attraction) or in opposite directions (repulsion). This laid the foundation of electrodynamics. The field of electromagnetism thus opened up, Ampère explored with characteristic industry and care, and developed a mathematical theory which not only explained the electromagnetic phenomena already observed, but also predicted many new ones.

Faraday's electricity

1825 Faraday had worked his way up to being laboratory director at the Royal Institution in London, and in 1833 he was made a professor of chemistry. In the lab, he had great success with electrochemistry, and he even has an electrical unit named after him (a 'faraday' is the amount of electricity measured during electrolysis). Faraday built the first  dynamo, a copper disk that rotated between the poles of a permanent magnet and produced an electromotive force (something that moves electricity). His work in electromagnetic induction led to the development of modern dynamos and generators. Faraday also discovered the compound benzene. Faraday's work contributed some of the essential building blocks for the emergence of television.

1827 In the 19th century, the subject of electrical engineering, with the tools of modern research techniques, started to intensify. Notable developments in this century include the work of Georg Ohm who quantified the relationship between the electric current and potential difference in a conductor.

1829 Robert Peel established the Metropolitan Police Force for London based at Scotland Yard. The 1,000 constables employed were affectionately nicknamed 'Bobbies' or, somewhat less affectionately, 'Peelers' (both terms are still used today).

The mechanical computer

1830 A well known British mathematician, named Charles Babbage, came up with the idea of a machine that could compute mathematical polynomials and this resulted in the creation of the first mechanical computer. Babbage called the machine a 'difference engine'. He made a small model of it and presented it at his evening cocktail parties, as the 'thinking machine'. However, he could not build the complete machine. At the time, even the most advanced technology available was far from satisfactory for the needs of such an invention. Babbage himself manufactured some of the parts necessary, and in addition to a generous fund granted to him by the British government for the purpose of building such a machine, Babbage also invested all of his savings in the project.

1830 Lord Palmerston

Although he had always been a member of Tory administrations, Lord Palmerston (a subsequent Prime Minister) accepted the offer to join Lord Grey and his Whig government in this year.

1831 Prime Minister, Earl Grey, The Whig Party.

Nearly two hundred year ago, the House of Lords was as powerful, if not more so, than the Commons; party allegiances were much more shifting and it was thought that a General Election might change the party balance in the Commons, but could not bring down a Government with a majority in the Lords. The Wigs, led by Earl Grey (who gave his name to the tea blend) won a landslide election this year – producing a Parliament overwhelmingly in favour of change. Both the electoral system and the political landscape of the time were rotten to the core, and in desperate need for reform. Every county was represented by two MPs, despite the fact that Yorkshire, for example, had 17,000 electors, while Rutland had just 600. The great Reform Act (see below) was finally pushed through the Lords only after a threat by the King to make enough new peers to give the Whigs a majority there too. The election this year, and the Act which followed, breached a dam of narrow self-interest and fear, and paved the way for gradual, British-style piecemeal reform.

During the 17th to 19th century period the political term 'Whig' became used to describe those Members of Parliament opposed to the religious policies of King Charles II (1630–1685) through to those of King George III (1760–1820.) All monarchs during this time had absolute rule of the Kingdom, with Parliament simply enacting the monarch's wish.

Charles II   George III

The Whigs supported the establishment of the Hanoverian settlement (the development of a constitutional monarchy – where Parliament agreed policy which was then given assent by the Sovereign through Royal Assent). By the 19th century, the Whig's rivals in Parliament, the Conservatives (Tories), became the supporters of the status quo.

Both political parties began as loose groupings or tendencies, but became quite formal by 1784, with the ascension of Charles Fox as the leader of the 'Whig' party. The Whigs opposed the governing party of the 'Tories' under William Pitt

the Younger who had become PM at the request of King George III in 1783. There followed many years of Parliamentary debate about the rights and wrongs of the supreme sovereign governing the country with absolute rule. The appointment of Whig Prime Minister, The Earl Grey in 1831 represented the major change in the political system whereby Parliament took the lead, with the monarch conducting a more ceremonial role and giving the Royal assent to new legislation. So – democracy, as we know it today, started less than 200 years ago in England. The aristocratic connotations surrounding the name 'Whig' caused some politicians to refer to themselves as Liberals, a term used by reforming politicians in Europe. However, the term Liberal was not used officially in the UK until 1868 when William Gladstone became Prime Minister. The term 'Liberal' remains today within the current political arena in the form of the third political party in Parliament (in the 21st century) known as the Liberal Democrats with Nick Clegg as the current leader. The current Conservative leader is David Cameron.

The electrostatic machine

1831 Georg Ohm constructed an early electrostatic machine – the homopolar generator – which was a DC electrical generator that is made when a magnetic electrically conductive rotating disc has a different magnetic field passing through it (it can be thought of as slicing through the magnetic field). This creates a potential difference between two contact points, one in the center of the disc the other on the outside of

the disc. It was the beginning of modern dynamos, that is, electrical generators which operate using a magnetic field. Joseph Henry's and Michael Faraday's subsequent work with electricity jumpstarted the era of electronic communication. Faraday became best known for the discoveries of electromagnetic induction and the laws of electrolysis. Faraday's biggest breakthrough in electricity was the invention of the electric motor which was key to the development of the electro mechanical television built by Baird in 1925. He made a start with the theory of electronic communication. Overall, Faraday's work laid the foundation for radio and television broadcast delivered through the radio spectrum.

The Reform Act

1832 The Reform Act – The Representation of the People Act 1832 – introduced wide-ranging changes to the electoral system of the United Kingdom. The Act was proposed by the Whigs led by the Prime Minster, The Earl Grey. The Act granted seats in the House of Commons to large cities that had sprung up during the industrial revolution, and took away seats from the 'rotten boroughs' – those geographic council areas of the United Kingdom with very small populations. The Act also increased the number of individuals entitled to vote, increasing the size of the electorate by 50–80%, and allowing a total of one out of six adult males to vote, in a population of some 14 million. These changes introduced proper general elections in the United Kingdom.

1835 and 1837 Whig Prime Minister, The Viscount Melbourne.

 **1837** Queen Victoria reigned from 1837 to 1901. Her reign as Queen lasted nearly 64 years, longer than that of any other British monarch before or since, and the longest of any woman monarch in British history.

1841 30 August, new Tory Prime Minister, Sir Robert Peel, Bt.

Samuel Morse

 In December, Samuel Morse had successfully tried his experiments with the telegraph and applied for a grant with the USA federal government, and even demonstrated his work in New York and Washington. But the process was delayed due to a recession in the economy. At the same time, Charles Wheatstone, a British physicist, along with William Cooke, patented a telegraph system in Europe. But the Morse model was efficient and much simpler to use than this system. By 1843, Morse was successful in getting the required grant and the first telegraph line of 40 miles was constructed from Washington to Baltimore. The line ran from the Supreme Court in the Capitol complex to the Baltimore railroad station. The first system made use of the Morse code, which was later accepted as a global standard for deciphering text. The significance of the telegraph to television is the achievement of the movement of electrical data from one place to another. It would be nearly 100 years after Morse code that the moving medium was pictures (1926).

1844 Samuel F B Morse transmitted the first electrical message "What has God wrought?" This message was conveyed from Washington to Baltimore on 24 May of this year.

1847 New Liberal Prime Minister, Lord Russell.

Alexander Graham Bell was born in Edinburgh (he died in 1922). Bell was credited with inventing the first practical telephone in 1876. The telephone (from the Greek: τῆλε, *tēle*, 'far' and φωνή, *phōnē*, 'voice') is a device that transmits and receives sound, most commonly the human voice.

1851 Queen Victoria visited the World's Fair in London and was so entranced by the stereoscopes on display that she precipitated an enthusiasm for three-dimensional photography that soon made it a popular form of entertainment world-wide.

1852 George Hamilton-Gordon, 4th Earl of Aberdeen styled Lord Haddo from 1791 to 1801, was a Scottish politician, successively a Tory, Conservative and Peelite, who served as Prime Minister of the United Kingdom from 1852.

1855 This year, Lord Palmerston, aged 70, became Prime Minister,

succeeding the Earl of Aberdeen. Queen Victoria found it difficult to work with him but their relationship gradually improved. She later wrote in her journal: "We had, God knows! terrible trouble with him about Foreign Affairs. Still, as Prime Minister he managed affairs at home well, and behaved to me well. But I never liked him." Palmerston's first period as Prime Minister lasted for three years. His second started in 1859 when he was 75 years old. The main foreign events that he had to deal with during this period included the American Civil War and Napoleon III's war with Austria. The main domestic issue involved the continuing debate over parliamentary reform. Palmerston was totally opposed to any extension of the franchise and during 1864 came into conflict with William Gladstone, his Chancellor of the Exchequer, who was a strong supporter of reform. Palmerston won the argument and Gladstone had to wait until he became Prime Minister before he could introduce these measures.

1857 🦃 Liberal Prime Minister, Lord Palmerston re-elected.

1859 🦃 Liberal Prime Minister, Lord Palmerston re-elected for a second time..

First still image transferred

1862 Abbe Giovanna Caselli invents his pantelegraph (French: pantélégraphe) and becomes the first person to transmit a still image over wires. It is a system of sending and receiving images over long distances by means of telegraph wiring. This system was actually a prototype of the fax machine.

1864 James Clerk Maxwell, a professor at Cambridge University talked about his theory of the existence of electromagnetic waves. Edison was later to show that an electric current could jump through space.

1865 🦃 General Election. Liberal Prime Minister, Earl Russell.

Jules Verne

For satellite television to become a
reality, space travel needed to be
conquered. Theoretically, space travel
was contemplated this year. 'From the
Earth to the Moon' was a humorous
science fantasy novel by Jules Verne. It
tells the story of the president of a
post-American Civil War gun club in

Baltimore, his rival, a Philadelphia maker of armour, and a
Frenchman, who build an enormous sky-facing columbiad cannon
to launch themselves in a projectile/spaceship from Earth to the
Moon. The story is also notable in that Verne attempted to do
some rough calculations as to the requirements for the cannon
and, considering the total lack of any data on the subject at the
time, some of his figures are surprisingly close to reality. However,
his scenario turned out to be impractical for safe manned space
travel since a much longer cannon muzzle would have been
required to reach earth escape velocity while limiting acceleration
to survivable limits for the passengers. Incredibly, the story bears
similarities to the real-life Apollo missions of the 20th century;
Verne's cannon was a type called a columbiad while the Apollo 11
command module was named Columbia. The spacecraft crew
consisted of three persons in each case. The physical dimensions
of the projectile are very close to the dimensions of the Apollo
Command Service Module. Verne's voyage blasted off from
Florida, as did all Apollo missions. Verne correctly states in the
book that objects launched into space are best positioned if they
are launched towards the zenith of a particular location, and that
the zenith would better line up with the moon's orbit from near

the Earth's equator. In the book, Florida and Texas compete for the launch, with Florida winning. The names of the crew, Ardan, Barbicane, and Nicholl, are vaguely similar to Bill Anders, Frank Borman, and Jim Lovell, the crew of Apollo 8, the first manned spacecraft to travel to the moon, although it didn't actually land.

1868 General Election. Liberal Prime Minister, William Gladstone.

The first telegraphy Act

1869 In this year, the Telegraphy Act this year gave the Post Office the exclusive rights to transmit telegrams within the UK.

1870 The idea of sending and receiving images along wireless routes was bouncing around between scientists in the 1870s

1871 Between 1861 and 1865, based on the earlier experimental work of Faraday and other scientists, James Clerk Maxwell developed his theory of electromagnetism, which predicted the existence of electromagnetic waves.

1872 In April, American William Henry Ward, received a US Patent for radio development. However, this patent did not refer to any known scientific theory of electromagnetism and could never have received and transmitted radio waves. A few months after Ward received his patent, Mahlon Loomis of West Virginia received a US Patent for a 'wireless telegraph'. This patent utilized atmospheric electricity to eliminate the use of the overhead wire used by the existing telegraph systems. It did not contain diagrams or specific methods and it did not refer to or incorporate any known scientific theory. It is substantially similar to William Henry Ward's patent and could not have transmitted and received radio waves.

1873 This year, James Clerk Maxwell had started a different path on the development of electricity with equations that described the electromagnetic field, and he predicted the existence of electromagnetic waves travelling with the speed of light. Heinrich R Hertz was to confirm this prediction experimentally.

1874 General Election. Conservative Prime Minister, Benjamin Disraeli.

Disraeli, aged 70, led the Conservatives to a clear majority for the first time in 33 years. He brought about a great expansion of the British Empire, especially in India. In the UK, there was a flood of modernising legislation with the Public Heath Act, Medicines Act, Factory Act and the Employers and Workmen Act, as well as legislation regarding peaceful picketing.

1875 Towards the end of this year while experimenting with the telegraph, Thomas Edison noted a phenomenon that he termed 'etheric force', announcing it to the press on 28 November. He abandoned this research when Elihu Thomson, among others, ridiculed the idea. The idea was not based on the electromagnetic waves described by Maxwell.

1876 Boston civil servant George Carey was thinking about complete television systems and the next year he put forward drawings for what he called a selenium camera that would allow people to see by electricity.

The telephone was invented in March this year by Alexander Graham Bell. The incident in which Bell spilled acid on himself and called out to his assistant, Watson, not realizing his voice was being carried over the telephone was on 10 March. The invention was patented be Bell on 30 January 1877. The telegraph and telephone are both wire-based electrical systems, and Alexander Graham Bell's success with the telephone came as a direct result of his attempts to improve the telegraph.

Thomas Edison

1877 An early format war was about recording media formats: cylinder records vs disc records. This year, American Thomas Edison invented sound recording technology using a tin cylinder record, and soon  thereafter mass-marketed the wax Edison cylinder. In 1886, Berliner invented disc records. By the late 1890s, cylinders and discs were widespread. Cylinders were more expensive to manufacture, but most cylinder players could make recordings. Discs saved space and were cheaper, but due to the constant angular velocity (CAV) of their rotation, the sound quality varied noticeably from the long outer edge to the short inner portion nearest the center; and disc record players could not make recordings. Edison refused to produce the discs until Berliner's patent expired in the late 1910s.

1878 American, Thomas Edison became the first person to apply the term 'filament' to a fine wire that glows when carrying an electric current.

1879 This year, Thomas Edison invented the first commercially  practical incandescent electric lamp. He also made radical improvements on the construction of dynamos, including the mica laminated armature and mica insulated commutator. Also in this year, Edison constructed the first electric motor ever made for a 110 to 120 volt line at Menlo Park, New Jersey. This device is still in existence and operative, and is located in the Edison Historical Collection in New Jersey. On 31 December, he gave the first public demonstration of an electric lighting system in streets and buildings at Menlo Park, New Jersey, utilizing underground mains.

George du Maurier drew a cartoon for Punch magazine in London showing a mother and father in London watching a flat screen on the wall displaying a live picture of their daughter playing tennis in Ceylon (now the Democratic Socialist Republic of Sri Lanka).

1880 General Election. Liberal Prime Minister, William Gladstone.

Inventors Alexander Graham Bell and Thomas Edison theorize about their telephone devices transmitting images as well as sound (today's videophone!) This year, Edison established the first incandescent lamp factory at Menlo Park, New Jersey, New York.

AC vs DC

1881 Another format war starts: AC vs DC electrical current. In alternating current (AC), the movement (or flow) of electric charge periodically reverses direction. An electric charge would for

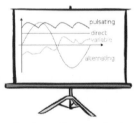

instance move forward, then backward, then forward, then backward, over and over again. In direct current (DC), the movement (or flow) of electric charge is only in one direction.

Used generically, AC refers to the form in which electricity is delivered to businesses and residences. The usual waveform of an AC power circuit is a sine wave, however in certain applications, different waveforms are used, such as triangular or square waves. Audio and radio signals carried on electrical wires are also examples of alternating current. In these applications, an important goal is often the recovery of information encoded (or modulated). A power transformer developed by Lucien Gaulard and John Dixon Gibbs was demonstrated in London in 1881. They also exhibited the invention in Turin in 1884, where it was adopted for an electric lighting system. AC systems overcame the limitations of the direct current system used by Thomas Edison to distribute electricity efficiently over long distances even though Edison attempted to discredit alternating current as too dangerous during the war of the currents.

Pantelegraph

The idea of using scanning to transmit images was put to actual practical use this year in the pantelegraph, through the use of a pendulum-based scanning mechanism. From this period onward, scanning in one form or another, has been used in nearly every image transmission technology to date, including television. This is the concept of 'rasterization', the process of converting a visual image into a stream of electrical pulses.

1882 Robida's Vision

French artist Robida produced drawings of moving pictures being transmitted onto the walls of people's livingroom.

Electrical Engineering

During the latter part of the 1800s, the study of electricity was largely considered to be a subfield of physics. It was not until the late 19th century that universities started to offer degrees in electrical engineering. This year, the Darmstadt University of Technology founded the first chair and the first faculty of electrical engineering worldwide. In the same year, under Professor Charles Cross, the Massachusetts Institute of Technology began offering the first option of Electrical Engineering within a physics department.

1883 Darmstadt University of Technology and Cornell University introduced the world's first courses of study in electrical engineering.

The Scanning Disk

1884 This year, Nipkow patented the use of a selium block as the heart of what he called the electric telescope. This year saw the invention of the mechanical scanning disc by the 20 year old German, Paul Nipkow which was a

major step forward. Using his electric telescope he managed to send images over wires using a rotating metal disc with 18 lines of resolution to make up the picture. The disc itself is nothing more than a mechanically spinning disc of any suitable material (metal, plastic, cardboard, etc.), with a series of equally distanced circular holes of equal diameter drilled in it. The disc is placed between the lens and the selenium to transform the light into a modulated electrical wave. This invention was well before that of the CRT (1921) and was only a limited success. The selenium was insufficiently sensitive for light to create a satisfactory image.

1885 🗳 General Election. Liberal Prime Minister, Marquess of Salisbury.

This year, University College London founded the first chair of electrical engineering in the United Kingdom.

Also in this year, the German Heinrich Rudolf Hertz became a full professor at the University of Karlsruhe where he discovered electromagnetic waves. Hertz helped establish the photoelectric effect (which was later explained by Albert Einstein) when he noticed that a charged object loses its charge more readily when illuminated by ultraviolet light.

1886 General Election. Conservative Prime Minister, William Gladstone.

In this year, the University of Missouri established the first department of electrical engineering in the United States. During this period work in the area increased dramatically. This year Edison switched on the world's first large-scale electrical supply network that provided 110 volts direct current to 59 customers in lower Manhattan.

Alternating Current

1887 Nikola Tesla filed a number of patents related to a competing form of electrical power distribution known as alternating current. In the following years, a bitter rivalry between Tesla and Edison, known as the 'war of currents', took place over

the preferred method of distribution. AC eventually replaced DC for generation and power distribution, enormously extending the range and improving the safety and efficiency of power distribution. The efforts of Tesla and

Edison did much to further electrical engineering – Tesla's work on induction motors and polyphase systems influenced the field for years to come, while Edison's work on telegraphy and his development of the stock ticker proved lucrative for his company, which ultimately became General Electric. (A polyphase system is a means of distributing alternating current electrical power. Polyphase systems have three or more energized electrical conductors carrying alternating currents with a definite time offset between the voltage waves in each conductor. Polyphase systems are particularly useful for transmitting power to electric motors. The most common example is the three-phase power system used for most industrial applications.)

By the end of the 19th century, other key figures in the progress of electrical engineering were beginning to emerge. German-American mathematician and electrical engineer, Charles Proteus Steinmetz helped foster the development of  alternating current that made possible the expansion of the electric power industry in the United States, formulating mathematical theories for engineers.

This year, Heinrich Rudolf Hertz made observations of the photoelectric effect and of the production and reception of electromagnetic (EM) waves, published in the journal Annalen der Physik. His receiver consisted of a coil with a spark gap, whereupon a spark would be seen upon detection of EM waves. He placed the apparatus in a

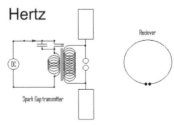

darkened box to see the spark better. He observed that the maximum spark length was reduced when in the box. A glass panel placed between the source of EM waves and the receiver absorbed ultraviolet radiation that assisted the electrons in jumping across the gap.

The experimental setup of Hertz' apparatus

1888 Heinrich Hertz first demonstrated the existence of electromagnetic waves this year. Marconi was to pick up on this discovery and relate it to moving point-to-point radio waves.

What is radio?

Radio (or wireless as it was known) is the transmission of signals by modulation of electromagnetic waves with frequencies below those of visible light. Electromagnetic radiation travels by means of oscillating electromagnetic fields that pass through the air and the vacuum of space. Information is carried by systematically changing (modulating) some property of the radiated waves, such as amplitude, frequency, phase, or pulse width. When radio waves pass an electrical conductor, the oscillating fields induce an alternating current in the conductor. This can be detected and transformed into sound or other signals that carry information.

1888 John Logie Baird

The birth of John Logie Baird on 13 August. He was a Scottish engineer (from Helensburgh, Dunbartonshire). When he was 12 years old he built his own telephone network. He had invested in chutney in the West Indies, artificial diamonds in Glasgow and soap in London. In 1918, he held the patent for the Baird 'undersock' – a sock worn beneath regular socks for extra warmth. Baird was forced to resign from his position as an electrical engineer through persistent ill health, and he retired early, in 1922, to Hastings, East Sussex. Under these circumstances, he used his time to research ways of transmitting pictures. By some, he was regarded as the inventor of television (including the world's first ever colour system – see 1926). This was despite previous work by others. Although Baird's electromechanical system was eventually displaced by a purely electronic system (not designed by him) his early successes of demonstrating working television broadcasts, and his colour and cinema television work earned him a prominent place in television's invention.

1890 At the World's Fair in Paris (the first International Congress of Electricity) Russian, Constantin Perskyi made the first known use of the word 'television'. The word television is derived from mixed Latin and Greek roots, meaning 'far sight': Greek tele (τῆλε), far, and Latin visio, sight.

1891 Edison invented and patented the first motion picture camera. This mechanism, with its continuous tape-like film, made it possible to take, reproduce, and project motion pictures as we see and hear them today.

David Sarnoff (Russian: Давид Сарнов) born on 27 February in Uzlian, a small Jewish village near the city of Minsk, Russian Empire (now in Belarus). Sarnoff became very influential in the

early development of radio and television in the USA in the 1920s and onwards for 50 years. He was to make his name by claiming that as a young radio operator he was first to report the sinking of the Titanic in 1912. Some historians doubt this suggestion.

1892 General Election. Liberal Prime Minister, William Gladstone.

1893 First remote control of an electrical device

Nikolai Tesla demonstrated the first remote controlled motorboat using radio waves.

1894 In wireless telegraphy, Oliver Lodge perfected and named the 'coherer', a radio-wave detector invented by the French physicist Edouard Branly. It was one of the most important types of detector developed before electronic tubes.

1894 This year, Guglielmo Marconi started his experiments to use radio waves to communicate voice signals.

1895 General Election. Conservative Prime Minister, Marquess of Salsbury.

The Electromagnetic Spectrum

The electromagnetic spectrum extends from low frequencies used for modern radio to gamma radiation at the short-wavelength end, covering wavelengths from thousands of

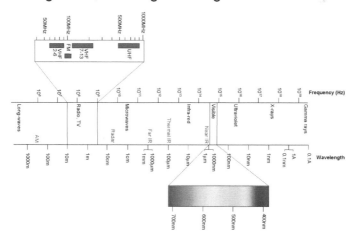

kilometers down to a fraction of the size of an atom. The long wavelength limit is the size of the universe itself, while it is thought that the short wavelength limit is in the vicinity of the Planck length, although in principle the spectrum is infinite and continuous.

It is important, therefore, at this stage in the book to explain the spectrum which inventors were trying to understand. Its use led to AM radio, FM radio and the analogue transmission of VHF, and then UHF television signals. AM stands for Amplitude Modulation. FM stands for Frequency Modulation. VHF stands for Very High Frequency. UHF stands for Ultra High Frequency. AM radio ranges from 535 to 1705kHz (kilohertz – or thousands of cycles per second of electromagnetic energy). FM radio ranges from 87.5MHz to 108MHz. These are the numbers seen on the radio dial. AM radio waves are of a lower frequency than either FM radio or television waves. When transmitted, the two types of frequency behave differently. How far an AM station's signal travels depends on such things as the station's frequency (channel), the power of the transmitter in watts, the nature of the transmitting antenna, how conductive

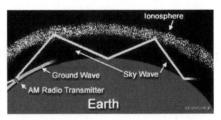

the soil is around the antenna (damp soil is good; sand and rocks aren't), and, a thing called ionospheric refraction. The ionosphere is a layer of heavily charged ion molecules above the earth's atmosphere. Please note that for AM radio stations the ground wave doesn't go very far. This means numerous stations can be put on the same radio frequency without interfering with each other – assuming they are far enough apart. The problem that arises, if you want to see it as a problem, is that the sky wave can end up in other states, provinces, or even in other countries. The ionosphere is much more effective in reflecting these radio waves at night. That's why at sunset most AM radio stations have to reduce power, directionalise their signal (send it more in some directions than others), or go off the air (sign off until sunrise the next day). This may explain why some AM radio station goes off the air at sunset, or becomes much harder to hear (because of reduced power).

FM radio and TV VHF and UHF airwaves don't act in the same way as AM radio waves. The FM radio band goes from 88 to 108MHz (megahertz, or millions of 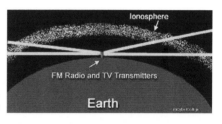 cycles per second). These are the numbers on the FM radio dial. FM stations must be 200kHz apart at these frequencies, which means that there's room for 200 FM stations on the FM band. But, unlike AM radio stations, FM stations don't end up being assigned frequencies with nice round numbers like 820 or 1240. Thus, an FM station may be at 88.7 on the dial. FM stations don't reduce power or sign off the air at sunset. Because of their higher frequency, ionospheric refraction doesn't appreciably affect FM or TV signals. For the most part, FM and TV signals are line-of-sight. Although this means that FM stations don't interfere with each other, this characteristic creates a couple of other problems. First, these waves go in a straight line and don't bend around the earth as AM ground waves do. Thus, they can quickly disappear into space. So, the farther away from the FM or TV station you are, the higher you have to have an antenna to receive the FM or TV signal. The signals will leave the earth after 50 miles or so. Since FM and TV signals are line-of-sight, they can be stopped or reflected by things like mountains and buildings. In the case of solid objects like buildings, reflections create ghost images in TV pictures and that 'swishing sound' when you listen to FM radio while driving around tall structures.

So what is the real difference between AM and FM signals? In fact, there is a lot of difference.

The first type of radio service was AM radio. The term 'modulation' refers to how sound is encoded on a radio wave called a carrier wave; or, more accurately, how the sound affects the carrier wave so that the original sound can later be detected by a radio receiver. In the top-left of this drawing, the RF energy (carrier wave) is not modulated by any sound. There would be silence on your radio receiver. Sound transmitted by an AM radio station affects the carrier wave by changing the amplitude (height) of the carrier wave. Unfortunately, this type of modulation is subject to static interference from such things as household appliances — and especially from lightening storms. AM also limits the loud-to-soft range of sounds that can be reproduced (called dynamic range) and the high-to-low sound frequency range (called frequency response, to be explained below). FM radio, which came along in the 1930s, uses a different approach than AM. It's virtually immune to any type of external interference, it has a greater dynamic range, and it can handle sounds of higher and lower frequencies. This is why music, with its much greater frequency range than the human voice, sounds better on FM radio.

When the carrier wave of FM radio is modulated with sound that the distance between the waves, or the frequency of the carrier wave, changes. Thus, AM radio works by changing the amplitude of the carrier wave and FM radio works by changing the frequency of the carrier wave. The professional radio dial comprises three groups of AM radio frequencies (RF) – Long wave (148.5–283.5KHz), Medium wave (526.5–1606.5KHz) and Short wave (3000–30,000KHz).

Photoconductivity

The origins of what would become today's television system can be traced back as far as the discovery of photoconductivity. Scientists May and Smith experimented with selenium and light. This revealed the possibility for inventors to transform images into electronic signals. James Maxwell this year published a unified theory of electricity and magnetism in his article on Electricity and Magnetism.

Cinematography and the Kinetoscope

This year, saw the launch of cinematography. Marconi first made use of electricity in developing radio. By the spring, Thomas Edison invented a crude Kinetoscope with phonographs inside their cabinets. The viewer would look into the peep-holes of the Kinetoscope to watch the motion picture while listening to the accompanying phonograph through two rubber ear tubes connected to the machine (the kinetophone). The picture and sound were made somewhat synchronous by connecting the two with a belt.

1896 The Italian, Guglielmo Marconi arrived in London and registered his application for a wireless patent in. He lived at 101 Hereford Road, Bayswater, London. Marconi said he could transmit a radio signal for 100 yards without wires using the Hertzian principles and Oliver (later Sir Oliver) Lodge's coherer. The coherer was a primitive form of radio signal detector used in the late nineteenth and early twentieth centuries, consisting of a capsule of metal filings in the space between two electrodes. It was a key enabling technology for radio, and was the first device

used to detect radio signals in practical spark gap transmitter wireless telegraphy. Its operation is based upon the large resistance offered to the passage of electric current by loose metal filings being decreased under the influence of radio frequency alternating current.

On 30 March this year, the famous British electrical engineer, A A Campbell-Swinton recommended Marconi to Presco, the engineer-in-chief at the Post Office, as inventing a new system of telegraphy without wires. Marconi demonstrated his radio device to the Post Office chief engineer who was later knighted. The Marconi Wireless Telegraph and Signal Company was formed the next year with capital of £100,000. There was great speculation in the press about what Marconi was up to – some called it (prophetically) 'space technology'.

Lord Northcliffe bought the Daily Mail as part of his belief in mass communication.

CRT

1897 Invention of the basic cathode-ray tube (CRT) by German, Karl Braun. In essence, the CRT would simply become the TV screen of television sets until the development of Plasma, LCD, LED and other screen technologies in the 21st century. A CRT has a stream of electrons leaving the negative electrode, or cathode, in a discharge tube (an electron tube that contains gas or vapour at low pressure), or emitted by a heated filament in certain electron tubes. A vacuum tube is an electron tube consisting of a sealed glass or metal enclosure from which the air has been

withdrawn. In essence, a CRT is a specialized vacuum tube in which images are produced when an electron beam strikes a phosphorescent surface.

1898 In Madison Square Garden, at the Electrical Exhibition of 1898, Nikolai Tesla staged a scientific first; a demonstration completely beyond the generally accepted limits of technology. His invention took the form of a radio-controlled boat, a heavy, low-lying, steel craft about four

feet long. Radio hadn't been officially patented yet (Tesla's basic radio patent was filed in September 1897, but granted in March 1900), and examiners from the US Patent Office were reluctant to recognize improbable claims made in the application 'Method of and Apparatus for Controlling Mechanism of Moving Vessels or Vehicles'. Confronted with a working model, however, examiners quickly issued approval. This demonstration showed a practical use of radio waves.

1898 John Logie Baird begins studies at Larchfield Academy which was a preparatory school for boys in Helensburgh, Scotland.

1899 First international radio communication between England and France.

This year, the Thomas Edison phonograph was the first device to record sound and to have taken off in the world of the audio marketplace.

20th Century

1900 General Election. Liberal Prime Minister, Henry Campbell-Bannerman.

This year, Russian David Sarnoff emigrated with his family to the east side of New York. After selling newspapers on the street, he became an office boy at the Commercial Cable Company. Six years later, on 30 September, when his line manager had refused him unpaid leave for Rosh Hashanah, he joined the Marconi Wireless Telegraph Company of America as their office boy. He learnt Morse code and telegraphy and became a radio operator with the company, and this started a career of over sixty years in electronic communications.

This year, the Slaby-Arco wireless system was developed by Adolf Slaby and Georg von Arco. In 1900, Reginald Fessenden made a weak transmission of voice over the airwaves. Around this time, Tesla opened the Wardenclyffe Tower facility and advertised services.

Soon after 1900, the momentum shifted from ideas and discussions to the physical development of television systems. Two major paths in the development of a television system were pursued by inventors. They attempted to build mechanical television systems based on Paul Nipkow's rotating disks (1884) or inventors attempted to build electronic television systems based on the cathrode ray tube developed independently in 1907 by English inventor A A Campbell-Swinton and Russian scientist Boris Rosing. American, Charles Jenkins and Scotsman, John Baird followed the mechanical model while Philo Farnsworth, working independently in San Francisco, and Russian emigrant Vladimir Zworkin, working for Westinghouse and later RCA, advanced the electronic model. As will be seen, electronic television systems eventually replaced mechanical systems.

1900 Formation of the Labour Party

The Labour Party was formed at a meeting in London on 26–27 February this year for the purpose of expressing working class opinion. The meeting was hosted by the Trades Union Congress with representation from the trade unions, the Fabian Society and others.

1901 First Transatlantic radio signal

In the UK, there were now 7.7m homes. On 1 December, Marconi sent the first radio signal from Cornwall, UK across the Atlantic to Newfoundland – a distance of 2000+ miles. He wanted to prove that radio waves could be sent beyond the horizon and keep to the curvature of the earth.

1901 Death of Queen Victoria

On 21 January, at the age of 81, Queen Victoria died. Her son, Edward VII reigned as monarch from 1901 to 1910.

Edward VII was brought up strictly under a very rigorous educational regime by his parents, who had unrealistic

expectations of his abilities. During his mother's reign, he undertook public duties (including working on Royal Commissions in the field of social issues), but he was excluded by his mother from acting as her deputy until 1898. Edward was 59 when he became king, having been heir apparent for longer than anyone else in British history. (At the time of publishing this book, Prince Charles has been waiting 64 years). Criticised for his social life, Edward's main interests lay in foreign affairs, and military and naval matters.

1902 General Election. Liberal Prime Minister, Arthur Balfour.

1902 Julio Cervera Baviera

Recent studies in Spain credit Julio Cervera Baviera as the inventor of the radio. Cervera Baviera obtained patents in England, Germany, Belgium, and Spain. In May-June 1899, Cervera had, with the blessing of the Spanish Army, visited Marconi's radiotelegraphic installations on the English Channel, and worked to develop his own system. He began collaborating with Marconi on resolving the problem of a wireless communication system, obtaining some patents by the end of 1899. Cervera, who had worked with Marconi and his assistant George Kemp in 1899, resolved the difficulties of wireless telegraph and obtained his first patents prior to the end of that year. On 22 March 1902, Cervera founded the Spanish Wireless Telegraph and Telephone Corporation and brought to his corporation the patents he had obtained in Spain, Belgium, Germany and England. He established the second and third regular radiotelegraph service in the history of the world in 1901 and 1902 by maintaining regular transmissions between Tarifa and Ceuta for three consecutive months, and between Javea (Cabo de la Nao) and Ibiza (Cabo Pelado). This was after Marconi established the radiotelegraphic service between the Isle of Wight and Bournemouth in 1898. In 1906, Domenico Mazzotto wrote: "In Spain the Minister of War has applied the system perfected by the commander of military engineering, Julio Cervera Baviera." Cervera thus achieved some success in this field, but his radiotelegraphic activities ceased suddenly, the reasons for which are unclear to this day.

1902 17 January this year saw the launch of the Times Newspaper Literary Supplement.

1903 2 November saw the launch of the Daily Mirror – the first daily newspaper illustrated exclusively with photographs. The Mirror was a broadsheet newspaper until the 1950s.

1904 This year, the US Patent Office reversed its decision, awarding Marconi a patent for the invention of radio, possibly influenced by Marconi's financial backers in the States, who included Thomas Edison and Andrew Carnegie. This also allowed the US government (among others) to avoid having to pay the royalties that were being claimed by Tesla for use of his patent.

The Telegraphy Act

In the UK, the Telegraphy Act this year gave the Post Office control over all point-to-point wireless telegraphy. John Ambrose Fleming invented the diode rectifier vacuum tube as a detector for the Marconi radio. Three years later, Lee De Forest made the diode into an amplifier by adding a third electrode, and electronics had begun. Theoretical understanding of electricity became more complete with the discovery of the electron by J J Thomson.

The intervention of British law started to govern the development of the communications industry. The Wireless Telegraphy Act established the need for all UK wireless telegraphy users to obtain a licence for transmitting and receiving radio signals. If it were not for developments in radio broadcast, the medium of television would not be broadcast as radio waves (the original way of sending pictures and sound). The Wireless Telegraphy Act regulated all wireless communication to ensure that the entire radio frequency spectrum would be used for the public good, and to allow the development and the enforcement of international agreements. Radio frequency (RF) is the rate of oscillation of electromagnetic radiation within the range of about 3Hz (Hertz) to 300GHz. (the spectrum).

1904 The diode value

Professor Sir Ambrose Fleming invented the thermionic valve this year – essential for the further development of wireless. The invention of the thermionic valve by Fleming at the Marconi Company was a significant development for electronics and radio  communication. The first transatlantic radio transmissions of 1901 threw up a significant problem: how to detect the incredibly weak radio signals at the receiving end. Fleming, inspired in 1904 by a 'sudden and very happy thought', turned to modified experimental filament lamps which he had investigated earlier, and found that they detected the high-frequency signals. His invention was a diode, the first in a line of devices which were to be a mainstay of electronics well into the solid-state era.

1906 General Election. Liberal Prime Minister, Henry Campbell-Bannerman.

Lee De Forest invented the Audion vacuum tube that proved essential to electronics. The Audion was the first tube with the ability to amplify signals. The second Wireless Telegraphy Act was passed making provision for the licensing of wireless telegraphy broadcast stations. Wireless telegraphy as a concept was now defined in British law as 'the sending of electro-magnetic energy over paths not provided by a material substance'. On Christmas Eve, Canadian engineer Reginald Fessenden first broadcast his voice shore-to-ship off the coast in Massachusetts, USA.

This year saw the first broadcast of music and speech together – by Canadian-born R A Fessenden.

1906 John Logie Baird was enrolled into the Glasgow Royal Technical College being a higher education institution. He received his Diploma in Electrical Engineering in 1914. He subsequently attended the University of Glasgow but his degree course was interrupted by World War I and he never returned to graduate.

Further work on the CRT

1907 Further developments in America on the amplification tube technology (CRT) was conducted by Lee De Forest (1873–1961, a Yale University PhD) with Arthur Kom. Separately in the same year, British scientist Campbell-Swinton (FRS (1863–1930)) discovered that the CRT could be used to pick up an image on a thin plate coated with a photosensitive substance. Russian, Boris Rosing filed a patent for his television system using the CRT.

1908 Campbell-Swinton wrote a letter to Nature magazine describing 'distance electronic vision' using the Rosing CRT principles – which remained the basis of the television receiver until Plasma, LCD and LED screens were developed in the 1990s. What Campbell-Swinton did NOT do was to put his theory into practice by way of achieving broadcast demonstration. Campbell-Swinton eventually replaced the spinning disk with his idea of an electronic device using two beams of cathode. (In Electrical Engineering the cathode is an electrode of a cathode ray tube, fluorescent lamp, diode, fuel cells, or lead storage batteries.)

The term radio was now being used by scientists as an alternative to wireless. This was a hangover from the earlier days of radio telegraphy and Morse code.

1909 The first demonstration of the instantaneous transmission of still silhouette images was by Georges Rignoux and A Fournier in Paris, using a rotating mirror drum as the scanner, and a matrix of 64 selenium cells as the receiver.

The ship RMS Republic was a steam-powered ocean liner built in 1903 by Harland and Wolff in Belfast, and lost at sea in a collision six years later while sailing for the White Star Line. A CQD ('Come Quick, Danger') telegraph distress call was transmitted in Morse code as — · — · — — · — — · · and was one of the first distress signals adopted for radio use. It was announced on 7 January 1904, by 'Circular 57' of the Marconi International Marine Communication Company, and became effective, for Marconi installations, beginning 1 February 1904. The CQD signal was issued on the new Marconi radio telegraph

device resulting in the saving of around 1200 lives. At the time, the RMS Republic was one of the largest and most luxurious liners afloat, although, ironically, she was designed more for safety and sturdiness rather than beauty. The distress signal CQD soon changed to become known as 'SOS'. The SOS signal is a prosign (short for

'procedural signals') meaning that its respective letters have no inherent meaning as such. It was simply chosen as it was easy to remember. The SOS signal has become the commonly used description for the international Morse code distress signal · · · — — — · · ·. This distress signal was first adopted by the German government in radio regulations effective 1 April 1905, and became the worldwide standard under the second International Radiotelegraphic Convention, which was signed on 3 November 1906 and became effective on 1 July 1908. Although the letters have no meaning, over time, the SOS signal became associated with phrases such as 'save our ship' or 'save our souls'.

1910 February and December

General Elections in February and again in December. Liberal Prime Minister, Herbert Asquith.

By this year, ship-to-shore wireless telegraphy messages were commonplace. This was mainly due to the work of Fessenden and De Forest with the USA taking the lead in wireless telephony.

George V reigned as monarch of the United Kingdom from 1910 to 1936. George V's reign began amid the continuing constitutional crisis over the House of Lords, which refused to pass a Parliament Bill limiting its powers (which would remove its

power to veto a Bill from the Commons).
After the Liberal government obtained the
King's promise to create sufficient peers to
overcome Conservative opposition in the
Lords (and won a second election in 1910),
the Parliament Bill was passed by the Lords
in 1911 without a mass creation of peers.

1910 Dr Crippen

For the first time a wireless telegraph transmission
assisted in a criminal arrest; that of Dr Crippen (and
Ethel le Neve).   During their sea voyage from
Antwerp to Canada, Ethel le Neve disguised herself
as a boy. The Montrose's Captain became suspicious
of the couple's affectionate behaviour, and radioed

his concerns back to London. Chief Inspector Drew boarded a
faster ship, the SS Laurentic, and arrested the pair on 31 July 1910
upon disembarkation. The SS Montrose was a transatlantic ocean
liner for Elder, Dempster & Company and the Canadian Pacific
Steamship Company. Crippen was hanged in Pentonville Prison,
London on 23 November 1910, for the murder of his wife, Cora

Crippen. He has gone down in
history as the first criminal to
be captured with the aid of
wireless communication.

1911 Russians Boris Rosing and his student Vladimir Zworykin at
the Petersburg Institute of Technology, created a television system
that used a mechanical mirror-drum scanner to transmit, in
Zworykin's words, "very crude images" over wires to the
electronic Braun CRT as the receiver. Moving images were not
possible because, in the scanner, "the sensitivity was not enough

and the selenium cell was very laggy". The further development of television technology slowed down after 1911 for a number of years.

In the world of wireless, Fleming wrote in the magazine 'The Marconigraph' that he was amazed at messages being received through the ether – rather than across wires.

1911 25 January saw the launch of the Daily Herald, the first newspaper to sell two million copies a day.

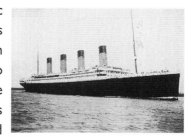

1912 14 April – the RMS Titanic disaster – telegraphy wireless failed to save the day through human error. Had the duty radio officer of the nearest ship, the Carpathia, not switched off his equipment the rescue would have saved many more lives. RMS Titanic was the largest passenger steamship in the world when she set off on her maiden voyage from Southampton, England, to New York City on 10 April 1912. Four days into the crossing, at 23:40 on 14 April 1912, she struck an iceberg and sank at 02:20 the following morning, resulting in the deaths of 1,517 people in one of the deadliest peacetime maritime disasters in history.

With the Marconi company in New York the young radio operator David Sarnoff was said to be the first to intercept the SOS call and to report that the Titanic was sinking. Aboard RMS Titanic radio operator Jack Phillips initially sent the 'CQD' signal, still commonly used by British ships. Harold Bride, the junior radio operator aboard ship, jokingly suggested the new code 'SOS' be used, thinking it might be the only time he would get to use it.

The synchronized Kinetscope

1913 The Wireless society was formed in London. This year, Thomas Edison introduced an improved version of his Kinetoscope. This time, the sound was made to synchronize with a motion picture projected onto a screen. A celluloid cylinder record measuring 5 ½ inches in diameter was used for the phonograph. Synchronization was achieved by connecting the projector at one end of the theatre and the phonograph at the other end with a long pulley. Nineteen talking pictures were produced this year by Edison.

1913 On 12 April, the New Statesman Newspaper was founded.

1914 The First World War started. The use and development of radio telegraphy during the war years was considerable. At a political level the value of point-to-point telegraphy was significant during the Great War. Manufacturers of wireless receiving equipment were keen to encourage the sale of receivers which became known as the wireless. Manufactures pestered government to allow regular entertainment broadcasts.

This year, Russian Isaac Shoenberg emigrated to London. He then joined the Marconi Wireless and Telegraph Company and soon became head of patents and then general manager. An enthusiast for music and sound recording, he moved to the Columbia Gramophone Company as general manager in 1928. Three years later, following a merger, the company assumed the name Electric and Musical Industries Ltd. (EMI) and Shoenberg became head of research and patents.

1915 14 March saw the launch of the Sunday Pictorial newspaper which became the Sunday Mirror in 1963.

1915 John Logie Baird was turned down for military service.

1918 🐾 The end of the Great War. The United Kingdom had a Liberal Prime Minister, David Lloyd George. He was the first Welshman to be Prime Minister, and the last Liberal Prime Minister.

1918 29 December saw the launch of the Sunday Express newspaper.

1919 David Sarnoff became a pioneer of American commercial radio and television. Throughout most of his career he led the Radio Corporation of America (RCA) in various capacities from office boy to President. He was to form the NBC television network and do important work during the Second World War. He was the first American to recognise the potential of the wireless for entertainment rather than just for information. In later years, he was to pioneer the development of television in the USA.

First USA radio

1920 The first American radio station goes on the air – KDKA in Pittsburgh.

The first official UK radio broadcast by Guglielmo Marconi who transmitted Dame Nellie Melba singing from Chelmsford on 15 June.

1920s Another format war took place. 78 rpm gramophone record format war: lateral vs vertical 'hill-and-dale' groove cutting.

When Edison finally introduced his 'diamond disc' (using a diamond instead of a steel needle), it was cut 'hill-and-dale', meaning that the groove modulated on the vertical axis as it had on all cylinders – unlike other manufacturers' disks which were cut laterally, meaning that the groove modulated on the horizontal axis. In 1929, Thomas Edison bowed out of the record industry altogether, ceasing all production of his disks, and cylinders which he had also manufactured up to that point. In addition, there were several more minor format wars between the various brands using various speeds ranging from 72 to 96 rpm. The Edison

A JOLLY EVENING IN YOUR OWN HOME.

disks rotated at about 80 rpm. In 1958, the stereophonic record was introduced which uses perpendicular modulations for each channel, providing backward compatibility to the lateral-cut monaural recording.

News for the general public came mostly through cinema screens. This period saw the newsreels' popularity increase significantly, and there was fierce competition among the production companies. There were also some new arrivals; Empire Screen News launched in 1926 and British Screen News opened in 1928. The latter title survived for about four years. The decade also saw several newsreel companies launching cine magazines, which offered audiences coverage of lighter stories and a wider range of subject matter. Some titles were created especially for female audiences, for instance, Eve's Film Review, which was launched by Pathe. The decade also saw the introduction of 'super' reels which, running for nearly 10 minutes, lasted almost twice as long as the ordinary newsreels. There were also changes in ownership; the British interests of the Gaumont, and later Pathe, both passed to British companies.

More work on the CRT

1921 Vladimir K Zworykin did more work on his CRT-type device that would convert patterns of light into electronic impulses – the kinescope. In later years, the eventual cathode ray tube – CRT had a vacuum tube containing an electron gun (a source of electrons) and a

fluorescent screen, with internal or external means to accelerate and deflect the electron beam, used to create images in the form of light emitted from the fluorescent screen.

How the CRT was to operate

1. Three Electron guns (for red, green, and blue phosphor dots)

2. Electron

3. Focusing

4. Deflection

5. Anode

6. Mask for separating beams for red, green, and blue part of displayed image

7. Phosphor layer with red, green, and blue zones

8. Close-up of the phosphor-coated inner side of the screen (television, computer monitor), radar targets and others.

Jack Demsey fight broadcast on RCA

David Sarnoff now at RCA (Radio Company of America), who bought Marconi America, contributed to the rising postwar radio boom by helping arrange for the radio broadcast of a heavyweight boxing match between Jack Dempsey and Georges Carpentier in July of this year. 300,000 listened to the fight on radio.

Albert Einstein

Albert Einstein is best known for his theories of special relativity and general relativity. He received the 1921 Nobel Prize in Physics for his services to Theoretical Physics, and especially for his discovery of the law of the photoelectric effect which is a phenomenon in which electrons are emitted from matter (metals and non-metallic solids, liquids or gases) as a consequence of their absorption of energy from electromagnetic radiation of very short wavelength, such as visible or ultraviolet light. Electrons emitted in this manner may be referred to as photoelectrons. As it was first observed by Heinrich Hertz in 1887 the phenomenon is also known as the Hertz effect although the latter term has fallen out of general use. Hertz observed and then showed that electrodes illuminated with ultraviolet light create electric sparks more easily.

1922 The Coalition Government breaks up and the BBC broadcasts the election results for the first time.

General Election. Conservative Prime Minister, Andrew Bonar Law. Poor health forced Bonar Law to resign in May 1923.

The first regular wireless broadcast in the UK was started this year by the Marconi Company from London. Wireless manufacturers talked to the Post Office on 18 May about the future of wireless broadcasting. (N.B. The term 'broadcasting' came from the original agricultural term, meaning 'scattering seeds widely'.)

1922 Radio manufacturers create the BBC

The cartel of radio manufacturers meeting at the Post Office in May was headed by Scotsman John Reith (1889–1971). He became the founder of the commercial BBC this same year, as Managing Director, concentrating only on the development of wireless broadcasting. The Chairman was Lord Gainsford. The BBC was formed as a result of agreements reached at the meeting. The first BBC broadcast on wireless was on 14 November – although the company was not formed until 15 December and not licensed until the next year. It had a staff of four, and was financed by a Post  Office licence fee of 10 shillings, payable by anyone owning a receiver, and supplemented by royalties on radio sales. The first broadcast came from London on 14 November, and 'listening-in' quickly became a popular pastime.

1923 John Logie Baird's early work on television in Hastings

Baird appears to have arrived in Hastings in the winter of 1922 when he fell ill and was advised to leave London. He came to Hastings to join his old Glasgow school friend, Guy Robertson, known as 'Mephy', with whom he had shared lodgings in London the previous year. Mephy was then living at 21 Linton Crescent

and this is where Baird joined him.
Over the following 18 months Baird
worked on his invention – albeit a
crude system. It was in Hastings that
Baird produced the first shadowy
outline of an object, the shape of a
Maltese Cross, in his lodgings (the home of Mr and Mrs Charles
Wheatley). An official blue plaque marks the house where this
took place. Hastings Museum now holds various pieces of related

 correspondence. During the spring of
1923, Baird seems to have developed
his apparatus with the help of Mephy
to the extent that, on 27 June, he put
an advert in The Times, 'Seeing by
wireless. Inventor of apparatus wishes
to hear from someone who will assist,
not financially, in making working
model'. As a result of this, the editor of 'Broadcasting' magazine
and the Chief Research Engineer at the BBC came down to
Hastings to visit him and, subsequently, sent down some
equipment. He was also contacted by a London cinema owner,
Will Day, and together, they entered a partnership and applied

for Baird's first patent for a system of
transmitting views, portraits and 'Scenes by
telegraphy or wireless telegraphy' on 26 July
1923. In November 1923, an account of his
experiments in Hastings appeared in Chamber's
Journal. It seems that by late 1923, Baird had
succeeded in transmitting shadowy images
although the receiver and transmitter were still
mechanically connected.

Others, around the world, were working on their version of television – in the USSR and the USA.

1923 🗳 General Election.Labour Prime Minister, Ramsay MacDonald. This was the first Labour Government working with the support of the Liberals. It was the beginning of the two party system of the UK. A Labour government or a Conservative government with the Liberals running in third place.

1924 New Conservative Prime Minister, Stanley Baldwin.

The creation of the BBC

The BBC was licensed on 18 January this year by the Postmaster General under the Wireless Telegraphy Act 1904, before being established as a public body by Royal Charter in 1927. The first BBC radio broadcast of the daily weather forecast occurred this year.

1924 Baird's plaque in Hastings

By April 1924, Baird had moved his workshop out of his lodgings at 21 Linton Crescent and moved to the upper floor of No 8 Queen's Avenue. He was able to do this because his father, John Baird, the retired Presbyterian Minister of West Parish Church, Helensburgh read in the national press of his demonstration and sent a £50 donation. In February this year, John Logie Baird had entered the shop of Hasting radio dealer Victor Mill and asked for assistance, saying "I've fitted up an apparatus for transmitting pictures and I can't get it to go." Mills accompanied Baird back to his laboratory/apartment and waved his hand in front of the neon when Baird shouted "It's here, it's here!"– the first real-time moving picture in world history had occurred. In July this year, Baird received a 1000-volt electric shock, but fortunately survived with only a burnt hand. His landlord in Hastings, Alderman Ben Tree (four times Mayor of Hastings), asked him to quit his workshop. Baird referred to Mr Tree as Mr Twigg. Baird moved to London to further develop his invention. Some years later the Hastings town council affixed a little plaque above the entrance to the attic over Mr Tree's shop – 'Queen's Arcade, Hastings. Television first demonstrated by John Logie Baird from experiments started here in 1924'.

1924 On 2 November, the Sunday Express published the first crossword in a British newspaper.

1924 The Sykes Committee

In this year, the Government set up the Sykes Committee to look at the regulation of wireless broadcast. It reported to Parliament in August with the following recommendations:

- A single broadcast licence of 10 shillings a year be charged to households buying or making receiver sets – the income being shared between the BBC and the Post Office.

- No advertising allowed.

- The setting up of a Board to whom complaints could be addressed.

- The BBC should move into public ownership at some time into the future – this took place in 1927.

This year saw 595,496 wireless licences bought from the Post Office. Wireless manufacturers reported that 'receiving sets' were being bought by the middle and upper classes. The cost of sets represented about

20 or so weeks wages for the working classes. Typically, a top-of-the-range four valve cabinet receiver would cost £50. Most commonly an outside aerial was also required for a good wireless signal.

Wireless listings begins

On New Year's Day, The Times newspaper started to list BBC planned broadcasts without charge – but by 13 January the BBC were asked to pay the normal advertising rates. John Reith refused because he believed that to include radio times in a newspaper listing would increase the circulation of the newspaper. Reith persuaded Gordon Selfridge (Selfridges Store) to include programme listings in its adverts in the London Pall Mall Gazette – and circulation rapidly increased. On 10 May, Reith persuaded his own board of directors to produce its own magazine. The first issue of the Radio Times (costing two pence – N.B. 240 pence to the pound) was on 28 September and sold 250,000 copies listing programme times for all six BBC stations:

- 2LO London
- 5WA Cardiff
- 5IT Birmingham
- 5NO Newcastle
- 2ZY Manchester
- 5SC Glasgow

1924 Television invention progresses

On 14 June this year American, Charles F Jenkins made his first experimental wireless television transmissions with a mechanical system (using the Nipkow (1884) disk) from the Navy radio station in Anacostia to his Jenkins Laboratories office in Washington.

This year, Vladimir Zworkin (see 1921) patented his iconscope; a TV camera tube based on Campbell-Swinton's ideas (see 1907). The iconscope, which he called an electric eye became the cornerstone for further television development. Zworkin later developed the kinescope for picture display.

John Logie Baird made his early crude apparatus of odds and ends and by this year he managed to transmit a flickering image across a few feet.

Also in this year Philo Farnsworth, an American, came up with his ideas for broadcast television, and Baird was granted a British patent for his 'system of transmitting views, portraits and scenes'.

This year saw 1,129,578 wireless licences bought from the Post Office.

1925 First public demonstration of television by Baird

On 25 March, through Gordon Selfridge Jr, John Logie Baird gave a series of demonstrations of his televised silhouette images in motion at Selfridge's Department Store in London. Baird was paid £60 for three demonstrations a day for three weeks.

1925 Francis Jenkins makes progress

The American company, General Electric began with mechanical scanning for television. For the company, Francis Jenkins was able to demonstrate on 13 June the transmission of the silhouette image of a toy windmill in motion from a naval radio station to his laboratory in Washington, USA, using a lensed disc scanner with 48 lines per picture transmitting 16 pictures per second. However, Jenkins never achieved transmission of television content to a viewing audience.

1925 The date of the invention of television

This year saw Baird improving his mechanical system to transmit

his image of the ventriloquist's dilapidated dummy 'Stookey Bill' with real detail. Baird is recorded as saying that the head formed itself on the screen with "almost unbelievable clarity". Baird then ran down to the office below and hauled office boy William Taynton upstairs and put him in front of the transmitter. Baird then went to the receiving end to see the flickering but clearly recognisable image of William's face – the first face to be seen on television. Baird paid William 2/6d. Baird achieved this on 30 October 1925 at 22 Frith Street, Soho, London W1. This is the date that most historians record as the date television was invented (but not broadcast). It is recognized that others played a key role in the developments of the components of television – especially the Paul Nipkow disk.

Looking for publicity (and funding) Baird visited the Daily Express newspaper offices to promote his invention. The news editor was terrified. Later he was quoted by one of his staff as saying:"For God's sake, go down to reception and get rid of a lunatic who's down there. He says he's got a machine for seeing by wireless! Watch him – he may have a razor on him."

1925 Television by different frequencies

Baird saw Dr Edmond Fournier D'Albe as his main competition. D'Albe's idea was to achieve the transmission of images by sending out every spot of the picture on a different frequency, But this approach proved to be impractical and was not pursed.

Baird was also aware of the work of A A CampbellSwinton and in his own words said "… perhaps fortunately for me (he) abandoned his work."

1925 Television invented in America?

Baird also knew of the work of Jenkins. In the United States, Charles Francis Jenkins (earlier a pioneer of the movie projector) was a leading inventor and promoter of mechanical scanning television and largely responsible for the strong and passionate interest in television in the 1920s and early 1930s. His work in mechanical television paralleled the work of John Logie Baird in England. Jenkins also provided a television demonstration in the USA on 13 June this year – less than three months after the similar demonstration by Baird in England. Jenkins' demonstration, using mechanical scanning at both the

transmitting and receiving ends, consisted of crude silhouette moving images called 'shadowgraphs'. This early work in mechanical scanning television helped lay the foundation for later all-electronic television. Jenkins was continually frustrated by the insensitivity of the photo-cells he used. In the USA, the first public demonstration was achieved by the American Telegraph Company in January 1926 (see later), some fourteen months after Baird's demonstration.

1926 Britain's only general strike, widely broadcast by BBC radio

On 14 July, the Postmaster General announced in the House of Commons the acceptance of the recommendations of the Crawford Committee (set up the previous year) and proposed the Royal Charter for the BBC. The Charter was granted for a 10 year period from 1 January of the following year. Whilst the new BBC did not have a monopoly, no other broadcaster had been licensed by the Post Office.

Radio in the USA

From the organization of the first true radio networks in the late 1920s, broadcasting in the United States was dominated by two companies, CBS and RCA's NBC. Before NBC's 1926 formation, RCA had acquired AT&T's New York station WEAF (later WNBC, now CBS-owned WFAN). With WEAF came a loosely organized system feeding programming to other stations in the northeastern United. States. RCA, before the acquisition of the WEAF group in mid-1926, had previously owned a second such group, with WJZ in New York as the lead station (purchased by RCA in 1923 from Westinghouse). These were the foundations of RCA's two distinct programming services, the NBC 'Red' and NBC 'Blue' networks. Legend has it that the colour designations originated from the colour of the push-pins early engineers used to designate affiliates of WEAF (red pins) and WJZ (blue pins).

Creation of NBC

This year in America, the RCA-owned NBC television network

was headquartered in the GE Building in New York City's Rockefeller Center with additional major offices in Burbank, California. It is sometimes referred to as the Peacock Network, due to its stylized peacock logo, created originally for colour broadcasts in later years. Formed this year by the Radio Corporation of America (RCA), NBC was the first major broadcast network in the United States.

The first true television system (with gradations of light and shade) was demonstrated by John Logie Baird to members of the Royal Institution and a reporter from The Times newspaper, on

January 26 this year. The demonstration took place at 22 Frith Street in the Soho district of London (see later). Some reported that the mechanical picture was of poor quality.

Leon Theremin

Leon Theremin increased his television resolution to 32 lines and eventually achieved 64 lines using interlacing. The interlaced scan refers to one of two common methods for 'painting' a picture image on an electronic display screen (the other being progressive scan) by scanning or displaying each line. This technique uses two fields to create a frame. One field contains all the odd lines of the image, the other contains all the even lines of the image. Thermin electrically transmitted and then

projected near-simultaneous moving images on a five foot square screen. The technology was first patented by German Telefunken engineer, Fritz Scroter in 1930.

Boris Grabovsky and Campbell-Swinton

Soviet inventor Boris Grabovsky claimed to have made the first electronic broadcast. Logie Baird thought his 'televisor' system, using mechanical picture scanning (with the Nipkow disk rather than electronic scanning (CRT) as developed by Campbell-Swinton), with electronic amplification at the transmitter and at the receiver, was still viable.

1926 Baird's public demonstration

Baird knew that two sources of light sensitive devices existed at that time – the photo-electric cell and the selenium cell. Baird chose the selenium route because he considered it was more sensitive. 30 Members of the Royal Institution and other visitors went to the laboratory in an upper room at 2 Frith Street, Soho, London W1 on 26 January. They saw a demonstration of apparatus invented by Baird. They were shown a transmitting machine, consisting of a large wooden revolving disc containing lenses, behind which was a revolving shutter and a light sensitive cell. It was explained that by means of the shutter and lens disc an image of articles or persons standing in front of the machine could be made to pass over  the light sensitive cell at 'high speed' – 30 lines per second. The current in the cell varies in proportion to the light falling on it, and this varying current is transmitted to a receiver where it controls a light behind an optical arrangement similar to that at the sending end. By this means, a point of light is caused to traverse

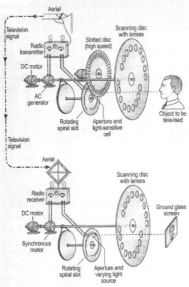

a ground glass screen. The light is dim at the shadows and bright at the highlights, and crosses the screen so rapidly that the whole image appears simultaneously to the eye. The diagram was used by Baird in an article for the Journal of Scientific Instruments in January 1927. This diagram was redrawn by Robert Britton of the National Museum of Scotland.

1926 The BBC reputation

The BBC was very wary of Baird's experiments, being concerned for their own reputation for high technical standards. There was talk of animosity between the two Scotsmen (Reith and Baird). When he discovered the unoffical use of the radio network to broadcast Baird's 30-line pictures Reith stopped it. Baird decided to build his own transmitter (callsign 2TV) and continued to conduct his broadcast experiments.

This year saw 2,178,259 wireless licences bought from the Post Office.

1927 Formation of the RTS (Royal Television Society)

The Society began as a meeting place for television engineers, and the earliest records chart the birth of television and document the

ROYAL TELEVISION SOCIETY

pioneering work of, amongst others, John Logie Baird. For 40 years the Society held regular meetings throughout the country where lectures were presented on the latest technical developments of the

television receiver. The importance of these lectures was acknowledged with awards from the television companies. These awards have since grown to become a key feature of the Society's work.

1927 Braille Radio Times

The BBC first published a Braille version of the Radio Times for the blind.

1927 Television over telephone wires

This year, Baird television was demonstrated over 438 miles of telephone line between London and Glasgow, and Baird formed the Baird Television Development Company (BTDC).

First video recorder

This year, John Logie Baird invented the world's first video recording system, 'Phonovision'. By modulating the output signal of his TV camera down to the audio range, he was able to capture the signal on a 10-inch wax audio disc using conventional audio recording technology. A handful of Baird's 'Phonovision' recordings survive and these were finally decoded and rendered into viewable images in the 1990s using modern digital signal-processing technology. Phonovision is a proof of concept format and experiment for recording a television signal on phonograph records. The format was developed in this year. The objective was not simply to record video, but to record it synchronously, as Baird intended playback from an inexpensive playback device, which he called a 'Phonovisor'.

1927 Herbert E. Ives

Ives of Bell Labs in America transmitted moving images from a 50-aperture disc producing 16 frames per minute over a cable from Washington, DC to New York City, and via radio from Whippany, New Jersey. Ives used viewing screens as large as 24 by 30 inches (60 by 75 centimeters). His subjects included the US Secretary of Commerce who commented, "... today we have, in a sense, the transmission of sight for the first time in the world's history. Human genius has now destroyed the impediment of distance in a new respect, and in a manner hitherto unknown."

Philo Farnsworth

Farnsworth invented an early television system, which he conceived of while ploughing his father's Idaho (USA) potato field at age 14. He filed for and was granted a patent which he called the Image Dissector. He also helped to develop radar. On 7 September in this year, he transmitted the first American image on television in San Francisco. The first person whose image appeared on TV was his wife, Pem Farnsworth.

BBC given its first Royal Charter

The BBC changed from a commercial organisation to a public company, through Royal Charter. Sir John Reith (later Lord Reith) was its first Director General as it became a corporation – the 'British Broadcasting Corporation' (formerly the British Broadcasting Company).

1927 BellTelevision

The American AT&T company – through its Bell Laboratories – demonstrated its television system this year. The first politician on TV was the American Herbert Hoover (later 31st USA President 1929–1933) giving a speech broadcast by wire (not by radio) from Washington and watched in New York by an invited audience. The New York Times reported that it was "like a photo come to life". The same year AT&T did achieve broadcast by radio from Washington to New York, both sound and pictures. In that same year, in Los Angeles, Philo Farnsworth produced an electronic system that worked in the laboratory.

As mentioned, this was also the year when Baird transmitted a long-distance television signal over 438 miles of telephone wires between London and Glasgow. Leon Theremin achieved an image resolution of 100 lines. The Japanese engineer Kenjiro Takayanagi transmitted his facial image. The Soviet Union was also experimenting with electronic systems at the Leningrad Polytechnic Institute.

1927 Echophone

This year saw Kurt Stille forming the Echophone Company in Germany with Karl Bauer, and contracting with Ferdinand

Schuchard to invent magnetic recording tape.

1927/8 Transatlantic television

This year, the BTDC (Baird Television) achieved the first transatlantic television transmission between London and New York, and the first transmission to a ship in mid-Atlantic.

1927 The mirror drum

At the Berlin Radio Exhibition, Hungarian D Von Mihaly demonstrated his mechanical system with a mirror-drum – later to be adopted by Baird himself. In America, there were now 18 experimental television stations, mostly comprising 48-line transmission.

1927 Videophone

Bell Laboratories in the USA constructed a mechanically scanned videophone which never went into production. Videophones haven't caught on – even today, although Skype became its equivalent in August 2003.

First Television in the USA

1928 The first regularly scheduled television service in the United States began on 2 July. The Federal Radio Commission authorized C F Jenkins to broadcast from experimental station W3XK in Wheaton, Maryland, a suburb of Washington, D.C. Separately, the CBS network had its origins in United Independent Broadcasters Inc., a collection of 16 radio stations that was bought by William S Paley in 1928 and renamed the Columbia Broadcasting System. Under Paley's guidance, CBS would first become one of the largest radio networks in the United States and then one of the big three American broadcast television networks.

1928 First mass-produced television set

This year, Baird built a television receiving set and demonstrated it at the National Radio Exhibition in London. One visitor to the exhibition, Percy Packman, who was an engineer at the Plessey Electrical Company, offered to

1930 Baird "Televisor"

make improvements to Baird's cabinet. Baird was very pleased with the result and Plessey built 1000 of the sets between 1929 and 1931. This was the first mass produced television set and was named by Baird as the 'Televisior'.

1929 🗳 General Election. Labour Prime Minister, Ramsay MacDonald.

First broadcast television by Baird

The BBC Radio Times announced a regular series of experimental television transmissions by the Baird process for half an hour every morning. The first broadcast was on 30 September from Baird's studio in Covent Garden.

Circulation of the Radio Times reached 1.147m. Radio had become one of the first social inclusion tools allowing equal access to those who could afford a wireless receiver.

RCA interested in television

When David Sarnoff was put in charge of radio broadcasting at RCA, he soon recognized the potential for television. RCA began daily mechanical/experimental television broadcasts in New York

City in March this year over station W2XBS. The 60-line transmissions consisted of pictures, signs, and views of persons and objects, but Sarnoff was not satisfied with the quality of the pictures. This same year, the young USA Russian immigrant Vladimir K. Zworykin had a meeting with RCA's David Sarnoff. He told Sarnoff that he could build an electronic television system

for $100,000. Sarnoff agreed to fund the development work, and commented later that Zworykin was as good a salesman as he was an inventor. Sarnoff was determined for his company to pioneer the medium and so he had agreed to meet with the Westinghouse engineer Vladimir  Zworykin who at the time was developing an all-electronic television system in his spare time on the company premises. Zworykin told Sarnoff he could build a viable television system in two years with the $100,000 grant, but the estimate was off by several orders of magnitude and by several years in time.

The final cost of this enterprise was closer to $50 million. On the road to success, they also encountered a battle with the young inventor Philo T Farnsworth, who had been granted patents in 1930 for his solution to broadcasting moving pictures. Eventually Sarnoff was ordered to pay him $1,000,000 in royalties.

This year, Sarnoff engineered the purchase of the Victor Talking Machine Company, the nation's largest manufacturer of records and phonographs, merging radio-phonograph production at Victor's large manufacturing facility in Camden, New Jersey.

The USA depression started this year and the value of RCA dropped to one fifth of its previous value.

1929 BBC interested in television

The BBC became involved in television
development from this year. In France, 30-line
pictures had been demonstrated. The first
experimental British television broadcast, in
September, was made by Baird Television's electromechanical
system over the BBC radio transmitter – just 30 lines of
resolution. Baird named his world's first television 'station' 2TV,
but this brand name was not recognized or used by the BBC.

1929 Acknowledged by Hastings

On 7 November, the Mayor of Hastings (Cllr.
Thorpe) unveiled a commemorative plaque to L
Baird in Queens Arcade, Hastings, West Sussex.

1930 Television sets on sale in the UK

Baird provided a limited amount of programming five days a week,
broadcast after the BBC radio broadcasts closed each night.
Optimistically, Baird installed a Baird 'Televisior' at 10 Downing
Street for Prime Minister,
Ramsey McDonald. The
following week (5 April
1930), Ramsey MacDonald
wrote to Baird: "When I look
at the transmissions I feel
that the most wonderful
miracle is being done under
my eye. ... You have put
something in my room which
will never let me forget how
strange is this world." Later

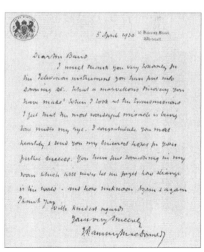

that year Baird Televisions went on general sale for 25 guineas (£26.25). The average weekly wage was £2.10s (£2.50). Only a few were sold to richer, more inquisitive people. BBC television in these early years had a very small reach to just a few hundred sets in the London region.

USA television

Philo Farnsworth was granted an American patent for electronic television – despite objections from David Sarnoff's RCA/NBC who (unsuccessfully) tried to buy the patent. The Leon Theremin work of 1926 was patented in Germany by the Telefunken engineer, Fritz Scroter.

David Sarnoff became president of RCA on 3 January this year succeeding General James Harbord. On 30 May, the company was involved in an antitrust case concerning the original radio patent pool. Sarnoff's tenacity and intelligence were able to negotiate an outcome where RCA was no longer partly owned by Westinghouse and General Electric, giving him the final say in the company's affairs. Initially, the Great Depression caused RCA to cut costs, but Zworykin's project was protected. After nine years of Zworykin's hard work, Sarnoff's determination, and legal battles with Farnsworth (in which Farnsworth was proved in the right), they had a commercial system ready to launch.

Hertz

In this year, the unit hertz (Hz) was established in honour of Heinrich Rudolf Hertz by the IEC for frequency, a measurement of the number of times that a repeated event occurs per unit of time (also called 'cycles per second' (cps)). It was to be adopted by the CGPM (Conférence générale des poids et mesures) in 1964.

1931  General Election. Conservative Prime Minister, Stanley Baldwin leading a National Government to deal with the Great Depression and General Strike which was a ten year world economic crisis that left millions unemployed.

In America, W2XCR television first aired their regular broadcasting debut in New York City on 26 April with a special demonstration set up in Aeolian Hall at Fifth Avenue and Fifty-fourth Street. Thousands waited to catch a glimpse of the Broadway stars who appeared on the six-inch (15 cm) square image, in an evening event to publicize a weekday programming schedule offering films and live entertainers during the four-hour daily broadcasts. Appearing were boxer Primo Carnera, actors Gertrude Lawrence, Louis Calhern, Frances Upton and Lionel Atwill, WHN announcer Nils Granlund, the Forman Sisters, and a host of others.

Vladimir Zworykin, now working at RCA had decided to develop a new type of cathode ray pickup tube, one described in French and British patents of 1928 priority by Hungarian inventor, Kalman Tihanyi, whom RCA had approached in July 1930, after the publication of his patents in England and France. Tihanyi's tube,

the 'Radioskop' was a system characterized by an operation based on an entirely new principle; the principle of the accumulation and storage of charges during the entire time between picture repetitions. RCA began experiments on these principles in April this year, and after the achievement of the first promising experimental cameras, on 23 October it was decided: this new camera tube would be named 'Iconoscope'. At this time, EMI was still considering investing in the development of television, but was unsure about taking such a risk. Being a patent expert, Shoenberg persuaded EMI management to fund a similar project, as development in England by the British firm EMI could also follow the original charge storage design. An excellent research and development team at EMI was quickly assembled by Shoenberg. His team succeeded in making their first electronic television picture-generating tubes in 1932. Schoenberg's team, Alan Dower Blumlein, J D McGee and W F Tedham, initially secretly, managed to transmit a picture all-electronically across their laboratory. The picture was crude but, undeterred, Shoenberg and the EMI team continued with further research.

Television in Russia

The USSR began 30-line electromechanical television test broadcasts in Moscow. RCA in America had by then developed an electromechanical television system with 120 lines.

1931 First BBC outside broadcast

In this year, Baird transmitted, for the BBC, live coverage of the Derby from Epsom. However, the picture was so poor that the viewer could not discern one horse or jockey from another.

1931 Baird changes his design

This year, Baird designed a new television camera to improve the picture quality. He replaced the Nipkow disc with a mirror drum. This was a rotating drum fitted to a series of mirrors – one for each line of resolution.

1932 The creation of EMI

EMI was created this year from a merger of companies with RCA as a shareholder.

1932 BBC moves offices

The BBC moved from its offices in Savoy Hill on the London embankment to its purpose built offices/studios at Broadcasting House in Portland Place, London.

First Empire Address by King George V, 25 December 1932

The first Christmas Day message by a British monarch was in 1932, when King George V broadcast live from Sandringham. In the speech, which was written by Rudyard Kipling, the King celebrated the power of the wireless to unite all the people of the Empire, and wished them a Happy Christmas. He began: "Through one of the marvels of modern science, I am enabled, this Christmas Day, to speak to all my peoples throughout the Empire."

Developments at EMI

Between 1932 and34, EMI's electronic television demonstrations were usually done in private and were proving relatively disappointing. The cameras were insensitive to light, and there were problems with secondary emission and 'tilt and bend'

distortion. The EMI mirror-drum cameras, approaching 180 lines, still provided a superior picture to the electronic cameras. In early 1934, EMI joined forces with the

Marconi Wireless and Telegraph
Company (MWT) to form the
Marconi-EMI Television Company.
MWT engineers would be able to
handle the transmitter side of the

television system. The more significant advantage of the
amalgamation however was that Shoenberg's team could use
RCA's electronic television patents and other technology
(including Zworykin's Iconoscope patents). By April 1934, after
further modifications, Marconi-EMI's experimental camera was
yielding vastly better pictures. They named their successful
camera tube the 'Emitron'.

3-D movies

Edwin H Land (co-founder of the Polaroid Corporation) patented
a process for producing polarized filters that eventually led to
the development of full colour 3-D movies. This was possible
because the left/right separation could be achieved using the
polarizing filters rather than the colour channel. Land also
perfected a 3-D photographic process called vectography. During
the Second World War vectographic prints were used widely for
military applications such as aerial photography.

Demonstrations to the BBC

This year, the UK government 'owning' the
radio spectrum employed for terrestrial
broadcasting wanted control of its use. The
BBC was licensed by the Postmaster General
to launch the experimental service using

Baird's 30-line electromechanical television system. EMI was most
annoyed – they demonstrated their electronic system to the

BBC. The new Chief Engineer, Noel Ashbridge inspected the equipment for the BBC and declared it to be "By far the best wireless television." Baird was said to be furious.

1932 BBC radio Empire Service

The British Broadcasting Corporation (BBC) first broadcast radio outside Britain in December. Overseas radio broadcasts on the 'Empire Service' (later to become the BBC World Service) were meant to unite the English-speaking peoples of what was then the British Empire.

British Movietone News

The first British cinema sound newsreel to be launched this year was British Movietone News. The Empire Screen News disappeared but its counterpart, Universal Talking News, launched. It dropped the 'Talking' from its banner in the mid-1930s. Pathe continued in business and produced several discrete silent and sound titles.  Gaumont British – the company had modified its name when its ownership had changed in the 1920s – produced Gaumont Graphic (a silent newsreel) and Gaumont Sound News (a sound version of the silent newsreel).

Baird v Marconi

There was increasing awareness by BBC engineers that the EMI system was much better than Baird's equipment.

The Iconoscope camera

Zworykin created his iconoscope camera for Sarnoff at RCA with 240 lines of resolution. The Iconoscope (from the Greek: εἰκών 'image' and σκοπεῖν 'to look, to see') was the name given to the early television camera tube in  which a beam of high-velocity electrons scans a mosaic of photo-emissive isolated granules. Some of the principles of this apparatus were described when Vladimir Zworykin filed two patents for a Television system back in 1923 and 1925.

Radio Luxembourg

1933 Radio Luxembourg started this year on frequency 1440 AM. It had a very powerful transmitter to reach across Europe – reaching parts of the east of the UK.  It was owned by a French company and promised international broadcasts which would not favour any nation. The English service was handled by an agency ('Radio Publicity Of London'). They appointed 23 year old Stephen Williams who had been directing English programmes at Radio Paris to be principal announcer from December this year, with several hundred records and a couple of hampers of musical arrangements.

FM radio

Radio's premier inventor, Edwin H Armstrong was responsible for the Regenerative Circuit (1912), the Super-heterodyne Circuit (1918), the Super-regenerative Circuit (1922) and the complete FM System by this year. His inventions and developments form the backbone of radio communication as we know it today in the analogue format. Previously radio broadcast was only in the AM frequency. Even though he had improved AM radio in significant ways, Armstrong was well aware of AM radio's major limitations: static interference from household appliances and lighting, limited audio quality (frequency response and dynamic range), nighttime interference between many stations (co-channel interference) because of ionospheric refraction, especially in rural areas.

Armstrong took his FM invention to a friend, David Sarnoff, who was head of RCA and had said he would help him develop it. RCA bought into the patents and helped Armstrong develop an experimental radio station. But it then became evident that Sarnoff and RCA were out to protect their existing AM radio empire and they didn't want the competition from a new and much better form of radio. Years of costly legal battles ensued that RCA could afford and Armstrong could not. Among other things, RCA closed down the FM station that they had helped Armstrong build. Strongly believing in his invention, Armstrong started to develop FM radio on his own. He

sold rights to manufacture FM radios to several companies. Although Armstrong tried to fight for his superior radio system, RCA continued to tie him up with years of legal battles. These both sapped his creative energies and drained his financial resources. On 31 January 1954, Edwin Armstrong gave up his long, taxing battle against Sarnoff and

RCA. He wrote a note to his wife apologizing for what he was about to do, removed the air conditioner from his 13th story New York apartment, and jumped to his death. A few weeks later RCA announced record profits. Armstrong never lived to see the great success of his invention. Nor will we know what other inventions this genius of electronics might have contributed if his personal and financial resources hadn't been devastated by years of legal battles. Once FM radio started to make money, RCA quickly started pushing its development and subsequently made millions of dollars from the sale of FM transmitters and equipment.

1934 Circulation of the BBC Radio Times reached 2.15m.

1934 German, Joseph Begun built the world's first sound tape recorder used for broadcasting.

1934 Marconi-EMI was formed.

1934 The BBC's first Director of Television was appointed – Gerald Cock, who predicted that feature films would not be broadcast on television.

1934 On 5 January, television listings appeared in the Radio Times for the first time.

1934 The earlier television newsreels were replaced this year by Gaumont British News.

First BBC test card

The first testcard 'Tuning Signals' was broadcast by the BBC, the earliest being a simple line and circle broadcast using Baird's 30-line system, and used to synchronise the mechanical scanning system. The test card literally was a card, a photograph with a camera pointing at it. And hence the name test card. When a television was installed in the home, the engineer would turn the set on and look at the test card to see that it was properly tuned in, properly focused and had the right sort of brightness and contrast. The test card would have been on our screens every day, even Saturdays and Sundays, when there were no programmes on, and was likely to have been eight hours a day.

1934 In August this year in America, Philo Farnsworth demonstrated an all-electronic system at the Franklin Institute in Philadelphia which pointed out the direction of television's future.

1934 On 18 October, the Daily Mail published the first photograph that was transmitted by beam radio (from Australia to London).

1935 📺 General Election. Conservative Prime Minister, Stanley Baldwin.

In the UK, the BBC was licensed to provide a public television service. The USA demonstrates television at the Radio City studios in New York. By this year, low-definition electromechanical television broadcasting had ceased in the United States except for a handful of stations, run by public universities, that continued to 1939. The Federal Communications Commission saw television in the continual flux of development with no consistent technical standards, hence all such stations in the United States were granted only experimental and not commercial licences, hampering television's economic development.

20th Century Fox

The 20th Century Fox film company was formed this year. It was one of the six major American film studios And was located in the Century City area of Los Angeles, just west of Beverly Hills. Fox was destined to become part of the News Corporation in the 20th Century and influential in the naming of Fox Television in the USA. The original Fox Film Corporation was founded by William Fox in 1915, and Twentieth Century Pictures, was

started in 1933 by Darryl F Zanuck, Joseph Schenck, Raymond Griffith and William Goetz.

1936 King Edward VIII inherited the monarchy on 20 January this year. Edward VIII became the only British sovereign to abdicate voluntarily. He stepped down on 11 December 1936, after almost a year, to marry the American divorcee Wallis Simpson. Edward was born on 23 June 1894 in Richmond, Surrey, the eldest child of the Duke of York. He was always known in his family as David, one of many middle names. In 1910, Edward's father came to the throne as King George V and Edward became Prince of Wales.

240-line television in the USA

In America, RCA demonstrated a working iconoscope camera tube and kinescope receiver tube (both made by Zworykin) to the press on 24 April . On 15 June this year, Don Lee Broadcasting began a one-month-long demonstration of high definition (240+ line) television in Los Angeles on W6XAO (later KTSL), with a 300-line image from motion picture film. By October, W6XAO was making daily television broadcasts of films. RCA and its subsidiary NBC demonstrated in New York City a 343-line electronic television broadcast, with live and film segments, to its licencees on 7 July.

1936 Coronation of King George VI

King George VI was crowned monarch on 12 May 1937 just five months after his brother abdicated, and on the date originally planned for Edward VIII's coronation, As the second son of King George V, he was not expected to inherit the throne and had spent his early life in the shadow of his elder brother Edward. King George VI and Queen Elizabeth had two daughters, Elizabeth (who succeeded her father as Queen Elizabeth II) and Margaret.

1936 Early electronic cameras

Working together this year three manufacturers, RCA/NBC (USA), Telefunken (Germany) and EMI (USA) developed a practical electronic camera system.

1936 BBC compares Baird to EMI

The Postmaster General, now controlling the broadcast of television in the UK through legislation, decided with the BBC that the EMI electronic and the Baird electro-mechanic television systems would be compared in over-air tests. Baird (240-line transmission) and EMI-Marconi (405-line definition) agreed with the BBC to become the first TV station anywhere in the world to broadcast daily and varied content to a 15,000 London television audience. The crude Baird mechanical system was used one week and the basic EMI-Marconi electrical system the next. The service went on the air at 3.00pm Monday 2 November.

First television listings

Also on 2 November the Radio Times first carried the first television listings. The BBC therefore began broadcasting a dual-system service from Alexandra Palace, London, alternating between Marconi-EMI's 405-line electronic standard one week and Baird's (now improved) 240-line electro-mechanical standard the following week – making the BBC Television Service the world's first regular, so-called 'high-definition' (as then defined) television service. It was broadcast in the analogue, radio wave format. The service went on the air with a speech from three speakers – the Postmaster General, Major the Right Hon G C Tryon MP,  Mr R C Norman, Chairman of the BBC, and the Right Hon. the Lord Selsden KBE, Chairman of the Television Advisory Committee. This was followed by the time and weather. At 3.20pm the British Movietone News was broadcast. At 3.30pm there was a variety progamme and close down was 4.00pm. The difference between the two broadcast systems was very clear from the beginning. The BBC Radio Times was now achieving a circulation of three million copies listing regional radio programmes and the London Television programmes – producing an annual surplus for the BBC of £600,000.

With the BBC now broadcasting television, Europe was well ahead of America in the development of television systems. In the UK, television was publicly owned. In America, television networks were all to be privately owned companies. In the USA, David Sarnoff the President of RCA/NBC was soon to make great strides forward.

1936 First thoughts for a flat screen television

This year saw the discovery of manuscripts, authored by Kálmán Tihanyi including a design of the first known flat-panel receiver. Tihanyi was a Hungarian physicist, electrical engineer and inventor. One of the early pioneers of electronic television, he made significant contributions to the development of cathode ray tubes

(CRTs), which were bought and further developed by the Radio Corporation of America (later RCA) and German companies Loewe and Fernseh.

EMI wins over Baird

In 1937, Reith left the BBC to become chairman of Imperial Airways. The improved 405-line monochrome analogue television broadcasting system began this year. The British government, on advice from a special advisory committee, decided that Marconi-EMI's 405-line electronic system gave the superior picture, and the Baird 240-line system was dropped (4 February).

Baird's television systems were therefore replaced by an electronic television system developed by EMI-Marconi under Isaac Shoenberg, similar to the system described by A A Campbell-Swinton, improved by Kalman Tihanyi in 1926, and initially developed by Vladimir Zworykin. Philo T Farnsworth's Image Dissector camera was available to Baird, however it was found to be lacking in light sensitivity. The last date for broadcast of the Baird system was 30 January this year.

The new BBC broadcasts were the first fully electronic television system to be used in regular broadcasting anywhere in the world. It was introduced with BBC support but suspended for the duration of World War II. The Marconi-EMI system was developed in 1934 by the EMI Research Team led by Sir Isaac Shoenberg (an electronic engineer born in Russia). The figure of 405 lines had been chosen following discussions over Sunday lunch at the home of Alan Blumlein (an English electronics engineer). The system was the first to use interlacing; the 405 scanning lines were broadcast in two complementary fields, 50 times

per second, creating 25 frames per second. Of the 405 lines, 377 were used for the image. By today's DVB nomenclature standards, it could be called 377i except that 405 line has never been broadcast or recorded digitally. Though articles at the time of its introduction referred to the 405-line system as 'high definition', that was in relation to the crude mechanical television systems that preceded it; this should not be confused with modern-day high-definition television.

1937 First BBC outside broadcast

Regular television news services began in the UK on 2 November this year. Broadcasting times were limited to two hours a day and were split equally between afternoons and evenings. In those early years, there were no BBC produced television news programmes. Instead, each week television broadcast on alternate evenings aired the latest Gaumont British News and then the British Movietone News cinema newsreels. Each evening's transmission ended with a recording of radio's nine o'clock news. Television did, however, cover some news events. It did so as live outside broadcasts. The first outside broadcast was on 12 May 1937, when BBC television broadcast live coverage of the return of King George VI's coronation procession from Westminster Abbey – from three camera positions at Hyde Park Corner. Television cameras had not been allowed inside the Abbey itself, although the service had been broadcast live worldwide by radio. A year later the return of Prime Minister Neville Chamberlain to Heston aerodrome on 30 September 1938, from the four-power Munich Conference on the Sudeten crisis was covered live. That transmission was an early television/radio 'simulcast' with commentary on both media given by Richard Dimbleby among others. Recording of the television coverage was not possible due to technical limitations of the equipment then in use, although the radio broadcasts were recorded.

1937 New Conservative Prime Minister, Neville Chamberlain, who is best known for his appeasement foreign policy, and in particular for his signing of the Munich Agreement in 1938, conceding the Sudetenland region of Czechoslovakia to Nazi Germany. When Adolf Hitler continued his aggression, Britain declared war on Germany on 3 September 1939, and Chamberlain led Britain through the first eight months of the Second World War.

Pre-war BBC television

This year, television broadcasts in London were on the air for an average of four hours daily from 1936 to 1939. There were only 12,000 to 15,000 receivers. Some sets, in restaurants or bars, might have 100 viewers for sport and other events such as the first BBC outside broadcast of King George VI's coronation. The BBC research department developed the world's first close-talking noise-cancelling ribbon microphone allowing clearer broadcast speech. This year saw the launch of another newsreel, National News, this time broadcasting in full colour. It was panned by the critics and soon went under. There were a few other entrants, but they too quickly met the same fate.

1937 The death of Marconi

On 20 July, Marconi died in Rome at the age of 63 – but his company continued under RCA in America and as Marconi-EMI in the UK.

1938 France was now achieving 455 lines of transmission. Experimental 240-line transmissions began in Leningrad. The BBC's first non-English language services (Arabic and Latin

American Spanish) started on radio this year.
At the beginning of the Second World War,
the BBC was broadcasting in seven languages.
The BBC was felt by many listeners to offer
a more balanced view of the world than other
broadcasters, and gained a reputation for
accuracy and impartiality during this time,
leading to a peacetime commitment to independent reporting.
By the end of the war, there were 45 separate language services
and the BBC's English Service was broadcasting 24 hours a day
around the world. Cable TV in the UK has its origins as far back
as 1938, when towns such as Bristol used wires to carry
television signals to homes that couldn't receive transmissions
over the air.

In America, Zworykin delivered a much improved CRT to David
Sarnoff at RCA/NBC.

1939 State of War

September saw the close-down of television for the duration of
the war to avoid the Crystal Palace transmitter becoming a
beacon for enemy 'planes. By the outbreak of war, television was
available only within a 25 mile radius of London's Crystal Palace,
and each set was priced at about £126 (the average weekly wage
was £2). Broadcast on radio continued. At 11:15am on 3
September the Prime Minister, the Rt Hon. Neville Chamberlain
made the declaration of war with Germany over BBC wireless.
This picture shows the new King, George VI, apparently delivering
his evening speech to the nation announcing war with Germany
on 3 September 1939. The picture was actually posed for
photographers after he had completed the speech live on air, in
private with his speech therapist. Before he ascended to the

throne, Albert, Duke of York, dreaded public speaking because he suffered from a severe stammer. His closing speech at the British Empire Exhibition at Wembley, West London on 31 October 1925 proved an ordeal for speaker and listeners alike. The Duchess found a speech therapist called Lionel Logue who was an

Australian. The two men met on 19 October 1926 at Logue's consulting room in Harley Street. The approach Logue pioneered was psycho-therapeutic – he suspected the problem for stammerers was not simply physical, but that there was something, usually a trauma, around the age of four or five, that created the condition. Some say the new King's father was over dominating. Logue successfully treated King George VI. What was ironically cruel of the age was that his reign coincided with a revolution in mass communication. For the first time in British history, subjects could listen to their monarch addressing them live through their wireless sets, as if he were with them in their living rooms. But the technology didn't allow George VI to pre-record his broadcasts, as would be the case for the generations that followed. When he addressed the nation, it had to be done through a live microphone, without editing. The speech was, however, recorded for posterity on a 78 rpm record for delivery to the very distant and isolated parts of the British Empire. Such a recording was simply a copy of what was transmitted live – there was no editing equipment so the technology did not help the King's problem with live speeches. After the war, Logue's pioneering work with the King was

recognised with the award of a CVO ('Commander of the Victorian Order' – an honour bestowed by the monarch alone). He was also acknowledged as a leading figure in the speech therapy world. Logue was not only medically unqualified as a therapist, he was actually an actor by training.

1939 Wartime brought huge challenges for the BBC – having to deal with the government's Ministry of Information while finding itself a target for German bombs.

1939 Electronic television

John Logie Baird made many contributions to the field of electronic television after mechanical systems had taken a back seat. This year, he showed colour television using a cathode ray tube in front of which revolved a disc fitted with colour filters; a method taken up by David Sarnoff's RCA/NBC in the United States.

1940 BBC bombed

Newsreader Bruce Belfrage was on air when 500lbs of explosives hit Broadcasting House in October 1940. He paused as he heard the bomb go off during his nine o'clock bulletin, but continued as normal, as he was not allowed to react on air for security reasons. Seven people were killed.

Entertainment and drama on the Home Service kept up morale – particularly 'It's That Man Again', featuring comedian Tommy Handley. Meanwhile, the Empire Service, settling into new headquarters at Bush House, broadcast to occupied Europe.

By the outbreak of war, some 20,000 television sets had been sold in the UK.

View-Master

Introduced in this year, View-Master became a popular 3D toy for children.

Regular broadcasts in the USA

In America, NBC officially began regularly scheduled television broadcasts in New York on 30 April, with a broadcast of the opening of the 1939 New York World's Fair. President Roosevelt opened the Fair on television. American politicians were soon to realise the political power of the television media. By June this year, regularly scheduled 441-line electronic television broadcasts were available in New York City and Los Angeles.

Suspension of television

Despite the suspension of UK television services, broadcasts continued in the USA. America progressed its development and research. RCA's technical standards continued to improve by employing Vladimir Zworykin and by using his iconoscope camera for scanning, and another of his inventions, the Kinescope, for receiving the pictures. President Roosevelt at the New York World's Fair became the first President to appear on television – channel RCA/NBC. There were only about 100 TV sets in the whole of the New York area. RCA put a TV set on sale at the World Fair – at $600 compared to a new car at $1,000.

Radio Times continues

In the UK, by September this year the Radio Times was devoting three pages a week to television, but when war was declared on

3 September, television closed down. The nation turned once again to the wireless. "Broadcasting carries on!" announced the first wartime Radio Times, but there was only one station, the newly christened Home Service, to inform, educate and entertain through the dark years ahead. By 1944, paper rationing had reduced the Radio Times magazine to 20 pages of tiny type on thin paper, but despite all the disruption of war, Radio Times never missed an edition.

1940 🗽 Conservative Prime Minister, Winston Churchill.

Baird Colour television

The World's First Baird so-called 'High Definition' Colour Television system was demonstrated. It was never broadcast and remained experimental. Table-top televisions went on sale in Leningrad. Production stopped after a few hundred were sold because of the war. In the USA, after only one year of broadcasts, the Federal Communications Commission (FCC) said that the NBC status would have to return to an 'experimental' station.

The FCC was looking for a common technical standard for the whole of America. RCA wanted 441-lines and the Philco company in Philadelphia wanted 605-line transmission. In WW2, France surrendered to Germany in June. The Germans used the Eiffel Tower to transmit propaganda to France. The transmitter was so powerful (30 KW) that the British Intelligence was watching the broadcasts.

NBC in the USA

1941 David Sarnoff at RCA/NBC was influencing the FCC (Federal Communications Commission) on the television national standards. The FCC adopted NTSC television engineering standards on 2 May, calling for 525 lines of vertical resolution, 30 frames per second with interlaced scanning, 60 fields per second, and sound carried by frequency modulation. Sets sold since 1939 which were built for slightly lower resolution could still be adjusted to receive the new standard. The FCC saw television ready for commercial licensing, and the first such licences were issued to NBC and CBS owned stations in New York on 1 July, followed by Philco's station WPTZ in Philadelphia. On 1 July, NBC television launched across America.

FM radio in the USA

By this year, 50 FM stations were on the air. Then the Japanese bombed Pearl Harbor. The ensuing war diverted resources and froze development. David Sarnoff and RCA still out to hold control of their radio empire, pressured the FCC to change all of the FM radio frequencies – a move they knew would instantly make obsolete all of the exiting FM radios, and cause Armstrong to lose his personal investment in FM radio. Listeners were understandably upset at having their radios suddenly rendered useless. And having been 'burned once', they were reluctant to immediately go out and buy new FM radios. Since most radio station owners didn't want to go to the expense of creating C allowed them to simulcast – simultaneously broadcast the same programming on both their AM and FM stations. Of course, this didn't show off FM's quality advantages and it did nothing to help the cause of FM. (Years later, the FCC ruled against the practice of simulcasting.)

Once TV started to evolve (to be covered in an upcoming module), interest in FM radio further diminished and by 1949, many FM stations had shut down.

1941 Pearl Harbour

Hawaii on the morning of 7 December 1941. The USA joined in the Second World War. At the onset of war, David Sarnoff served on Eisenhower's communications staff, arranging expanded radio

circuits for NBC to transmit news from the invasion of France. After the liberation of France, Sarnoff arranged for the

restoration of the Radio France station in Paris that the Germans had destroyed, and oversaw the construction of a radio transmitter powerful enough to reach all of the allied forces in Europe, called Radio Free Europe. Thanks to his communications skills and support, he received the Brigadier General's star in December 1945, and thereafter was known as 'General Sarnoff'. The star, which he proudly and frequently wore, was buried with him.

The world at war

1942 The USA television audience all but petered out. Britain and the Soviet Union were already off the air. The limited German television service continued in Berlin and Hamburg with 3,000 viewers – mostly in the reichspost (post offices), although about 350 homes had privately-owned receivers. The Radio Times reached its 1000th edition on 29 November, and still costing 2d.

Radio Times grows

1943 Circulation of the BBC Radio Times reached 3.179m.

German television

Allied bombers scored a direct hit on the Berlin transmitter, and German television broadcasts promptly ended.

BBC start up

This year in the UK, the Hankey Committee (Chairman: Lord Hankey – published 29 December 1944, and presented to Parliament in March 1945) was appointed to oversee the resumption of television broadcasts after the war. Baird persuaded them to make plans to adopt his proposed 1000-line Telechrome electronic colour system as the new post-war broadcast standard. The picture quality on this system would have been comparable to today's HDTV. The Hankey Committee's plan lost all momentum partly due to the challenges of post-war reconstruction. The monochrome 405-line standard remained in place until 1985 in some areas, and it was three decades until the introduction of the 625-line system in 1964 and (PAL) colour in 1967.

ABC in the USA

The American Broadcasting Company (ABC) is an American television network. Created this year from the former NBC Blue radio network, ABC is owned by The Walt Disney Company and is part of Disney-ABC Television Group. Its first broadcast on television was achieved in 1948. Corporate headquarters are in the Upper West Side of Manhattan in New York City, while programming offices are in Burbank, California, adjacent to the Walt Disney Studios. The formal name of the operation is American Broadcasting

Companies, Inc., and that name appears on copyright notices for its in-house network productions and on all official documents of the company, including paychecks and contracts. A separate entity named ABC Inc., formerly Capital Cities/ABC Inc., is that firm's direct parent company, and that company is owned in turn by Disney. The network is sometimes referred to as the Alphabet Network, due to the letters 'ABC' being the first three letters of the Latin alphabet.

David Sarnoff

General David Sarnoff anticipated that post-war America would need an international radio voice explaining its policies and positions. This year, he tried to influence Secretary of State Cordell Hull to include radio broadcasting in post-war planning.

After the United States entry into the Second World War , the FCC reduced the required minimum air time for commercial television stations from 15 hours per week to 4 hours. Most TV stations suspended broadcasting. On the few that remained, programs included entertainment such as boxing and plays, events

1948 Automatic - TVP490 7in

at Madison Square Garden, and illustrated war news, as well as training for air raid wardens and first aid providers. In 1942, there were 5,000 television sets in operation, but production of new TVs, radios, and other broadcasting equipment for civilian purposes was suspended from April 1942 to August 1945.

Baird's colour television

1944 Baird gave the world's first demonstration of a fully electronic colour television display with his improved 600-line colour system using triple interlacing, using six scans to build each picture. This was not adopted by any broadcaster.

625-line television

The world's first 625-line TV standard was designed in the Soviet Union in this year. In France, after the liberation, French television broadcasts resumed. From December this year until his death in 1946, John Logie Baird lived at a house in Station Road, Bexhill on Sea – immediately north of the station itself. The house was named 'Baird Court', and in 2006 Rother District Council gave permission for this property to be demolished and the land used for a modern block of flats, despite the efforts of many local residents who believed that it should have been listed and preserved due to its historical importance.

1945 End of the Second World War. General Election. Labour Prime Minister, Clement Attlee.

Nurses in line at the Polling Place on 5 July this year

Post-war USA television – towards colour

After the war, monochrome television production in the USA began in earnest. Colour television was the next major development and NBC once again won the American battle. CBS also had their electro-mechanical colour television system approved by the FCC. At RCA/NBC David Sarnoff's tenacity and determination to win the 'Colour War' pushed his engineers to perfect an all-electronic colour television system that used a signal that could be received on existing monochrome sets, and this finally won the day. CBS was now unable to take advantage of the colour market, due to lack of manufacturing capability and sets that were triple the cost of monochrome sets. A few days after CBS had its colour premiere on 14 June 1951, RCA demonstrated a fully functional all-electronic colour television system and became the leading manufacturer of colour Television sets in the United States.

1945 Satellite Television

This year saw Sir Arthur C Clarke's most famous prediction on the future; his proposal of geostationary satellite communications orbiting at 22,300 miles high which was published in the Wireless World magazine in February. It was not  considered seriously at the time but the prediction became a reality within 20 years with the launching of Intelsat I (Early Bird) on 6 April 1965 – becoming the first commercial satellite. This event marked the true beginning of satellite television. Sir Arthur C Clarke had the vision to foresee a satellite travelling at a speed and at a height which would mean that it effectively remains in the

 same position over the earth – capable of casting a 'footprint' over a given area of the earth's surface. It was later calculated that if a satellite follows an orbit parallel to the equator in the same direction as the earth's rotation, the satellite will appear stationary with respect to the earth's surface. Satellites in the geostationary orbits are located at a high altitude of

36,000 km (22,369 miles) and travelling at a speed of 11070 km/h (6880 mph) – slightly faster than the rotation speed of the earth turning on its own axis over 24 hours.

1946 Sony was founded this year. It became a multinational conglomerate

corporation headquartered in Minato, Tokyo, Japan, and one of the world's largest media conglomerates with revenue exceeding ¥ 7.730.0 trillion, or $78.88 billion US. Sony remains one of the leading manufacturers of electronics, video, communications, video game consoles, and information technology products for the consumer and professional markets. Its founders Akio Morita and Masaru Ibuka derived the name from sonus, the Latin word for sound, and also from the English slang word 'sonny', since they considered themselves to be 'sonny boys', a loan word into Japanese which in the early 1950s connoted smart and presentable young men.

1946 Television starts again in the USA and the UK

This year, 10,000 television sets were sold in the USA. Regular network television broadcasts began again on the DuMont Television Network this year, on NBC in 1947, and on CBS and ABC in 1948. By 1949, the networks stretched from New York to the Mississippi River, and by 1951 to the West Coast.

The British VHF television broadcast standard was for 405 line monochrome resolution. Television broadcast resumed from Alexandra Palace on 7 June 1946 with a speech from the Postmaster General, The Earl of Listowel. The next

day the BBC broadcast live television coverage
of the war victory parade in London. Broadcast
was limited to a few hours every day, just in the
London area. About 10,000 homes only had TV
sets and radio was still dominant. On radio, the
BBC's Home Service offered news and popular
entertainment such as Saturday night theatre. The
Light Programme had Mrs Dale's Diary, Housewife's Choice, panel
games and quizzes. In 1946, the Third programme was launched
for the 'alert and receptive listener'. This year saw the death of
Baird on 14 June 1946 in Bexhill-on-Sea, Sussex, England, at the
age of 57.

Russian television

The transmission mode of 625 lines became the national standard
in Moscow.

1946 Watch with Mother

Watch with Mother became the BBC's
'umbrella' title of individual children's
programmes shown on television to
compliment   the   popular   radio
programme 'Listen with Mother'. On
television, this year saw the start of
Muffin The Mule with Annette Mills.

UK television news

Television news was still simply a relay of the late-evening radio
news accompanied by a still picture of a clock in vision. The BBC's
charter was due for renewal by Parliament in 1946 and there
were political rumblings as to whether the BBC's monopolistic
broadcasting position should be ended. Prime Minister Clement

Attlee's government indicated that renewal would not be accompanied by an extensive review – a decision that drew much criticism at the time.

1946 Licence increased to £1 p.a. TV licencing began this year – incorporated as part of the existing licence.

The changing radio and radio/television UK licence over the years:

Broadcast Receiving Licences: 1922–2009

Date	Radio	TV B&W (with radio)	TV Colour (with radio)
November 1922	10s	—	—
June 1946	£1	£2	—
June 1954	£1	£3	—
August 1957	£1	£4	—
October 1963	£1	£4	—
August 1965	£1 5s	£5	—
January 1968	£1 5s	£5	£10
January 1969	£1 5s	£6	£11
July 1971	—	£7	£12
April 1975	—	£8	£18
July 1977	—	£9	£21

November 1978	—	£10	£25
November 1979	—	£12	£34
December 1981	—	£15	£46
March 1985	—	£18	£58
April 1988	—	£21	£62.50
April 1989	—	£22	£66
April 1990	—	£24	£71
April 1991	—	£25.50	£77
April 1992	—	£26.50	£80
April 1993	—	£27.50	£83
April 1994	—	£28	£84.50
April 1995	—	£28.50	£86.50
April 1996	—	£30	£89.50
April 1997	—	£30.50	£91.50
April 1998	—	£32.50	£97.50
April 1999	—	£33.50	£101
April 2000	—	£34.50	£104
April 2001	—	£36.50	£109
April 2002	—	—	£112
April 2003	—	—	£116
April 2004	—	—	£121
April 2005	—	—	£126.50
April 2006	—	—	£131.50

April 2007	—	—-	£135.50
April 2008	—	—-	£139.50
April 2009			£142.50

1947 Testcard

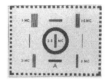

The first post-war BBC testcard, Testcard A, is broadcast on the BBC network.

First Party Political Broadcast

This year saw the first British Party Political Broadcast on 18 March. In America, MGM's Metro News emerged onto the scene, although seemingly only to enable it to share in the coverage of the 1948 London Olympics. BBC radio first broadcast of Mrs Dale's Diary. This year saw 14,560 television licences bought from the Post Office.

In the USA, RCA's David Sarnoff lobbied Secretary of State George Marshall to expand the roles of Radio Free Europe and Voice of America.

Why aren't there many recordings from the early days of BBC television?

There aren't any, or many, recordings from the early days of television because firstly the programmes were all live, and secondly there was no way to record them. Of course, live television must have been a truly terrifying experience for people back then. They would have four or five cameras, three or four sets, and so were quite restricted in what they could do, although they did achieve amazing things. It must have been stomach-churning and there are stories of people being physically sick just before they went on screen. They did develop a way of recording television pictures in this year which may seem very crude nowadays, but essentially they would put a film camera in front of a monitor, and record the pictures off the monitor onto film. So when you see clips from things like the coronation in the trial, those were done using film recording, and sometimes that's why they don't look the most fantastic quality – the original picture would have been much better.

1948 The BBC superior testcard C is released. Lack of specification means that there were many variants released with subtle differences. This is the latest television set

Radio Luxembourg started with the UK Top Twenty in the Autumn of this year (at 1293 m. long wave).,,

1948 News on BBC television

5 January saw the regular broadcast of the television version of the cinema newsreel. This was the forerunner to Television which began in 1954. It was a BBC-produced newsreel, which adopted many of the conventions of the cinema newsreels.

Some of the personnel who produced it had been recruited from the cinema newsreel companies. Initially, one edition of the newsreel was produced each week. It was broadcast on Monday

 and Wednesday evenings, and Saturday afternoons and evenings. Unlike its cinema counterparts, the programme was longer; each edition ran for about 10–15 minutes and comprised fewer discrete items. Later, bi-weekly editions were produced. Its coverage of the war in Korea lent the newsreel a more serious edge.

625 line standard

The concept of 625 lines per frame was implemented in the European standard. In the UK, proposals were discussed for five television 405-line channels in the band 40–68MHz. This was accepted by the Scientific  Advisory Committee and the Radio Industries Council.

BBC Newsreel

First transmission in the UK of BBC Newsreel – the first regular TV news programme.

Vinyl

 This year saw the start of the Vinyl record format war: Columbia Records' 12-inch (30 cm) Long Play (LP) 33S! rpm microgroove record vs RCA Victor's 7-inch (17.5 cm) 45 rpm Extended Play (EP), during the years 1948–1950. The format war ended in a compromise because each format found a separate marketing niche, and eventually record players were designed to play both types. Vinyl records are still used by niche audiences such as disc jockeys and audiophiles.

ABC television in the USA

In 1948, faced with huge expenses in building a radio network, ABC in America was in no position to take on the additional costs demanded by a television network. To secure a place at the table, though, in 1947, ABC submitted requests for licences in the five cities where it owned radio stations (which together represented 25 percent of the entire nationwide viewing audience at the time). All five requests were for each station to broadcast on channel 7; ABC chief engineer Frank Marx thought at the time that the low-band (channels 2 to 6) TV channels would be reallocated for military use, thus making these five stations broadcasting on VHF channel 7 the lowest on the TV dial and therefore the best channel positions. (Such a move never occurred, although fortuitously, 60 years later the channel 7 frequency would prove technically favorable for digital television transmission, a technology unanticipated at the dawn of TV broadcasting.)

1948 ABC on-the-air

On 19 April this year, the American ABC television network went on the air. The network picked up its first primary affiliates, WFIL-TV in Philadelphia (now WPVI-TV) and WMAL-TV in Washington (now WJLA-TV) before its flagship owned and operated station ('O&O'), WJZ-TV in New York (now WABC-TV) signed on in August of that year. The rest of ABC's fleet of owned-and-operated major market stations, in Detroit, Chicago, San Francisco and Los Angeles, would sign on during the next 13 months, giving it parity with CBS and NBC in the important area of big-city presence, as well as a long term advantage in guaranteed reach over the rival DuMont network, by the winter of 1949.

Growth of television in the USA

For the next few years, ABC was a television network mostly in name. Except for the largest markets, most cities had only one or two stations. The FCC froze applications for new stations in 1948 while it sorted out the thousands of applicants, and rethought the technical and allocation standards set down between 1938 and 1946. What was meant to be a six-month freeze lasted until the middle of 1952. Until that time there were only 108 stations in the United States. Some large cities where TV development was slow, like Pittsburgh and St. Louis, had only one station on the air for a prolonged period, while many more of the largest cities such as Boston only had two, and many sizable cities including Denver, Colorado and Portland, Oregon had no television service at all until the second half of 1952 after the freeze ended. For a late-comer like ABC, this meant being relegated to secondary status in many markets and having no reach at all in some. ABC commanded little affiliate loyalty, though unlike fellow startup network DuMont, it at least had a radio network on which to draw loyalty and revenue. It also had a full complement of five O&Os, (owned-and-operated station) which included stations in the critical Chicago (WENR-TV, now WLS-TV) and Los Angeles (KECA-TV, now KABC-TV) markets. Even then, by 1951 ABC found itself badly overextended and on the verge of bankruptcy. It had only nine full-time affiliates to augment its five O&Os – WJZ, WENR, KECA, WXYZ-TV in Detroit and KGO-TV in San Francisco. In the USA, TV set sales had increased TV ownership to 4 million homes.

Review of the BBC

1949 In Britain, an extensive review of the future of the BBC commenced (reporting in 1951). The famous cheery bandleader and ex-racing driver, Billy Cotton, was the star of his Sunday lunchtime series on the BBC Light Programme from 1949. By 1962, he had bellowed his weekly "Wakey-

Wakey!" 500 times, and the show still had six more years to run.

More television licences

This year saw 126,567 television licences bought from the Post Office in the UK. In the USA, 2,000,000 television sets were sold this year.

1950 General Election. Labour Prime Minister, Clement Atlee. Presented by Richard Dimbleby, this was the first time General Election results were reported on BBC television.

Colour television in the USA

CBS (Columbia Broadcasting System) first demonstrated colour television, in a former Tiffany & Co. building in New York City this year – thus earning it the name 'Color Broadcasting System' back when such a feat was innovative.

First television remote

The first television remote control was introduced this year in the USA; the 'Lazy Bones'. It was connected to the television by means of a long wire.

1950 Margaret Thatcher

Margaret Thatcher (née Roberts) fought (and lost) her first general election seat in Dartford, Kent, as the youngest UK candidate ever. Margaret Thatcher is mentioned in the context of television because she became significant in the development, in statute, of cable and satellite television later in the 20th century. She believed in the market economy.

1950 Listen with Mother – "are you sitting comfortably?"

Listen with Mother was a BBC radio programme for children which ran between 1950 and 1982. It was originally produced by Freda Lingstrom and was presented over the years by Daphne Oxenford, Julia Lang, Eileen Browne, Dorothy Smith and others

1950s Baird television

Baird's name continued to brand television sets in the 1950s.

Cinema audiences declining

Cinema newsreels came under increasing stress; costs continued to rise and the companies struggled to remain competitive. Some cinemas ceased taking newsreels – such as the Sidney Berstein's Granada cinemas. But the biggest threat to cinema news came from television itself. The emerging and growing medium was able to offer effortless immediacy through pictures broadcast straight into viewers' homes. At the same time, cinema audiences were declining and tastes were changing. Some newsreels did however try to compete. Gaumont British News experimented with the device of an on-screen reporter (Peter Lee).

1951 General Election. Conservative Prime Minister, Sir Winston Churchill. Although Labour polled more votes than in 1950 the Conservatives formed the Government after gaining more seats.

This was one of only three elections where this happened – the others being 1929 and 1974.

1951 Colour television in the USA

Commercial colour television broadcasts began on CBS in 1951 with a field-sequential colour system that was suspended four months later for technical and economic reasons. The television industry's National Television System Committee developed a colour television system that was compatible with existing black and white receivers, and commercial colour broadcasts reappeared in 1953

1952 Watch with mother – Andy Pandy and others on television

In this year, British children's television started with the experimental transmission of the puppet show Andy Pandy – under the banner '... for the very young'. Some 26 black-and-white episodes of Andy Pandy were shown repeatedly.

Live European Broadcast

This year, on 27 August, saw the first live broadcast in the UK from the European continent. The first political discussion programme was broadcast on the BBC – 'In the News'.

Children's television in the USA

The American Broadcasting Company (ABC) first aired Saturday morning television shows for children on 19 August this year. The network introduced two shows; Animal Clinic featured live animals, while the variety show Acrobat Ranch had a circus theme. Placed against a Western backdrop, acrobats audience competed for merchandise prizes. Tumbling Tim and Flying Flo lent an air of spectacle to Acrobat Ranch. In one segment, Host Uncle Jim presided over a game in which children from the studio

1950s Commercial Television on the way

The spirits of the nation were lifted by the Festival of Britain in 1951 and two years later by the Coronation. An extra 100,000 TV sets were sold to watch the event. Television was becoming the focus for family entertainment. For the youngest children there was a diet of puppets, like Muffin the Mule, Andy Pandy, Rag Tag and Bobtail, the Woodentops and Sooty with his xylophone. When commercial television was launched in 1955, a whole new innovation was born in the United Kingdom. The TV jingles started to lodge in the minds of the population – the Esso sign means happy motoring, Murray Mints, Murray Mints, too good to hurry mints and Double Diamond works wonders. By the end of the decade, a third of the population had television.

The Archers

BBC radio first aired The Archers based in Ambridge, a programme that is still broadcast today. This year, the BBC's Midlands Home Service broadcast five pilot episodes of a new, experimental drama series: The Archers. The producer, Godfrey Baseley had  previously worked mainly on agricultural programmes. He hoped that farmers would listen to the stories, but along the way pick up messages that would help them feed a Britain still subject to food rationing. Episode 15,674 was broadcast on 1 January 2009. The programme continues 60 years later.

Three quarters of a million television licences

This year saw 753,941 television licences bought from the Post Office.

First broadcast VTRs

In the UK, there were now 13.7m homes. Before the days of commercial VCRs (video cassette recorders – see 1974), there were broadcast video machines called VTRs (Video tape recorders). These machines were similar to reel-to-reel audio tapes, with large spools of multi-track magnetic tapes, from ½ inch to 2 inch wide by 7,000 feet long, moving at high lineal tape speed (20 to 30 feet per second for the early machines). This high speed was necessary to fit all of the black and white picture information onto the tape.

This year, American Charles Ginsburg led the research team at the Ampex Corporation in developing the first practical videotape recorder (VTR) for broadcasters. This year also saw the first VTR capturing live images from television cameras by converting the information into electrical impulses and saving the information onto magnetic tape.

Review of the BBC

On the completion of the review of the BBC (1949 to 1951), Lord Beveridge concluded that the Corporation should neither be broken up nor be subjected to competition. One of the committee's members, the Conservative MP Selwyn Lloyd, disagreed with these conclusions and issued a minority report recommending the end of the BBC's broadcasting monopoly. When the Conservatives won the 1951 election Lloyd's ideas were gradually incorporated into government policy. Over the next three years, and following two broadcasting white papers, the government introduced a bill which, when passed in July 1954, would see the establishment of an independent television network, which was to be overseen by an Independent Television Authority (ITA).

Newsreel of the week

The BBC introduced Newsreel Review of the Week, which was broadcast on Sunday evenings. It showed selected stories from the previous week's newsreels and was introduced by Edward Halliday, who sometimes appeared in vision. Lord Beveridge reported that the BBC should keep its monopoly.

I love Lucy in the USA

I Love Lucy first aired. I Love Lucy was an American television sitcom, starring Lucille Ball and Desi Arnaz. The monochrome series ran from 15 October on network CBS.

Korean War

Colour television production in America was suspended in October this year for the duration of the Korean War. As more people bought monochrome sets, it was increasingly unlikely that CBS could achieve any success with its incompatible system.

1952 Death of King George VI

King George VI died in his sleep on 6 February.

BBC television in Scotland

The official launch of BBC television in Scotland.

More progress

This year saw the Stockholm Conference to discuss VHF TV and Radio Frequency allocations in Europe. A twin-channel version of the first standards converter used to convert French 819-line pictures to the 405-line UK standard, enabling British viewers to see pictures simultaneously with the French over a temporary Paris to London link. The Flowerpot Men joined the afternoon slot for children. Watch with Mother was now showing programmes for pre-school children five days a week. The UK exploded its first nuclear bomb. The first dish washer went on sale, and the first underwater camera was developed in the UK.

BBC television reach

On 1 January this year, in the UK, BBC television could be received in 78% of the country, reaching some 3m television sets.

NTSC in USA

The NTSC in America was reformed and recommended a system virtually identical to RCA's in August this year

1953 The Coronation Queen Elizabeth II

After her marriage in 1947, Princess Elizabeth paid formal visits with The Duke of Edinburgh to France and Greece, and in autumn 1951 they toured Canada. Princess Elizabeth also visited Malta four times while Prince Philip was stationed there on naval duties, and enjoyed the life of a naval

wife and young mother. This way of life was not to last long, as her father's health was deteriorating. In 1952, King George VI's illness forced him to abandon his proposed visit to Australia and New Zealand. The Princess, accompanied by Prince Philip, took his place. On Wednesday, 6 February 1952, Princess Elizabeth received the news of her father's death and her own accession to the throne, while staying in a remote part of Kenya. The tour had to be abandoned, and the young Princess flew back to Britain as Queen. She was greeted at the airport by Prime Minister Sir Winston Churchill and other officials.

Broadcast of Coronation

The broadcast of the Coronation of Queen Elizabeth II in Westminster Abbey on 2 June achieved 27m UK viewers – a first. BBC tele-recordings were flown across the Atlantic to America. Around the world 220m viewers saw the coronation on television. The UK announcer was Peter Dimmock. (He was the first host of the long-running BBC Grandstand and also the first host of the BBC Sports Personality of the Year Awards.) Suppressed-frame tele-recording equipment was designed this year and used to record pictures of the Queen's Coronation.

BBC ident

The BBC made its first attempt at a proper brand image when Abram Games was commissioned to design an on-air image.

In this year, America was obsessed with the threat of Communism. On the American CBS (Columbia Broadcast System) television network, penetrating news was spearheaded by broadcast journalist Ed Murrow (born Egbert Roscoe Murrow, 25 April 1908–27 April 1965). He first came to prominence with a series of radio news broadcasts during the Second World War, which were followed by millions of listeners in the United States and Canada. A pioneer of television news telecast, Murrow produced a series of networked television news reports

that helped lead to the ultimate censure of US Senator Joseph McCarthy. This was the first time that a news presenter had managed to compromise a politician. At the end of

each broadcast Murrow delivered his byline –"good night and good luck". The 1950s CBS ident was designed by William Golden. This year saw television cameras on sale to the public in the USA.

The Light and Third Radio programmes

The years following the end of the war saw a steady expansion in radio broadcasting, and the Radio Times flourished with it, announcing the introduction of the Light Programme, the Third Programme, and the return of television. The Radio Times grew to meet the need with a number of regional editions to keep abreast of the changes. Television was the medium of the future, and in 1953 its growth was recognised when the TV listings were moved from the back of the magazine and integrated day-by-day with radio. It was suggested that the BBC should register the name 'TV Times' but the general manager of BBC publications rejected the idea on the grounds that television wouldn't catch on. It was subsequently used by the independent broadcasters on ITV.

Approval of RCA by FCC in the USA

On 17 December this year in America, the FCC approved RCA's system as the new standard for colour television.

1954 BBC Sportsview

Sir Peter Fox and Peter Dimmock, respectively the editor and presenter of BBC 'Sportsview' created the programme this year, and the first awards were held. The winner was Christopher Chataway who had recently broken the 5,000m world record. He later became a Member of Parliament and subsequently a Tory minister.

New Television Act 1954

After much debate both in the British Parliament and the British Press, the new Television Act (30 July) became law this year. This Act paved the way for the establishment of a commercial television service in the UK, creating the Independent Television Authority (ITA). The first director general was Sir Robert Fraser and the first Chairman was Sir Kenneth Clark

The ITA's responsibility was to regulate the new service, ensuring that it did not follow the same path taken by American television networks (which were perceived as 'vulgar' by some commentators). For example, it was made obligatory that commercials be clearly distinguishable from programmes. There would be no sponsorship or product placement within programmes. At the time, American shows were normally sponsored by a single company, so it was not uncommon for a game show host to step away from his podium after a round to sell cars. The term soap opera was first used this year. In the USA, comedy series of programmes were often sponsored by washing soap powder companies. It should be noted that in the USA all television broadcast was commercial and relied on advertising revenue. In the UK, television (the BBC) was effectively state owned and sponsored by a television licence payable by viewers. There was no advertising on British television until the emergence of ITV commercial channels on 22 September 1955. The first commercial was screened for Gibbs SR toothpaste.

1954 BBC News

At 7:30pm on 5 July, Richard Baker introduced the first television News Broadcast in the UK from Alexandra Palace. It was a 20-minute bulletin. The presenter's face was not visible on screen. In effect, it was illustrated Radio News. Initially, the newsreaders did not appear on screen following concerns that if they did it might lead to the news becoming in some way personalised. The BBC continued at that time to uphold its objective of broadcasting the news of the day 'accurately, fairly, soberly and impersonally'. Instead of showing the newsreader the programme made use of still images in vision, accompanied by some film inserts.

1954 First BBC weather forecast

This year saw the very first weather forecast to be televised. It featured a shadowy hand sketching isobars on a chart while an off-screen voice, backed by a segment of

soothing music, supplied some pertinent information. A sad-faced Yorkshireman by the name of George Cowling contributed the first in-vision forecast on 11 January this year. "The change", explained the Radio Times, "is designed to stress the continuity of the reports provided; the forecaster will show, for example, how the weather expected tomorrow is conditioned by the weather experienced today."

1954 The respectability of the BBC

The BBC was still regarded by many as a slow-moving, highly bureaucratic organisation and with no appetite for taking risks or giving offence. This feeling was the embodiment of respectability – "I want you to see yourself as an officer in a rather good regiment," was how Robin Day (later Sir Robin) was welcomed to the radio talks department this year. News bulletins remained pillars of grammatical rectitude.

1954 First regulator for commercial television

The Independent Television Authority (ITA) was an agency created under the 1954 television act to supervise the creation of  'Independent Television' (ITV), the first commercial television network in the United Kingdom. The ITA was responsible for determining the location, construction, building, and operating of the transmission stations used by the ITV network, as well as determining the franchise areas and awarding the franchises for each regional commercial broadcaster. The Authority began its operations on 4 August this year and achieved broadcast in the London area on 22 September 1955. Postmaster General, Charles Hill was working with the ITA to provide a second television service of regional broadcasters. At this point it is important to remember that the BBC had a monopoly on the television airwaves for some 18 years.

Colour television in the USA

When American 'colorcasting' began this year, there were few colour programmes and the receivers were prohibitively expensive for most American families. A colour TV set in the 1950s was extremely rare.

1954 Britain linked to the Eurovision television system for the first time.

1954 Further developments

A special 16 mm colour film and slide scanner was designed and built for TV cameras. The 405-line NTSC colour  demonstrations were given to the Technical Sub-Committee of the Television Advisory Committee, the BBC Board of Governors, and to many other people from the General Post Office, the radio industry, and from other interested countries.

The creation of ITN and its first Editor

The new ITA was not to be the overseer of the BBC. The 'regulator' for the BBC remained its own Board of Governors. The ITA, after much debate, during which it was advised by a committee that included an ex-newsreel senior executive, decided that news bulletins ought to run for thirteen and-a-half minutes and should be delivered by 'personality newsreaders'. The news company would initially be owned and operated by the four successful ITV regional contractors (broadcasters), although the ITA would also have a strong stake. The new company, Independent Television News

Ltd. was formally set up on 4 May. Independent Television News Ltd. operated as an independent news organization. The first Editor-in-Chief, Aidan Crawley, a former broadcaster and junior minister in Clement Attlee's government, was appointed on 8 February. Crawley had studied how television news was delivered in the USA and began translating what he had learned into practice. He believed that television news should be visual and, in contrast to the BBC's newsreaders, wanted his presenters, who would be called newscasters, to be journalists. They would share in writing and compiling the news and adapt the scripts to suit their natural speaking patterns. Crawley wanted the news to have a human touch and was keen that like their Fleet Street counterparts, the journalists should not shy away from 'scoops' and 'exclusives'. Crawley was also keen that the journalists should interview news personalities in a direct and pointed way and that they should follow up evasive responses. No longer were politicians and personalities to be accorded gentle, deferential interviews. The new team also pioneered the 'vox pop' principle in which ordinary citizens were canvassed for their opinions.

Reporting Politics

1950s The coverage of political issues by television continued to be a sensitive area for Government, particularly in the 1950s as the new medium developed. Politicians of all parties were concerned that television, being a powerful medium of communication, might eclipse the role of Parliament by becoming an alternative debating chamber. After the Second World War a 'gentleman's agreement' between the political parties led to the creation of a device called the 14-day rule. Under this agreement television was banned from covering or commenting on any political issues that were going to be debated in Parliament during the forthcoming 14 days. This was extended to inviting MPs to discuss on air any Bill that was before either house. With the advent of ITV it became a formal rule. Suez, however, was too big an issue to work within the rule; ITN ignored it, and every interview that ITN carried out broke it. When the rule was before Parliament for renewal in early 1957 its lack of logic was clearly evident and it was dropped. The rule's disappearance coincided with ITN's pioneering of a more aggressive and expansive coverage of politics.

Ownership of television

1950s There was debate in many countries on how to develop television broadcast. The three main alternative headings seemed to be:

- Public Service Television with no political influence.

- Commercial Television with no political influence.

- State-owned Television with political control of content.

It was obvious to all that only the first and second options would be viable in the UK.

1955 General Election. Conservative Prime Minister, Sir Anthony Eden.

BBC newsreaders in vision

The BBC newsreaders did not appear in vision until the beginning of September this year, just weeks before the launch of ITV's promised revolutionary news coverage. Kenneth Kendall was the first to appear in vision on September 4th.

1955 First ITV channels

This year saw the launch of the 'independent' television broadcasters (22 September) following the 1954 Television Act and a successful tendering process. ITV was made up of 15 broadcasting regions with each region run by a separate company. The ITV broadcasters were to be launched incrementally. Each region would broadcast its own content – especially local news.

Some content was shared nationally between the regions. ITV was a public service broadcaster (PSB) regulated by the Independent Television Authority (ITA) to provide competition to the BBC.

ITV programming

A whole range of new programming emerged onto the UK market. ITV launched on 22 September concluding a long public debate. The general population could now afford TV sets, many buying after the coverage of the Coronation in 1953, as post-war austerity gave way to a new consumer boom in Britain. A coalition of Tory MPs, advertisers, and industry won the case for a commercial channel, against the BBC's and others' claims that it would cheapen culture. The Independent Television Authority was created to act as both controller and regulator of a regional structure of franchises. ITV proved an immediate hit, although initially coverage was only in London, quickly followed by the Midlands and the industrial North. As the service gradually rolled

out across the nation, its audiences grew
and grew; the working class in particular
were attracted by the chance of having
popular, visually exciting entertainment in
the home. This was reflected in a huge
corresponding decline in cinema
audiences. Beginning this year and finally
ending in 1976, Dixon of Dock Green
was a popular series although its
homeliness would later become a

benchmark to measure the 'realism' of police series such as Z
Cars and The Bill. PC Dixon was played by Jack Warner. The series
was set in a suburban police station in the East End of London
and featured uniformed police engaged with routine tasks and
low-level crime. The ordinary, everyday nature of the people and
the setting was emphasised in early episodes by the British music-
hall song 'Maybe it's because I'm a Londoner' with its sentimental
evocations of a cosy community, being used as the series theme
song.

1955 Formation of ITN

As stated, ITN was founded in 1955 as part of the new
British commercial television network, referred to as
'Independent Television' by the ITA. It began as a
consortium of the initial broadcasters, with former MP
Aidan Crawley as Editor-in-Chief. The first ITN
newscaster was Christopher Chataway (later Sir Christopher).
This picture shows Chris Chataway breaking the world record
for the three mile on 30 July 1955. Soon afterwards he joined
ITN. ITN's first news programme was broadcast at 10.00pm on
the new channel's opening night on 22 September. Its new

approach to television news won early
critical and audience approval and had an
impact on how BBC television news itself
subsequently developed. Almost as soon as the new company
went on air, ITN's shareholder companies exerted pressure for
the bulletin running times to be reduced, for the company's costs
to be trimmed back, and made it clear that they did not support
Crawley's desire to extend ITN's remit to include current affairs.

Sir Robin Day

Sir Robin Day, OBE (24 October
1923 – 6 August 2000) was a British
political   broadcaster   and
commentator. His obituary in the UK
Guardian newspaper stated that 'he was the most outstanding
television journalist of his generation. He transformed the
television interview, changed the relationship between politicians
and television, and strove to assert balance and rationality into
the medium's treatment of current affairs'.

1955 Picture Book

February saw the BBC with Patricia Driscoll turning the very first
pages of "Picture Book" (initially just the Monday programme in
the Watch with Mother cycle). The Woodentops arrived in
December to complete the week with a different programme
shown each day. From this year to 1957 Patricia Driscoll
introduced the show. The programme encouraged children to
make things. She had a catch phrase: Do you think you could do
this? – I am sure you could if you tried. Driscoll left Picture Book
in 1957 to play the part of Maid Marian with Richard Greene in
the ITV series, The Adventures of Robin Hood. Her place in

Picture Book was taken by Vera
McKechnie in a further series in 1962–
63.

The Watch with Mother schedule was
as follows:

- Picture Book – Mondays (from 1955), presented by Patricia
  Driscoll, and by Vera McKechnie in the 1963 series.
- Andy Pandy – Tuesdays (from 1950).
- Flower Pot Men – Wednesdays (from
  1952).
- Rag, Tag and Bobtail – Thursdays (from
  1953).
- The Woodentops – Fridays (from 1955).

When ITN launched, lunchtime news programmes were a feature
of its scheduling. However, as the years advanced these
disappeared from the schedules, except at weekends, when they
were embedded into ITV's Saturday sports coverage and Sunday
afternoon family broadcasting. Lunchtime news programmes
disappeared completely from schedules in the second half of the
1960s.

The variety show and game show era was introduced by ITV:

1955 Sunday Night at the London Palladium

Sunday Night at the London Palladium (100 years old on 26 December 2010) launched on ITV and played for nearly 20 years (1955–74). The comperes included: Tommy Trinder, Dickie Henderson, Bob Monkhouse, Hughie Green, Alfred Marks, Robert Morley, Bruce Forsyth, Norman Vaughan, Jimmy Tarbuck, Jim Dale and Ted Rogers.

1955 Take Your Pick

Take Your Pick launched on ITV this year, hosted by Michael Miles

'Yes/No' interlude

1955 Double Your Money

Double Your Money was a British Quiz Show hosted by Hughie Green. Originally broadcast on Radio Luxembourg, it transferred to ITV in 1955, a few days after the commercial channel began broadcasting. Female  hostesses included Monica Rose, a former accounts clerk from White City, London, who was a chirpy and popular teenage contestant, subsequently recruited by Hughie Green.

1956 Crawley leaves ITN

The ITV companies saw current affairs programming being firmly within their territory. Ultimately, Crawley felt that he had no option but to resign and he did so on 13 January 1956. That evening the Chair of the ITA, Sir Kenneth Clark, was interviewed by ITN's Robin Day about the resignation, live on air in the 10:45pm ITN news bulletin (channel 3). While the encounter between Day and Clark was not recorded for posterity the now digitised script offers a glimpse of what transpired, as the archived bulletin script includes the newscaster's typed introduction and one page of manuscript notes. With Crawley gone, ITN quickly recruited an experienced Fleet Street journalist as its next editor-in-chief; Geoffrey Cox had been a foreign correspondent for the Daily Express before the Second World War, and afterwards had taken a senior post with the News Chronicle. He brought to the independent television company a hard news 'nose' and was sympathetic to Crawley's approach. Cox was to stay with the company for 12 years and oversee its development into an established news broadcaster. In the year that Cox arrived, two international crises developed that provided opportunities for the new company to establish its credentials. From the early summer through until the end of the year a crisis developed centred around the Suez Canal. Cox had discovered that it was possible to extend the time allotted to the late evening news bulletin. He exploited this to ensure that both Suez and the other crisis, Hungary, were well covered and attracted audiences eager to learn and see more, including footage back from Port Said and the Hungarian border.

Radio Times

1956 In the UK, 15.6m homes now had television. Circulation of the BBC Radio Times reached 8.591m – the highest to be achieved until 1984.

Further developments

American Charles Ginsburg (inventor of the VTR) at Ampex, sold the first VTR to the television industry for $50,000. The world's first broadcast via Videotape – CBS airing of the Douglas Edward and the News program on 30 November from New York. CBS Television City in Hollywood replayed the broadcast three hours after it was received on the West Coast. The show was in black and white (the VR-1000 was designed for B&W and could not handle colour broadcasts).

1956 BBC vs ITN news

Robert Dougall, joined the BBC news team to meet the challenge from ITV. Only at this stage did the BBC allow the newscasters' names to be known. These were the days before Autocues and Teleprompters, with the newsreaders reading directly from a script. ITN is frequently cited as the pioneer of a new, considerably less-deferential style of interviewing; and today Newsfilm Online has digitised some of them. These including a series of interviews that Robin Day conducted from Suez in late November and early December 1956, and an interview with Lord Altrincham that was conducted by Robin Day on 6 August 1957. Brian Inglis fronted the new weekly review programme – 'What the papers say'. New ITV channels launched – ITV West, ITV Central and Granada.

Billy Cotton Band Show

As seen from 1949, the Billy Cotton Band Show was a popular Sunday afternoon radio programme on the BBC Light Programme from 1949 to 1968. The show transferred to BBC Television in 1956 usually playing Sunday evenings at 7.00pm. It ran, under various names, to 1965. There were 128 episodes in total. Regular entertainers included Alan Breeze, Kathie Kay, Doreen Stephens and the pianist Russ Conway.

1956 First infra-red remote control

Robert Adler invented the first practical remote control called the Zenith Space Commander. It was preceded by wired remotes and units that failed in sunlight.

1957 New Conservative Prime Minister, Harold
Macmillan.

Sputnick

The start of the satellite era. Sputnik I (Russian: 'Спутник-I'
Russian pronunciation: [ˈsputnʲɪk], , 'Satellite-I (PS-I, that is,
'Простейший -I   Спутник',   or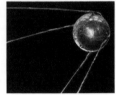
Elementary Satellite-I)) was the first Earth-
orbiting artificial satellite. It was launched
into an elliptical low earth orbit by the
Soviet Union on 4 October this year.

Roving Report

ITN ventured into current affairs programming, with the launch
of a half-hourly series called Roving Report. It first appeared in
March and was broadcast weekly. Launch of STV Central. First
experimental 625-line television transmissions at UHF in Band V
from Crystal Palace.

Cinema newsreel in further decline

The Cinema newsreel industry was in terminal decline. British
Paramount News closed for ever on 10 February 1957.

Television coverage of elections

ITN began developing ways of covering elections. Initially the
company was cautious and was careful to avoid encroaching upon
what was considered to be the political parties' territory. It
carefully planned its early coverage, by using by-elections as a test
bed. Throughout 1957 and 1958 the company increasingly found
its feet and identified the things that worked, and those that didn't.
Its coverage quickly evolved into one that is immediately

recognisable as a prototype
of the coverage with which
audiences are familiar today.
By all accounts, the political
parties considered the
coverage to have been fair,
and this enabled television to
develop further its coverage
of elections. The lessons learned in covering the by-elections
were to prove invaluable preparation for ITN in covering its first
general election, which was held in October 1959. It did so by
bringing reports from several constituencies, prepared for an
election night all-night programme to report the results, and
interviewed the Prime Minister, Harold Macmillan two days
before the election. In that interview, he was finally asked to
describe the 'actual mechanics' of resuming the reins of power, if
he were to be successful. He smiled and said, "I don't do anything!
That's what's so splendid about it. I don't even have to shift my
house ..."

The ITN News programme Roving Report first appeared in
March. The magazine Picture Post closed because of reduced
circulation. The ITV recruited journalists such as Fyfe Robertson
and Trevor Philpott. Alan Wicker joined ITV from the Telegraph.
The BBC meanwhile launched the Tonight programme; a daily
magazine programme with Cliff Michelmore as the anchorman.

1958 Ed Murrow

On 25th October, at an American awards ceremony, CBS news
presenter, Ed Murrow famously said "... I began by saying our
history will be what we make it. If we go on as we are then

history will take its revenge and  retribution will not limp in catching up with us. Just once in a while let us exult the importance of ideas and information. Let us dream to the extent of saying a given Sunday night (a time normally occupied by Ed Sullivan) is given over to a clinical survey of the state of American education, and a week or two later, the time normally used by Steve Allen (an hour-long CBS television variety show) is devoted to a thorough-going study of American

 policy in the Middle East, would the corporate image of their respective sponsors be damaged? Would the stockholders rise up in their wrath and complain? Would anything happen other than a few million people would have received a little illumination on subjects that may well determine the future of this country and therefore the future of the corporations. To those who say people wouldn't look, they wouldn't be interested, they are too complacent, indifferent and insulated, I can only reply, there is in one reporter's opinion considerable evidence against that contention. But even if they are right, what have they got to lose? Because if they are right, and this instrument (television) is good for nothing but to entertain, amuse and insulate, then the tube (CRT) is flickering now and we will soon see that the whole struggle is lost. This instrument can teach, it can illuminate; and yes it can even inspire. But it can do so only to the extent that humans are determined to use it towards those ends. Otherwise, it is only wires and lights in a box. Good night. And good luck."

1958 4 January 'Sputnik 1', which had been launched on 4 October 1957, falls to Earth from its orbit.

Microprocessing

In electronics, an integrated circuit (also known as IC, microcircuit, microchip, silicon chip, or chip) is a miniaturized electronic circuit. Itconsists mainly of semiconductor devices, as well as passive components, manufactured in the surface of a thin substrate of semiconductor material. Integrated circuits are used in almost all electronic equipment in use today (especially television technology) and have revolutionized the world of electronics. The integrated circuit can be credited as being invented by both Jack Kilby of Texas Instruments and Robert Noyce of Fairchild Semi-conductor, working independently of each other. Kilby recorded his initial

ideas concerning the integrated circuit in July this year and successfully demonstrated the first working integrated circuit in September.

1958 International News

This year saw the launch of ITV Meriadan. The BBC Tonight programme now had achieved an audience of seven million. The first UK by-election (Rochdale) was broadcast by ITV and the BBC. ITN was keen to ensure that it was able to cover international stories, allowing for its slim financial resources. The company sent out its own film crews to capture the big and developing news stories, for instance, its reporter Brian Connell covered events in Paris in May 1958, where political events were pointing to a return to power of Charles de Gaulle. Connell covered de Gaulle's press conference (translating the general's remarks on the fly) and a demonstration in which he interviewed its leaders while they were marching. One of its stringers (freelance cameramen) managed to film the landing in Beirut of battle-prepared US marines in 1958. The troops landed on a pleasure beach among bemused onlookers and children. There are countless other examples of ITN's international coverage available for download today from Newsfilm Online, including footage of aircraft blown up by Palestine Liberation Front guerillas in Dawson's field, Jordan, in 1970.

More television homes over radio homes

By this year, more homes had TV instead of just radio.

Further developments

The first BBC videotapes were made of broadcast material. The ITV region, Associated-Rediffusion, showed the first (non-live) programme broadcast from an Ampex VTR (video tape recorder). The first investigations into stereophonic broadcasts (Crosby system) began. Launch of American NASA this year to plan for space exploration.

First STD call in UK

1958 On 5 December, HM The Queen made the first STD (subscriber trunk dialling) telephone call to the Lord Provost of Edinburgh, Sir Ian Anderson Johnston-Gilbert, from Bristol central exchange at Marsh Street, Bristol. The call cost 10d – 4p in today's currency. Bryan Fox was 18 and had finished his apprenticeship three months before he stood next to the Queen when she made the historic call. Mr Fox, 71, from Downend, in Bristol, who retired from BT in 1991, said: "It was one of the most important days ever in telecommunications history and a huge amount of work went into making sure the day went without a hitch."

1959 General Election. Conservative Prime Minister, Harold Macmillan.

Margaret Thatcher enters Parliament

Margaret Thatcher entered Parliament as the Member for Finchley, North London. Personal Computers and microcomputers (see 1976) were made possible because, in the field of microelectronics, the integrated circuit, or IC, was developed this year.

Ivy Fox

The author's mother, Ivy Fox, this year with the latest UK television set. In America, 73% of all homes had monochrome or colour television sets.

More ITV channels

Launch of more ITV channels: ITV Tyne Tees, ITV Anglia and UTV. Both UK BBC and ITV channels covered the General Election.

1959 More change

In the cinema, both Gaumont British News and Universal News closed in January. Both were replaced by a cine-magazine called Look at Life. This year saw the first transatlantic television transmission by telephone cable using slow-speed transmission equipment constructed by the design group of the Research Department of Cablefilm. The occasion was the opening of the St. Lawrence Seaway jointly by the Queen and President Eisenhower.

Audio tape format war

1960s Portable audio format war: 8-track and 4-track cartridges vs Compact Cassette.

8-track above and cassette below

While notably successful into the mid-to-late 1970s, the 8-track eventually lost due to technical limitations, including variable audio quality and lack of fine control. Similarly, the smaller formats of microcassette developed by Olympus and minicassette developed by Sony for applications requiring lower audio fidelity such as dictation and telephone answering machines.

FM radio broadcast format war

The Crosby system vs the GE/Zenith system. The Crosby system was technically superior, especially in transmitting clear stereo signals, due to its use of an FM subcarrier for stereo sound rather than the AM subcarrier employed by GE/Zenith. Many radios built in this period allowed the user to select Crosby or GE/Zenith listening modes. However, the Crosby system was incompatible with lucrative SCA services such as in-store broadcasting and background music. FM station owners successfully lobbied the FCC to adopt the GE/Zenith system in 1961, which was SCA-compatible.

1960 Coronation Street

The longest running and most successful British soap opera was first transmitted on ITV on Friday 9 December this year. Made by Granada Television, the Manchester based commercial company, 'the Street,' as it is affectionately known, has been at the top of the UK ratings for over 50 years. The programme is perhaps best known for its realistic depiction of everyday working-class life in a Northern community. Set in the fictional area of Weatherfield in a working class region of north-west England, it grew out of the so-called 'kitchen sink' drama style popularized in the late 1950s. The series, originally called Florizel Street by its creator Tony Warren, began as a limited thirteen episodes, but its cast of strong characters, its northern roots and sense of community immediately created a loyal following. These factors, combined with skilfully written and often amusing scripts have ensured its continued success.

1960 The BBC Television Centre

The BBC Television Centre at White City in West London is now the headquarters of BBC Television – officially opened on 29 June this year. It was one of the world's first buildings designed specifically for the making and transmission of TV programmes. It remains one of the largest. The site was once used for the Franco-British exhibition of 1908.

The building features a distinctive circular central block (officially known as the main block, but often affectionately referred to by staff as the 'doughnut') around which are studios, offices, engineering areas and the new News Centre. It was built as a circle so that when cables were laid from each studio to the

central apparatus room (CAR), through the centre of the circle, the cabling distance between all studios was the same. In the centre of the main block is a

statue designed by T B Huxley-Jones, of the Greek god of the sun, Helios (Greek: "Ηλιος, Latinized as Helius, meaning 'sun') which is meant to symbolise the radiation of television light around the world. At the foot of this statue are two reclining figures, symbolising sound and vision, the components of television. (This structure was originally a working fountain but due to the building's unique shape it was too noisy and was deactivated.) Even though there is a foundation stone marked 'BBC 1956' in the basement of the main building, construction had begun on the site in 1951. Over time various extensions have been added to the building to maximise the site's potential. Increasingly the corporation has had to seek further accommodation elsewhere, such as the nearby BBC White City. This new complex comprises White City One, a 25,000 square metre office building, and the linked Broadcast and Media Centres.

The overall design for Television Centre, from the air, appears to be like a question mark in shape. The architect, Graham Dawbarn (Norman & Dawbarn), drew a question mark on an envelope (now held by the BBC Written Archives Centre) while thinking about the design of the building, and realised that it would be an ideal shape for the site. However, an article in The B.B.C. Quarterly, July 1946, proposed a circular design for a new television studio complex, several years before Dawbarn drew up his plans.

The centre's studios range in size from 110 square metres (1074 ft²) to the vast Studio TC1 at 995 square metres (10,250 ft²). It is the third largest television studio in Britain (following The Fountain Studios' Studio A&B and The Maidstone Studios' Studio 5), and is equipped for HDTV production (as are TC4 and TC8). The studios have been home to some of the world's most famous

TV programmes including Fawlty Towers, Monty Python's Flying Circus, Blue Peter, Absolutely Fabulous, The Hitchhiker's Guide to the Galaxy and the classic, Doctor Who.

1960 Live Grand National and further developments

First live transmission of the Grand National with commentary by Peter Dimmock. The first split screen broadcast occurred on the Kennedy–Nixon debates. The first prototype multi-standard converter was used to convert pictures of Princess Margaret's Wedding to the American standard. Demonstrations of pictures using different television line standards were shown to a party from the GPO (The General Post Office – the 'owner' of the telephone public switched network), headed by its Director General, Sir Gordon Radley, as part of the Pilkington Committee deliberations to select the line standard for BBC 2.

1961 Hancock

In the UK, there were now 16.2m homes. 'The Blood Donor' was an episode from the final series of the BBC television comedy series Hancock (formerly Hancock's Half Hour). First transmitted this year, it has become one of the most famous situation comedy half-hour programmes ever broadcast in the UK. The show starred Tony Hancock. Supporting Hancock were Patrick Cargill, Hugh Lloyd, Frank Thornton and June Whitfield. It is certainly the best known of Hancock's many half-hours, but not completely on its artistic merits.

Computer packet switching

Leonard Kleinrock of MIT published the first paper on the computer packet switching theory for the concept of the Internet (see 1969). Since networking computers was new to begin with, standards were being developed incrementally. Once the concept was proven, the organizations involved started to lay out some ground rules for standardization.

Further ITV channels

Further ITV channels opened: West Country, STV North and Border. The Stockholm Conference on VHF/UHF planning was convened. Detailed proposals for frequency allocations in Bands I, II, III, IV and V were submitted by the BBC Research Department to the Conference via the Post Office.

1961 The Sunday Telegraph newspaper launched on 5 February.

1962 Z cars

Since 1955 a policeman's lot had been depicted as a happy one by the BBC's 'community copper' series Dixon of Dock Green. But when Z Cars came along in 1962, television finally got the chance to show the British public a different outlook altogether.

667 episodes of Z Cars, 25/50 minute duration were broadcast by the BBC 1962–65 and 1967–78.

In 1962, the writer Troy Kennedy Martin was confined to bed with mumps and decided to pass his time listening in to the police  wavelength on his radio. What he heard was a far cry from what was being depicted on television. As a result he created Z Cars, a series set on Merseyside at a time when Liverpool was on the verge of significant social changes. To combat the growing crime wave policemen were taken off the beat and placed in fast response vehicles, the 'Z Cars' of the series title (so called because the cars were Ford Zephyrs), and put on patrol around the old district of Seaport and the modern 'high rise' development of Kirkby Newtown.

1962 Walter Leland Cronkite, Jr.

Walter Cronkite (4 November 1916 to 17 July 2009) was an American broadcast journalist, best known as anchorman for the CBS Evening News for 19 years (1962–81). During the heyday of CBS News in the 1960s and 1970s, he was often cited as 'the most trusted man in America' after being so named in an opinion poll. Although he reported many events from 1937 to 1981, including bombing in Second World War, the Nuremberg trials, combat in the Vietnam War, the death of President John F Kennedy, Watergate, and the Iran Hostage Crisis, he was known for extensive TV coverage of the US space program, from Project Mercury to the Moon landings (with co-host Wally Shirra), to the Space Shuttle. He was the only non-NASA recipient of a Moon-rock award. The Beatles' first American TV broadcast was with Walter Cronkite.

This year saw the BBC Radio Times reach its 2000th edition on 10 March – costing 5d. Further ITV regions opened: Wales and the Channel. BBC Wales opened.

TW3

The sartorial programme 'That
Was The Week That Was'
(TW3) started. The idea for the
satire came from the Director

General, Hugh Greene. In November this year, Britain was
changing. Deference was on the way out. The Beatles were on
their way in. The 'satire boom' was in full swing and the revue
'Beyond the Fringe' had stormed to success on both sides of the
Atlantic. Private Eye had just launched and the Establishment club
was up and running in Soho. TW3 became the highlight of Sunday
nights in the UK.

Slow motion replay

This year saw the first video tape slow-motion sports replay
broadcast.

BBC2 and further developments

The Pilkington Report was published, recommending a second
BBC channel, a separate BBC service for Wales, a change of line
standard from 405 VHF to 625 lines, colour on 625-line UHF, and
the restructuring of ITV. A new ident for the BBC was introduced.

1962 Telstar satellite

This year, on 10 July, saw the launch of the
Telestar I satellite. This was NOT a
geostationary satellite but orbited the world
allowing time slot allocations to broadcasters.
First transatlantic colour television link by
satellite from Goonhilly Downs, Cornwall,
England to Andover, Maine, using BBC

Research Department slide scanner. 16 June saw the UHF monochrome and colour television field trials from Crystal Palace to determine, among other things, the problems involved in transmitting more than one channel from the same site using the 625-line transmission standard. Experimental transmissions of the Zenith-GE stereophonic system on a single VHF channel from the Wrotham transmitter took place.

Steptoe and Son

1962 Steptoe and Son was a British sitcom written by Ray Galton and Alan Simpson about two rag and bone men living in Oil Drum Lane, a fictional street in Shepherd's Bush, London. Four series were broadcast on the BBC from this year to 1965, followed by a second run from 1970–1974.

1962 Roving Report

The current affairs programme Roving Report was broadcast until November when it was replaced by a new programme called ITN Reports. The new weekly programme ran until December 1965, when it in turn was replaced by Reporting '66. In January 1967, the programme was restyled Reporting '67. 20 April saw the launch of BBC2 on the 625-line UHF (ultra high frequency) transmission mode.

BBC2 started a news review programme for deaf viewers. The live satellite broadcast of the opening of the Olympic Games, Tokyo was achieved.

1962 Completion of the ITV network

As stated earlier, after much debate both in the British Parliament and the British Press, the Television Act became law in 1954. This

Act paved the way for the establishment of a commercial television service in the UK, creating the Independent Television Authority (ITA). The ITA's responsibility was to regulate the new service, ensuring that it did not follow the same path taken by American television networks (which were perceived as 'vulgar' by some

commentators). For example, it was made obligatory that commercials be clearly distinguishable from programmes. At the time, American shows were normally sponsored by a single company, so it was not uncommon for a game show host to step away from his podium after a round to sell cars or The Flintstones or launch into an advert for cigarettes, with no perceived change from show to advert.

The ITA service, so-called because of its independence from the BBC (which previously had held a monopoly on

 Independent Television Authority

broadcasting in the UK), was to be made up of regions, with each region run by different companies. The network was built from 1955 to 1962. The three largest regions (London, the Midlands and the North of England) were subdivided into weekday and weekend services, with a different company running each. Space for commercials, shown during and between programmes, was always sold on a region-by-region basis by each ITV company, and not on a nation-wide basis throughout the United Kingdom. The reason for this seemingly over-complicated arrangement was to fulfil the 1954 Act's requirement for competition within the ITV system (as well as against the BBC) and also to help prevent any individual company obtaining a monopoly on commercial broadcasting.

The ITV companies were required, by the terms of their licences from the ITA, to provide a local television service for their particular region, including a daily local news bulletin and regular local documentaries. However, national news bulletins, covering events in the UK and the rest of the world, were (and still are) produced by Independent Television News (ITN). Until 1990 ITN was jointly owned by all the ITV companies.

Each company also produced programming that would be shown across the network, although the decision as to when or if to show each programme remained with the individual contractors. The four largest franchise operators, known as the 'Big Four', were Associated Rediffusion (London weekday), ATV (Midlands weekday and London weekend), Granada (North of England weekday) and ABC (North of England and Midlands weekend) and produced the bulk of this output. Each regional service had its own on-screen identity to distinguish it from other regions, since there was often a sizeable overlap in reception capability within each region.

The first ITV contractor to begin broadcasting was the London Weekday contractor Associated-Rediffusion, on 22 September 1955 beginning at 7.15pm local time. On the first night of telecasts, the BBC, who had held the monopoly on broadcasting in Britain, aired a melodramatic episode of their popular radio soap opera The Archers on the Home Service. In the episode, core character Grace Archer was fatally injured in a fire, and it

was seen as a ploy to keep loyal viewers and
listeners away from the new station. The first full
day of transmissions was 23 September 1955
when Britain's first female newsreader Barbara
Mandell appeared.

The weekend London contractor, ATV London (initially known
as 'ABC' until the Midlands' and North's weekend contractor,
Associated British Corporation, complained), began two days
later. The other regions all launched later:

Date	Region	Company
22 September 1955	London (Weekday)	Associated-Rediffusion
24 September 1955	London (Weekend)	Associated TeleVision (ATV London)
17 February 1956	Midlands (Weekday)	Associated TeleVision (ATV Midlands)
18 February 1956	Midlands (Weekend)	Associated British Corporation (ABC – not to be confused with the American Broadcasting Company, Associated Broadcasting Company, Australian Broadcasting Corporation or Asahi Broadcasting Corporation)
3 May 1956	North of England (Weekday)	Granada Television
5 May 1956	North of England (Weekend)	Associated British Corporation (ABC)

31 August 1957	Central Scotland	Scottish Television
14 January 1958	South Wales and West of England	Television Wales and the West (TWW)
30 August 1958	South Central and South East England	Southern Television
15 January 1959	North East England	Tyne Tees Television
27 October 1959	East of England	Anglia Television
31 October 1959	Northern Ireland	Ulster Television
29 April 1961	South West England	Westward Television
1 September 1961	English–Scottish Border and Isle of Man	Border Television
30 September 1961	North East Scotland	Grampian Television
1 September 1962	Channel Islands	Channel Television
14 September 1962	North and West Wales	Wales (West and North) Television (Teledu Cymru)

1963 Doctor Who

The programme originally ran from 1963 to 1989. The first Doctor was 55-year-old character actor William Hartnell.

Doctor Who was a British programme produced by the BBC. The programme depicted the adventures of a mysterious and eccentric humanoid alien known as the Doctor who travelled through time and space in his spacecraft, the TARDIS (an acronym for Time And Relative Dimensions In Space), which normally appeared from the

exterior to be a blue 1950s British police box. With his companions, he explored time and space, faced a variety of foes, saved civilizations, defeated alien, human and technological enemies of sorts, helping others and righting wrongs, as well as improving the way people, aliens and robots chose to live their lives. A new series was launched in early 2005 and still runs today.

1963 New Conservative Prime Minister, Sir Alex Douglas-Home.

First home VCR

This year, in America, Ampex introduced their VR-1500 video recorder, the world's first 'home' video system. Actually it wasn't very practical for home use at all. The camera and TV monitor were large (the camera weighed in at 100 pounds), and the cost was about $30,000 – not something a consumer could afford. And professionals who took the leap into this new technological pool had to drive the equipment around in trucks. It was anything but portable.

The early Beatles

The years up to 1963 were the years of hard graft for The Beatles. From the first meeting of John Lennon and Paul McCartney on 6 July 1957 there were hundreds of local club gigs in and around their home town of Liverpool. By the end of 1962, local radio and television stations were starting to notice and a number of local TV spots followed. Alas, these would now all seem to be lost, but these appearances marked the first recognition of what was to become a world-wide television phenomenon.

Top of the Pops

1964 In the UK, 17m homes had television. Top of the Pops, also known as TOTP, was a British music chart television programme, made by the BBC and originally broadcast weekly from 1 January 1964 to 30 July 2006.

Sir James Wilson Vincent Savile OBE, KCSG (born 31 October 1926), commonly known as Jimmy Savile (often misspelled 'Saville'), was the English DJ, actor and media personality, best known for his BBC television show Jim'll Fix It, and for being the first and last presenter of the long-running BBC chart show Top of the Pops. He was also noted for his support of various charities and fundraising efforts. The show was traditionally shown every Thursday evening on BBC1, before being moved to Fridays in 1996, and then moved to Sundays on BBC Two in 2005.

Each weekly programme consisted of performances from some of that week's best-selling popular music artists, with a rundown of that week's singles chart. Additionally, every year there was a special edition of the programme on Christmas Day featuring some of the best-selling singles of the year. Although the weekly show was cancelled, the Christmas special has continued. It was also survived by TOTP2, which began in 1994 and featured vintage performances from the Top of the Pops archives. In the 1990s, the show's format was sold to several foreign broadcasters in the form of a franchise package, and at one point various versions of the show were shown in nearly 100 countries.

1964 First commercial broadcaster to fail.

The first (and only) ITV company to fail was Wales West and North (WWN). It was taken over by Television Wales and West (TWW).

New BBC testcards

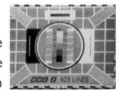

The BBC testcard D was released in 405-line format. Music as well as test tones were regularly used to accompany this image on BBC1. The very first prototype for a plasma display monitor was invented in July at the University of Illinois by professors Donald Bitzer and Gene Slottow, and then graduate student Robert Willson. However, it was not until after the advent of digital and other technologies that successful plasma televisions became possible. According to Wikepedia 'a plasma display is an emissive flat panel display where light is created by phosphors excited by a plasma discharge between two flat panels of glass'. BBC testcard E (TCE) was released to comply with the BBC's new 625-line

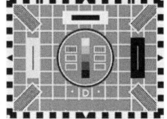

standard. Numerous television vendors complained that the image made on screen was unattractive – its sinusoidal frequency gratings looked soft – and TCE was withdrawn after only five days of service.

1964 On 15 September, the Daily Herald became the Sun newspaper.

1964 Biggest TV audience so far

The Beatles first tour of the USA in February saw the biggest American TV audience ever (73m) from New York on the Ed Sullivan Show. The broadcast was in black and white although it was filmed in colour.

1964 General Election. Labour Prime Minister, Harold Wilson.

Harold Wilson said he would use 'the white heat of technology' to boost British prosperity and this included television broadcast. Wilson really believed in television. He wanted to televise Parliment and advanced ministerial interviews by TV journalistics.

Television Act 1964

The ITA's existence was continued under the Television Act 1964. The BBC started its first studies into digital techniques for television broadcast. This year also saw the introduction of the 625-line broadcast system in the UK.

1964 First Pirate radio station

Britain's first offshore radio station, Radio Caroline, began broadcasting at Easter this year from a ship anchored just outside UK territorial waters. She was followed by a host of other radio stations based on boats and marine structures dotted around the coast. These 'pirates' rapidly won an enormous and enthusiastic audience.

The Tokyo Olympics broadcast to the UK via the Earlybird satellite.

1964 First home VCR

The Philips EL3400 is a good contender for the first domestic video recorder as it is a relatively compact stand alone unit. It still weighed 45 Kg and did not contain a  TV tuner or timer which might be considered essential for the domestic '1st' title. It used 1 inch tape.

1964–5 National Viewers' and Listeners' Association

Mary Whitehouse CBE (13 June 1910 to 23 November 2001) was a British campaigner against the 'permissive society' particularly as the media portrayed and reflected it. The motivation for her activities derived from her traditional Christian  beliefs and her work as a teacher of sex education. She became a public figure via the 'Clean-Up TV' pressure group, established in 1964, in which she was the most prominent figure. Mrs Whitehouse particularly found a lack of accountability in the BBC, describing it as, "an organisisation pursuing radical changes in its broadcasting policies at this time." She was the founder in 1965 and first president of the National Viewers' and Listeners' Association – later becoming Mediawatch-UK.

1965 Ban on cigarette advertising on television.

1965 Intelsat 1 Early Bird

6 April saw the launch of Intelsat 1 Early Bird, the first commercial geostationary communication satellite, marking the true beginning of satellite television into the future.

Telstar 2 was launched on 7 May and became operational on 16 May. Belonging to AT&T, the original Telstar was part of a multinational agreement between AT&T, Bell Telephone Laboratories, NASA, the British General Post Office, and the French National PTT (Post, Telegraph and Telecom Office) to develop experimental satellite communications over the Atlantic Ocean. Bell Labs held a contract with NASA, reimbursing the agency three million dollars for each of the two launches, independent of success. The US ground station was

Andover Earth Station in Andover, Maine, built by Bell Labs. The main British ground station was at Goonhilly Downs in Cornwall, south-western England, and it was used by the BBC. The BBC was the international coordinator and the standards 525/405 conversion equipment (filling a large room) was researched and developed by the BBC and located in the BBC Television Centre, London. The French ground station was at Pleumeur-Bodou in north-western France.

The Telstar 2 satellite was built by a team at Bell Telephone Laboratories, including John Robinson Pierce who created the project, Rudy Kompfner who invented the traveling wave tube transponder used in the satellite, and James M Early who designed the transistors and solar panels. The satellite is roughly spherical, measuring 34.5 inches (876.30 mm) in length, and weighed about 170 pounds (77 kg). Its dimensions were limited by what would fit in one of NASA's Delta rockets. Telstar was spin-stabilized, and its outer surface was covered with solar cells to generate electrical power. The power produced was a tiny 14 watts.

Death of Sir Winston Churchill

The BBC ran a live outside broadcast for the State funeral of Sir Winsaton Churchill. The commentary was by Richard Dimbleby.

1965 Reel to reel VTR portable

Domestic or profession 1-inch reel to reel video tape recorder (VTR). The VR 5003 was the international version of the Ampex 5000 (US version). Ampex was founded in 1944 and incorporated in California in 1946. In 1947, they  introduced their first audio tape recorder – the model 200A. In 1956, they introduce their first (reel to reel) video tape recorder, the VR 1000. This was a quadruplex VTR. It was the first production VTR ever sold (as opposed to earlier prototypes). It was a large floor-standing unit on wheels and cost $50,000. The VR 5003 (and the 5000) available from 1965 was called a 'portable VTR!' One person could carry it with a little effort. The build quality was very high. Ampex is still in business today.

1966 General Election. Labour Prime Minister, Harold Wilson.

1967 BBC colour television announced

The BBC announced colour television to be launched in the following year. 625-line PAL colour television system to be adopted by the UK. Colour pictures of the General Election were relayed from the BBC Television Centre to the USA via the 'Early Bird' satellite.

This year, Sony brought camcorder portability into reality when they introduced their first portable system, the DV-2400 Video Rover. It filmed in black and white only, and required a separate unit for playback. Panasonic and JVC followed soon after with their own portable models.

Testcard F (the most famous and widely used testcard) was released by the BBC to coincide with colour transmissions that started this year on 1 July on BBC2. Only  limited programmes were available in colour from the start. The full output became colour on BBC2 on 2 December this year. The testcard features a picture of Carole Hersee (daughter of BBC engineer George Hersee) playing noughts and crosses This design came about after Hersee was asked to intervene by the committee charged with the creation of technical standards for the new colour TV services.

The Marine Broadcasting Offences Act of this year was laid down on the statute book to suppress broadcasting from ships, aircraft and certain marine structures.

ITV Yorkshire opened on 1 July with colour in 625 lines UHF PAL launched. The occasional BBC 1 News at 10 broadcast in colour. The first regular colour pictures in the UK were broadcast by BBC2 in 1967 when it covered Wimbledon. From 2 December, BBC2 was broadcasting about 25 hours a week of colour material – 80% of its content.

The Wireless Telegraphy Act was placed on the statute book. It was an Act to enable the Postmaster General to obtain information as to the sale and hire of television receiving sets; to enable him to prohibit the manufacture or importation of certain wireless telegraphy apparatus.

First 400m TV audience

The first 400 million worldwide TV audience was achieved with 'All You Need Is Love' – a song written by John Lennon and credited to writers Lennon/McCartney. It was first performed by The Beatles on Our World, the first live global television link. The Broadcast reached 26 countries and was watched by 400 million households. The programme was broadcast via satellite on 25 June. The BBC had commissioned the Beatles to write a song for the UK's contribution.

1967 30 September, launch of Radio One with DJ Tony Blackburn

The first record Tony Blackburn played was 'Flowers in The Rain' by The Move. He chose it because of the crashing noise at the beginning. The DJ has kept the record to this day.

1967 Sony CV-2000

Many web sites and Sony themselves claimed this to be the first domestic video recorder. It is a stand alone VTR and used $\frac{1}{2}$ inch tape. It is certainly the first ever $\frac{1}{2}$ inch tape domestic video recorder, but is it really the first stand alone VTR?

1968 ITV London Weekend Television

ITV London Weekend opened. Radio coverage of the House of Commons started. ITV franchise changes: LWT replaces ATV London, Yorkshire TV forms a new region from part of the old Granada area, Harlech replaces TWW, and Thames formed by the merger of ABC and Rediffusion. ATV takes on the all-week Midland franchise.

1968 Philips LDL1002

This unit was marketed by Philips as a domestic video recorder and it was sold in relatively large numbers. It could be considered as the first mass produced domestic video recorder. It used ½ inch reels and the unit was no larger than audio tape recorders of that time. (It is compact at 43.5 cm wide by 36 cm deep by 19 cm high) Philips marketing  brochures were very definitely aimed at the domestic consumer. The unit is remarkably light, indeed it is even lighter than many audio reel to reel recorders of that time at only 13.55 Kg. It was housed in an attractive wood-appearance case to match a domestic setting.

1968 Concorde

Concorde made its first flight and broke the sound barrier travelling at 1,350 mph. Martin Luther King was assassinated. Star Trek started and it featured the first inter-racial kiss on television. The Forsyth  Saga aired on BBC 1 and was not only the last period costume drama to be filmed in monochrome, but also the most expensive series so far. The Liver Birds first aired on television and was the first soap to have two female leads. Dad's Army first aired and ran for nine years and is the most repeated series in television history. Themed toys began to appear in the shops for example, Batman and James Bond.

1969 Man first lands on the Moon on 20 July. Concorde goes into service.

1969 The Queen authorises a documentary

In June this year, the Queen authorised a documentary by inviting the television cameras into her life to film her family. This was a public relations move to try to counter republican talk from Cabinet factions and public opinion which said 18% of the population wanted an end to the Monarchy. This gave way to a public debate as to whether the Queen should pay income tax which eventually happened. The Prime Minister, Harold Wilson supported the Queen but members of his cabinet were against Royal spending. Harold Wilson believed in television saying that it "binds the nation together". He influenced the Queen to allow television to make the programme which was well received.

1969 Early Internet

The first practical use of the Internet was originally developed by DARPA, the American Defence Advanced Research Projects Agency, as a means of sharing information on defence research between involved universities and defence research facilities. Originally it was just email and FTP (file transfer protocol) sites as well as the Usenet where scientists could question and answer each other. It was originally called ARPANET (Advanced Research Projects Agency NETwork). The concept was developed starting in 1964, and the first messages passed were between UCLA and the Stanford Research Institute this year.

1969 ITV goes colour, using the PAL 625-line system on UHF

1969 Live television from the moon – Apollo 11

British television coverage of Apollo 11, man's first
mission to land on the moon, lasted from 16 to 24
July 1969. All the then three UK channels, BBC1,
BBC2 and ITV provided extensive coverage. Most of
the footage covering this historic event from a British perspective
has now been either wiped or lost. The Lunar module plaques
 were rectangular stainless steel plaques attached
to the ladders on the lunar modules used from
Apollo 11 through to Apollo 17. The picture shows
the upload transmitter dish used to beam back
television pictures to Earth. James Burke, one of
the main presenters of the BBC's coverage of the
Apollo 11 mission, reviewed its launch earlier in the day on 16 July
1969. The BBC television coverage of Man's first landing on the
moon consisted of 27 hours of coverage
over a ten day period. The programmes
titled 'Apollo 11' were broadcast from Lime
Grove Studios in London. The BBC2 sections
were broadcast in colour and the BBC1
sections in black and white (full colour television in Britain being
a few months away). Its main presenter was Cliff Michelmore,
with James Burke and Patrick Moore concentrating on scientific

 and technical explanations and
analysis. In America, Michael
Charlton reported live from
Cape Kennedy and Mission
Control in Houston. There had
been a big build up to the
coverage.

1969 Colour broadcast

ITV and BBC now broadcast completely in colour. The BBC introduced the first version of the then famous 'mirror globe' – a rotating globe with a flat

globe as a visual behind it. The inclusion of the word 'colour' in the station ident would be viewed as a subtle reminder to the vast majority of viewers still watching in black and white to buy a colour TV set. Live monochrome pictures were broadcast from the moon. (Colour pictures of the launch and splashdown were also achieved.) The BBC transmitted a full colour service from 15th November.

International News reporting

Towards the end of the 1960s reporters were still sending their filmed reports back to London by overnight flights for broadcast the next day. Satellites were soon to arrive allowing live reporting.

1970s Format Wars

More format wars took place during this decade. Various Quadraphonic encoding methods; CD-4, SQ, QS-Matrix, and others. The expense (and speaker placement troubles) of quadraphonic, coupled with the competing formats requiring various demodulators and decoders, led to an early demise of quadraphonic, though 8-track tape experienced a temporary boost from the introduction of the Q8 form of 8-track cartridge. Quadraphonic sound returned in the 1990s substantially updated as surround sound, but incompatible with old hardware.

More format wars

JVC VHS (video home system) vs Sony Betamax vs Philips Video 2000, the videotape format war. The competition started in 1976 and by 1980, VHS controlled 70% of the North American market. VHS' main advantage was its longer recording time. From the consumer perspective, VHS blank media held more hours and therefore was less expensive.

Vinyl record vs Compact Cassette. The popular 33&1/3 record dominated most of the 20th century, from the 1940s to the 1980s until newer technologies supplanted it. Its main rival, the compact cassette, was slow in growth but with the advent of boom boxes and Walkmans in the 1970s and early 1980s, cassettes eventually outsold vinyl records in the 1980s. Cassettes provided convenient mobile operation, playback free of scratches or skips, and near-CD quality on Type II pre-recorded music encoded with Dolby B.

Capacitance Electronic Disc (CED) vs LaserDisc (LD) vs VHD (Video High-Density), non-recordable video disc formats. All of these ultimately failed to achieve widespread acceptance, although LD found a small videophile market that appreciated its high quality images. The Laser Disc remained available until the arrival of the DVD. Mainstream consumers preferred the recordable videotape for capturing live television and making home movies, quickly making VHS the de-facto standard video format for almost 25 years (circa 1979–2002).

Dolby vs DBX noise reduction systems for audio cassettes, developed by Dolby Laboratories and DBX respectively. These two were mutually incompatible. Dolby B became the de-facto standard for store-bought, pre-recorded cassettes.

Viacom formed

In America, one of the largest media companies in the world was formed – Viacom Inc. It operated numerous subsidiaries in six segments: cable networks,
television, radio, outdoor; entertainment, and video. Well known to later cable viewers were television channels: MTV, Nickelodeon, Nick at Night, VH1, and Showtime. Television holdings included the CBS and UPN television networks, King World Productions, and Paramount Television. Infinity Radio owned and operated a wealth of radio stations. The entertainment segment included: Paramount Pictures, a producer and distributor of motion pictures since 1912, venerable publisher Simon & Schuster, and Paramount Parks' theme attractions. Viacom Outdoor was engaged in display advertising. Blockbuster Inc. operated and franchised video stores around the globe.

Viacom began with 70,000 stockholders and yearly sales of $19.8 million. It had about 90,000 cable subscribers, making it one of the largest cable operators in the United States. It also had an enviable stable of popular, previously-run CBS television series, including I Love Lucy, available for syndication, which accounted for a sizable percentage of Viacom's income.

1973 Cable TV in the USA

By 1973, there were about 2,800 cable systems in the United States, with about 7.5 million subscribers. This market fragmentation, along with the lack of an infrastructure in many communities and tough federal regulations, slowed the development of cable television. In 1973, Viacom had 47,000 subscribers on Long Island, New York, but a drive to find 2,000 more added only 250.

Pay-TV in the USA

In 1976, to compete with Home Box Office (HBO), the leading outlet for films on cable, Viacom established the Showtime movie  network, which sought to provide its audience with feature films recently released in cinema. Viacom retained a half interest in the network while Warner Amex owned the other half. Despite a federal ruling that removed many restrictions on the choice of movies and sports available on pay-TV during this time, and allowed a wider variety of programming, Showtime lost $825,000 in 1977. Nevertheless, Viacom earned $5.5 million that year on sales of $58.5 million. Most of the company's earnings represented sales of television series, but it also reflected the growth of its own cable systems which at that time had about 350,000 subscribers.

Showtime continued to compete aggressively with HBO. In 1977, it began transmitting its programming to local cable stations via satellite, at a cost of $1.2 million a year. The following year it worked out a deal with Teleprompter Corp., then the largest cable systems operator in the United States, with the result that Teleprompter offered its customers Showtime rather than HBO. Showtime also began offering a service channel called Front Row. Dedicated to family programming, including classic movies and children's shows, Front Row cost consumers less than $5 a month and was aimed at smaller cable systems where subscribers could not afford a full-time pay-TV service.

Viacom's forays into the production of original programming in the late 1970s and early 1980s had mixed results. Competition was stiff, the odds of producing a successful television series or film were long, and Viacom experienced several failures. The Lazarus Syndrome and Dear Detective series were failures, and CBS cancelled Nurse after 14 episodes.

Andy Pandy in colour

1970 In the UK, 18.4m homes now had television. Thirteen new colour episodes of Andy Pandy were made and first shown on the BBC from 5 January. In the cinema, Pathe news closed in February.

In America, General David Sarnoff retired as President of RCA this year at the age of 79, and died the following year.

1971 This year, Sony came up with another first in video recorder technology. The U-Matic – a recorder that used ¾ inch tape rather than the 2 inch tape first used in video recording. The machine wasn't portable, but its big advantage was that users could just pop in a cassette – no more threading tape. Meanwhile, Sony and JVC were both working to develop smaller ½ inch tape machines for home use.

In the UK, there were now 18.8m homes. Personal Computers and microcomputers were made possible (see 1976) by the development of the microprocessor by Ted Hoff (at the Intel Corporation in the Santa Clara Valley south of San Francisco). The microprocessor is a tiny machine which combines the equivalent of thousands of transistors (see 1827) on a single, tiny silicon chip. The BBC undertook its early experiments on digital video recording.

1971 Independent local radio

Although the BBC local radio stations had proved to be a success for community radio, there was still a demand from listeners for a form of commercial radio independent from the BBC, represented most strongly by the commercial radio lobby. A change of government occurred in 1972 which saw the passing of Harold Wilson's Labour administration to Edward Heath's Conservative government The new government looked upon the introduction of commercial radio much more favourably. In March 1971, a white paper, 'An Alternative Service of Radio Broadcasting' was published. The Sound Broadcasting Bill followed, becoming the Sound Broadcasting Act 1972. This new act transformed the ITA into the IBA (Independent Broadcasting Authority) giving it the additional responsibility for sound broadcasting in the UK.

1973 The radio only licence was abolished in February 1971. Buying a TV licence now covered radio.

The commercial radio lobby, and possibly the potential listeners, would be disappointed with the government's plans for commercial radio. The potential operators had hoped for a national pop station that would be cheap to run, generate large audiences and therefore make large sums of money from advertising. What they got was as far removed from that scenario as anyone could have possibly imagined. Instead of a station that would have the owners drowning in oceans of easy money, what they got was a system in which they would almost drown in oceans of government and IBA (The Independent Broadcasting Authority) bureaucracy!

It would be a very highly regulated system with tight programming requirements and extremely high technical standards. The IBA was given a plan to introduce 19 local stations in 18 areas and began advertising the initial franchises in 1972, anticipating that the first stations would be on air by 1973 and development would continue until 1976. The IBA plan did not refer to commercial radio, instead it was given the title Independent Local Radio (ILR). The new stations would be required to provide a public service radio funded by advertising, rather than the non-stop pop and 'DJs' that the offshore stations had provided eight years earlier. The stations would have a remit to appeal to all sections of the potential audience – they would be expected to be all things to all people – a resource that anyone could tune in to and find something of interest or pleasure. Some wavelengths had to be re-organised to accommodate new local BBC and ILR medium wave transmitters, for example, Radio Four lost 206m (1457kHz) and 261m (1151 kHz) and Radio Three had to hand over 194m (1546kHz).

BBC local radio initially started life serving small, or tightly defined areas but gradually evolved into more regional or county-wide stations, serving larger areas with bigger transmitters. ILR was to start life as BBC local radio had done, as a number of small services serving a main city and its surrounding area, often with smaller transmitters than BBC local radio currently used. One particular exception to this rule was the London area which would have two ILR stations, rather than one, and serve the whole of the Greater London area and much of the Home Counties with a wide-ranging signal.

1972 ▓ General Election. Conservative Prime Minister, Edward Heath.

More power to the ITV regulator

The BBC developed the log-periodic and this became the workhorse of the UHF television transmitter network.

16 October saw ITN launching a new weekday lunchtime news

programme. It was initially called First Report and ran for 20 minutes and went on air at 12.40pm each weekday. Its presenter was Robert Kee and the programme soon acquired an authority and gravitas. The programme shifted to a 1.00pm time slot in September 1974, and in September 1976 was re-named News at One and extended to run for a full half-hour, with Leonard Parkin as the presenter. The programme and its successors, allowed for changes in presentation style and broadcast timing.

Teletext

1973 The Teletext system was demonstrated by the BBC. The IBA also developed a teletext system. The Independent Broadcasting Act consolidated the Television and Sound Broadcasting Acts 1964 and 1972.

 1973 In the UK, the Handportable telephone (now known as the mobile) improved. It was launched by Philips.

1974 General Election. Labour Prime Minister, Harold Wilson.

BBC Ceefax and IBA Oracle

1974 BBC Ceefax and ITV Oracle were launched this year. These teletext systems were devised in the early 1970s by engineers

 from the BBC and the Independent Broadcasting Authority (IBA), at first working independently, but later as a combined force. Teletext allowed a viewer to display a large number of pages containing information about the

news, current events, weather, traffic, travel information, stock market, and so on. It was transmitted along with standard TV signals. This made used of the fact that about 30 of the 625 scan lines on a TV screen are not actually used, to allow time for the scanning beam to return to the top of the screen when it has reached the bottom. Initially, some of these unused lines were used to broadcast test signals, but it was soon realised that they could also be used to provide a public information service available on the TV. The initial BBC and IBA systems were slightly different. The BBC version originally called Teledata, but later changed to Ceefax (See Facts) was based on a page containing 24 rows of 32 characters per row whilst the IBA version, called ORACLE (for Optional Reception of Announcements by Coded Line Electronics), allowed 22 rows of 40 characters per row. Ceefax was to close in 2012.

The Independent Broadcasting Authority Act made further provision regarding the payments to be made to the IBA by television programme contractors. A new BBC 1 logo appeared

1974 ITN news expands

News reporting was now breaking more boundaries – an ITN report from Cyprus showed Turkish paratroopers in the course of landing to occupy part of the island. These reports have now all been digitised by Newsfilm Online and are available for download. Perhaps one remarkable piece of film shot by ITN was a deliberate re-staging of the invasion of Sinai by Egyptian armed forces. It was arranged specially for ITN – at a cost of countless £millions to the Egyptian defence ministry – and was carried as a special report in News At Ten on 16 July. The reporter was Keith Hatfield.

In America, this year also saw the Columbia Broadcasting System dropping its full name and becoming known simply as CBS, Inc.

1975 Rear projection television sets.

Rear projection television (RPTV) has been commercially available since the 1970s, but at that time could not match the image sharpness of the CRT. Such screens were attractive to some because they had much bigger screens than say 28 inch CRT television. A rear projection television uses a projector to create a small image from a video signal and magnify this image onto a viewable screen. The projector uses a bright beam of light and a lens system to project the image to a much larger size.

The war between VHS and Betamax

1975 On 10 May, Sony's Betamax video standard was introduced, followed a year later by JVC's VHS format (September). For around a decade the two standards battled for dominance, with VHS eventually emerging as the winner. The victory was not due to any technical superiority (Betamax is arguably a better format), but to several factors. Exactly how and why VHS won the war has been the subject of intense debate. The commonly-held belief is that the technically superior Betamax was beaten by VHS through slick marketing. In fact, the truth is more complex and there were a number of reasons for the outcome.

Sony's founder, Akio Morita, claimed that licensing problems between Sony and other companies slowed the growth of

 Betamax and allowed VHS to become established. However, most commentators have played down this issue and cited other reasons as being more important. It is certainly true that VHS machines were initially much simpler and cheaper to manufacture, which would obviously be an attraction to companies deciding which standard to back. It has also been reported that Sony inadvertently gave its competitors a helping hand by revealing key aspects of Betamax technology which were then incorporated into VHS. Manufacturers divided themselves into two camps: On the Betamax side were Sony, Toshiba, Sanyo, NEC, Aiwa, and Pioneer. On the VHS side were JVC, Matsushita (Panasonic), Hitachi, Mitsubishi, Sharp, and Akai. Picture to the left is an early 'piano key' VHS VCR. For consumers, the most immediately obvious difference between the two formats was the recording length. Standard Betamax tapes lasted 60 minutes – not long enough to record a movie. Conversely, the 3-hour VHS tapes were perfect for recording television programmes and movies. Sony did adapt and offer various solutions for longer recording, but it was too late. Picture to the right is an early Betamax VCR.

The issue of recording time is often cited as the most defining factor in the war. Rental movies on VHS became better than Betamax. In the early days, Sony (Beta format) never realized people would rent movies. It is arguable how the format war came to be, but once it happened, there was no turning back. Bitter Betamax owners cringed in their ever-decreasing corner of the video store while VHS owners gloated. The war was over by the late 1980s, although supporters of Betamax have helped keep the format going in a small niche market. Betamax production in America ended in 1993, and the last Betamax machine in the world was produced in Japan in 2002. Of course, both Betamax and VHS analogue machines will eventually be made obsolete by digital technology.

1976 General Election. Labour Prime Minister, James Callaghan.

The first PC

The first personal computer was invented by Steve Jobs and Steve Woznak. The first PC was an Apple computer. Colour TV sets now outnumbered monochrome sets. VHS became the video standard and JVC improved on it by introducing colour VHS.

Arabsat

Establishment of the Arab Satellite Communications Organization (ARABSAT) in order to design, execute and operate the first Arab space system of its kind.

This year, the development of the VHS tape format helped to complete the technology that has gained so much popularity.

1977 The PC industry began this year, when Apple, along with Radio Shack and Commodore, introduced the first off-the-shelf personal computers as consumer products.

The UK was granted five direct broadcast satellite channels (DBS) by the World Administrative Radio conference.

Eutelsat

The satellite television industry started. Eutelsat SA a French-based satellite provider was founded this year. Eutelsat was the first satellite operator in Europe to broadcast television channels direct-to-home. Eutelsat started operations six years later in 1983 with the launch of its first satellite – 1F1. Its satellite fleet was set to provide coverage over the entire European continent, as well as the Middle East, Africa, India and significant parts of Asia and the Americas. It became one of the world's three leading satellite operators in terms of revenues. By the turn of the century, Eutelsat's satellites were destined to be used for broadcasting 3,200 television and 1000 radio stations to more than 187 million cable and satellite homes. The first 1983 satellite was retired to a junk orbit in 1996. Other now disused Eutelsat spacecraft are:

Satellite	position	launched	inclined	retired
1F1	13° East	1983	1989	1996
1F2	7° East	1984	1990	1993
1F4	13° East	1987	1993	2002
1F5	10° East	1988	1994	2000
2F1	13° East	1990	1999	2003
2F2	10° East	1991	2000	2005
2F3	16° East	1991	2000	2004
2F4	7° East	1992	2001	2003

1978 Anna Ford became the latest female television newsreader. The television licence increased to £25. 'Teletrack' special effects equipment was used for World Cup football for the first time. This year saw yet another piece of legislation to govern television. The Independent Broadcasting Authority Act extended (until 31 December 1981) the period during which television and local sound broadcasting services were to be provided by the IBA and exclude section 4(2) and (5) of the Independent Broadcasting Authority Act 1973 in relation to proceedings in Parliament and proceedings of local authorities and committees and joint committees local authorities.

CCTV entryphone systems

In London, Shepherds Bush in the London Borough of Hammersmith & Fulham was the first UK social landlord to  introduce Closed Circuit Television (CCTV) to effectively create a television entryphone system to counter burglary and vandalism. The live CCTV pictures were modulated through the blocks analogue television distribution system to tenants and leaseholders own television sets. When the entryphone buzzer went off the resident simply changed channel to see who was calling – just the same as living in a house and peeping through the curtains before opening the front door. In an national policy review two years later, Peter Fox, The Estates Manager, who pioneered the systems in the Inner London Borough, explained to the Institute of Housing that, "the success of the system had three factors,

- Good PR through tenant involvement,
- Getting the technology right, and
- Good caretaking."

1979 🗳 **General Election**. Conservative Prime Minister, Margaret Thatcher.

The election of Margaret Thatcher led to a decade of policy development in television. Under Thatcher, the principle that broadcasting should be organised as a public service designed to serve the informational, educational and entertainment needs of the UK, was replaced with a market driven industry with public service increasingly less central.

The Broadcasting Act

The latest Independent Broadcasting Act this year conferred greater power on the Independent Broadcasting Authority to equip them to transmit a television broadcasting service additional to those of the British Broadcasting Corporation, and to that provided by the Authority under the Independent Broadcasting Authority Act 1973. BBC live stereo link via INTELSAT satellite from Moscow to London, using 704 kbit/s NICAM-1 equipment designed by the BBC Design Department, was achieved. In the cinema, the British Movietone News ceased on 27 May.

1980 BBC2 saw its first animated ident. In the UK, 20.4m homes had television.

PC peripheral compatibility

1980s The governments of the 1980s wanted rapid development in satellite television services to boost UK industrial competitiveness, but were unwilling to provide the finance for a UK satellite service and insisted on cable and satellite services being financed by private investment. In 1981, the Home Secretary Willie Whitelaw announced that DBS would start in 1986.

More format wars

At this time home computers often had incompatible peripherals such as joysticks, printers, or data recording (tape or disk). For example if a Commodore 64 user wanted a printer he would need to buy a Commodore-compatible unit, or else risk not being able to plug the printer into his computer. Similarly, disk formats were not interchangeable without third party software, since each manufacturer (Atari, IBM, Apple, et al.) used their own proprietary format. Gradually computer and game systems standardized on 'Atari 2600 connectors' for joysticks and mice with parallel ports for printers (mid-1980s), the MS-DOS-derived FAT12 format for floppy disks (mid-1990s), and so on. The main standards used on today's post-2000 computers for inter-compatibility are USB for external devices or FAT32 for pre-formatted hard drives. Some incompatibilities still exist between computers with Windows-based machines and Macintosh file formats, due to the restrictions on filename length and which characters are allowable as part of the filename.

More format wars

- AM stereo was capable of fidelity equivalent to FM but was doomed in the USA by competing formats during the 1980s with Motorola's C-QUAM competing vigorously with three other incompatible formats including those by Magnavox, Kahn/Haseltine, and Harris. It is still widely used in Japan, and sees sporadic use by broadcast stations in the United States despite the lack of consumer equipment to support it.

- Video8 vs VHS-C and later Hi8 vs S-VHS-C camcorder tape formats. This is an extension of the VHS vs Betamax format war, but here neither format won widespread acceptance.

Video8 had the advantage in terms of recording time (4 hours versus 2 hours maximum), but consumers also liked VHS-C since it could easily play in their home VCRs, thus the two formats essentially split the camcorder market in half. As of 2007, the Japan Victor Company (JVC) still makes VHS-C and S-VHS-C camcorders; Sony announced its last Hi8 camcorder – the TRV238.

- Compact Cassette vs CD. The Compact Disc was a clear improvement in audio quality and media durability over all prior magnetic (tape) media. Although CD players were rapidly adopted for home use in the mid-1980s, early portable CD players had problems with skipping due to vibrations and shock. Cassettes continued to dominate the portable player market. By the early 1990s, CD player memory buffering allowed skip-free performance and CD sales finally eclipsed cassettes. CDs are still the main method of pre-recorded distribution in the 2000s – although downloading music to PCs, laptops and ipods will probaby win this future format war.

- Several different versions of the Quarter Inch Cartridge used for data backup.

- Composite video and RF channel 3 F-connectors were two ways of connecting entertainment devices to television sets.

1981 On 1 August, BARB (Broadcasters' Audience Research Board) commenced reporting television viewing figures of **BARB** BROADCASTERS' AUDIENCE RESEARCH BOARD BBC1, BBC2 and ITV. The Chairman was Sir Stewart Crawford. The venture was underwritten by the BBC and ITV. It commenced with a 3,000 panel of homes who reported their viewing choices.

The BBC Radio Times reached its 3000th edition on 9 May – costing 20p. In the UK, there were now 20.9m homes. The Broadcasting Act 1981 amended and consolidated certain provisions of law – such as the extension of the IBA's functions to the provision of programmes for Channel 4 and the establishment of the Broadcasting Complaints Commission.

1981 IBM PC goes on sale

Type	Personal computer
Release date	August 12, 1981
Discontinued	April 2, 1987
Operating system	IBM BASIC / PC-DOS 1.0
	CP/M-86
	UCSD p-System
	CPU Intel 8088 @ 4.77 MHz
Memory	16 kiB ~ 256 kiB

It was the first to wear the 'PC' label, but that was IBM's only innovation. The IBM PC, is the original version and progenitor of the IBM PC compatible hardware platform. It was the IBM model number 5150. It was created by a team of engineers and designers under the direction of Don Estridge of the IBM Entry Systems Division in Boca Raton, Florida, USA. Alongside 'microcomputer' and 'home computer', the term 'personal computer' was already in use before 1981. It was used as early as 1972 to characterize Xerox PARC's Alto. However, because of the success of the IBM Personal Computer, the term came to mean more specifically a microcomputer compatible with IBM's PC products.

1981 The BBC Micro

This was the first computer to use the television as its screen. The BBC Microcomputer System, or BBC Micro, was a series of microcomputers and

associated peripherals designed and built by Acorn Computers for the BBC Computer Literacy Project, operated by the British Broadcasting Corporation. Designed with an emphasis on education, it was notable for its ruggedness, expandability and the quality of its operating system. In the early 1980s, the BBC started what became known as the BBC Computer Literacy Project. The project was initiated partly in response to an extremely influential ITV documentary series The Mighty Micro, in which Dr Christopher Evans from the National Physical Laboratory predicted the coming microcomputer revolution and its impact on the economy, industry, and lifestyle of the United Kingdom. The BBC wanted to base its project on a microcomputer capable of performing various tasks which they could then demonstrate in their 1981 TV series The Computer Programme. The list of topics included programming, graphics, sound and music, Teletext, controlling external hardware and artificial intelligence. It decided to badge a micro, then drew up a fairly ambitious (for its time) specification and asked for takers. The BBC discussed the requirement with several companies including Sinclair Research, Newbury Laboratories, Dragon and Acorn. The Acorn team had already been working on an upgrade to their existing Atom microcomputer. Known as the Proton, it included better graphics and a faster 2MHz MOS Technology 6502 CPU. The machine was only in prototype form at the time, but the Acorn team, largely made up of students including Sophie Wilson and Steve Furber, worked through the night to get a working Proton together to show the BBC. The Acorn Proton not only was the only machine to come up to the BBC's specification, but also exceeded it in nearly every parameter.

JVC wins over Betamax

1982 Sony and JVC were still running neck and neck in the format war. The first combinations were introduced – the camera recorder, or camcorder. Actually, JVC won the race, because in June of this year, they brought out their mini-VHS camcorder. A few months later, in November, Sony offered their Betamovie Beta, which came with the slogan 'Inside This Camera is A VCR'.

Changes at ITV

Channel 4 was launched on 2 November. Some ITV franchises changed; ATV, Southern and Westward give way to Central, TVS and TSW. This year saw the start of S4C (Sianel Pedwar Cymru/Channel 4 Wales), with all Welsh language programmes, both BBC and Independent, moving to this new channel. There had been growing debate that independent television should have an opportunity to open a second television channel. That debate was won and legislation was put in place by Margaret Thatcher's government.

ITN at Channel 4

The first transmission of Channel 4's 55-minute news programme. Channel 4 awarded ITN the contract for producing the programme news but said that it wanted it to be different from other television news programmes. Initially the programme's ratings were poor, as the programme struggled to find a format and approach that was consistent with what Channel 4 wanted. However, after a change of editor and a complete overhaul, the programme began to develop its own style and voice and, more importantly, to grow its audience. Channel 4 News went on to become an award-winning news programme with a reputation for providing penetrating news analysis and authoritative journalism. The Channel gradually added weekend news bulletins to its schedule and early in the new century lunchtime bulletins became a regular feature of its schedules as well.

BBC starts on HDTV

This year, the BBC High Definition Television (HDTV) studies commenced in earnest. HDTV was the new television broadcast standard bringing picture quality that is closer  to a cinematic experience. Many old movies were filmed on 35mm celluloid film – some of which have high resolution pictures. When digitally re-mastered for broadcast the films require an HD television screen with a resolution above 760 lines (as opposed to 625 lines for standard digital broadcast). The HD television screens must be supplied with an HD signal from a digital broadcaster or another HD source.

1981 Rupert Murdoch buys the Times and Sunday Times newspapers.

1982 Arabsat first satellite

Arabsat enters into a contract with the American Space Agency NASA for the launch into orbit of the first Arab satellite; Arabsat-1A. 982. The planned footprint touches the southern UK.

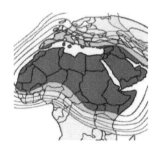

1983 General Election. Conservative Prime Minister, Margaret Thatcher.

The first launch of Windows

In this year, Microsoft announced the development of the first release of Windows 1.0, a graphical  user interface (GUI) for its own operating system (MS-DOS), which had shipped for IBM PC and compatible computers since 1981. The product line subsequently changed from a GUI product to a modern operating system over two families of design, each with their own codebase and default file system. This software facilitated the further development of the PC and its final convergence with television in the 21st century. Bill Gates (founder of Microsoft) had been shown a Macintosh prototype of a GUI by Steve Jobs early in its development, around 1981, and Microsoft was partnered by Apple to create some of the important early Mac software, such as MultiPlan and Word.

Eutelsat starts broadcast

 Eutelsat was originally set up in 1977 as an intergovernmental organisation to develop and operate a satellite-based telecommunications infrastructure for Europe. Eutelsat started operations this year with the launch of its first satellite followed by a further 30 satellite launches, creating one of the leaders in the Fixed  Satellite Services industry, with a 14% global television market share by the end of 2005.

1983 Start of breakfast television

Breakfast television started on 1 February this year on BBC, (known as Breakfast Time 1983–1989 and Breakfast News 1989–2000). The presenters were, Selina Scott, Frank Bough and Francis Wilson, the weatherman. The style was sofa-based and relaxed. This was followed by TV-am (1983–1992) on the ITV network broadcasting to the UK from 1 February this year until 31 December 1992. It made history by being the first national operator of an ITV franchise at breakfast-time, and was broadcast every day of the week, for most or all of the period between 6.00am and 9.25am. TV-am was also

sofa-based but a little more formal with Angela Rippon, Anna Ford, David Frost, Robert Kee and Michael Parkinson, 'The Famous Five', as they were known, as they set out with their 'mission to explain'. The mission never really got off the ground, and it wasn't long before 'The Famous Five' had been replaced by Anne Diamond, former sports presenter Nick Owen, weather girl Wincey Willis and Roland Rat, the puppet.

The first 2 inch television

1984 The first modern 2 inch screen handheld television (Sony Watchman) appeared on the UK market this year. The FD-210 had a grayscale five centimeter display. The device weighed around 650 grams, with a measurement of 87 x 198 x 33 mm. Also this year saw the audio CD Walkman and the Sony dictaphone .

This year, the circulation of the BBC Radio Times reached 10.050m. Also in this year, Sony video cameras competed with the first digital still cameras with their MAVICA, a video camera that recorded images on semiconductors, instead of film. This camera used freeze-frame technology to produce still photos.

 The BBC testcard F was converted to an electronic format. Cable broadcast and satellite broadcasts were the subject of the Cable and Broadcasting Act. This year and next were key years in the development of cable services. In this year, Swindon Cable was the first operator to be licensed under the new regime that would see cable franchises being scattered around the UK. The Telewest cable story began this year in Croydon operating under the name of Croydon Cable.

1985 New BBC 1 animated ident.

The old monochrome 405-line broadcast standard remained in place in the UK from 1936 until this year and it had taken three decades to complete the introduction of the 625-line system in 1964 and (PAL) colour in 1967.

Camcorders

The new camcorders on the market were a hit with the public. This year, half a million were sold. Within three years, that number had multiplied to three million, with Sony, JVC and Matsushita (Panasonic) as leaders in the market. This year, Sony came out with their first Handicam, the Video 8 system. JVC also introduced a smaller videocassette, the VHS-C (compact), which allowed them to make a smaller camcorder.

1985 405-line television ceases

Closure of 405-line VHF television broadcasting.

1985 The cable authority

This year saw the establishment of the UK Cable Authority (Jon Davey first Director General), which started to advertise more licences around the country. The first to go operational was Aberdeen Cable. The Telecommunications Act provided legislation that established regulation of the airwaves.

1985 Arabsat

8 February saw the launch of the first-generation satellite Arabsat-1A, by an Ariane rocket. Launch of the second of the first-generation satellites Arabsat-1B by the American space shuttle was on 18 June.

1985 ASTRA created

SES ASTRA (Société Européenne des Satellites), Europe's first private satellite operator, was incorporated in Luxembourg and headquartered in Betzdorf. SES was formed on the initiative and support of the Luxembourg Government this year. The Luxembourg State remains a major shareholder today. As Europe's first private satellite operator, SES launched ASTRA 1A, its first satellite, in 1988. ASTRA 1A entered service at the orbital position 19.2° East in 1989. Rupert Murdoch's SKY TV, along with German broadcasters Pro7, Sat. 1, and RTL were among ASTRA's first major customers.

1986 Another ident for BBC 2. The BBC's NICAM 728 system for digital stereo sound with television, was accepted by the Department of Trade and Industry as the  British Standard. The provisional specification, drawn up jointly with the IBA and in consultation with BREMA, was published. The European Community announced the setting up of Eureka Project 95 to establish a European HDTV standard. HDTV picture store and high line-rate picture monitor was demonstrated at the International Broadcasting Convention, Brighton.

1986 Launch of NICAM digital stereo sound on television.

1986 The IBA awarded DBS (Digital Broadcast Satellite) contract to BSB (British Satellite Broadcasting) for a three-channel service.

1986 Fox News in the USA

Launched this year in America, the Fox Television Network which is owned by Fox Entertainment Group, part of Rupert Murdoch's News Corporation. The  network is named after sister company 20th Century Fox.

1986 NBC changes hands

This year, control of the American network NBC passed to General Electric (GE), with GE's $6.4 billion purchase of RCA. GE had previously owned RCA and NBC until 1930, when it had been forced to sell the company as a result of antitrust charges. After the acquisition, the chief executive of NBC was Bob Wright, until he retired, giving his job to Jeff Zucker.

Another format war

1987 Format war: Sony's Digital Audio Tape (DAT) vs Philips' Digital Compact Cassette (DCC) vs Sony's MiniDisc. DAT was introduced in 1987, and both DCC and MD in 1992. Since affordable CD-R was not available until 1995, DCC and MD were an attempt to bring CD-quality recording to the home consumer. Restrictions by record companies fearful of perfect digital copies had limited DAT to professional use. In response, Sony introduced MiniDisc which provided compressed recordings that seemed to allay record companies' fears. Philips' DCC was discontinued in 1996, however MD successfully captured the Asia Pacific market (for example, Japan, Hong Kong and Singapore). Consumers in other parts of the world chose neither format, preferring to stick with analog Compact Cassettes for home audio recording, and eventually upgrading to CD recordable disks and compressed MP3 formats.

General Election. 🐗 Conservative Prime Minister, Margaret Thatcher.

1987 Digital Light Processing (DLP)

This year saw the introduction of another type of television screen. Digital Light Processing (DLP) is a display technology developed by Texas Instruments. DLP imaging systems employ either one or three large chip devices called

Digital Micro Mirror Devices, or DMDs. The micro mirrors are mounted on the DMD chip and tilt in response to an electrical signal. The tilt directs light toward the screen, or into a 'light trap' that eliminates unwanted light when reproducing blacks and shadows. DLP was invented in this year by Dr Hornbeck of Texas Instruments Inc. He developed the DMD: an optical semiconductor capable of steering photons with unparalleled accuracy. This digital micro-mirror, greatly refined, is the basis of modern DLP technology. (In 2002 Dr Hornbeck was elected Fellow of the International Society for Optical Engineering. The first commercial sub-systems using DLP were shipped in 1996 by nView for use in projectors.)

1987 Wendy Henry (News of the World) and Eve Pollard (Sunday Mirror) become the first women editors of newspapers in the UK.

First ASTRA satellite

 1988 On 11 December, the Société Européenne des Satellites (SES ASTRA) successfully launched and positioned its first satellite, ASTRA 1A, at 19.2° East. It was launched using an Ariane rocket. The satellite provided television coverage to Western Europe and was revolutionary as one of the first medium-powered satellites, allowing reception with smaller dishes than before. Among the channels carried in the first years was the entire four channel Sky Television (later British Sky Broadcasting, after the merger with rival British Satellite Broadcasting on the Marcopolo satellite) service consisting of Sky One/Sky Channel, Sky News, Sky Movies and Eurosport, the Scandinavian TV3 and TV1000, the German Pro7, Sat.1, RTL plus, 3sat and Teleclub, the

Dutch RTL4 as well as FilmNet, Screensport, MTV Europe, The Children's Channel and Lifestyle. Astra IA began television broadcasts on 5 February 1989. Until 1998 all of SES Astra's satellites were co-located with IA at 19.2° East, leading that position to be known mostly as Astra I (later, Astra 19.2°E), although Astra 2C also used to operate there, before it moved to 28.2° East in the autumn of 2007.

1988 Murdoch announces Sky News

On 8 June this year, Rupert Murdoch announced to the British Academy of Film and Television Arts that he would provide a new television news service (later to be called 'Sky News').

Cable merger

In London, Croydon Cable Television was acquired by United Cable of Denver, USA. They had franchises in Edinburgh, and Avon and the south east were added to the new network. The world administrative radio conference 'ORB-88', was convened in Geneva. The BBC Research Department provided technical support for geostationary television satellite orbit plans, and assisted with the first public demonstration of an advanced digital sound broadcasting technique under the auspices of the EBU. A 12GHz radio-camera antenna was developed with Television Outside Broadcasts for the Seoul Olympic Games and proved highly successful. The National Radiological Protection Board published new guidance on human exposure to electromagnetic radiation hazards and intensified the search for better measurement methods close to broadcasting antennas. The BBC Research Department advised on measurement techniques. The Research Department contributed in a major way to the Eureka

Project 95 HDTV demonstrations at the International Broadcasting Convention in Brighton. Full NICAM 728 Specification was published. Conditional access television VCR downloading experiments with British Medical Television commenced. The BBC RDS service was publicly launched at the Earls Court Radio Show. Digital audio editing equipment went on trial at Broadcasting House.

1988 BSB formed

Formation of the British Satellite Broadcasting (BSB) consortium by ITV Granada, Pearson, Virgin, ITV Anglia, and Amstrad.

Early this year, the BSB consortium was awarded a licence to operate three channels by the Independent Broadcasting Authority (IBA). Around the time of the licence award, Amstrad withdrew its backing and Australian businessman Alan Bond joined the consortium along with Reed, Chargeurs and London Merchant Securities among others. The BSB service would prove to be technically superior, broadcasting in the D-MAC (multiplexed analogue components type D) system dictated by the European Union regulation with potentially superior picture sharpness, digital stereo sound and the potential to show widescreen programming, rather than the existing PAL system. To distance itself from Sky and its dish

antennas, BSB announced a new type of flat-plate satellite antenna called a 'squarial' (that is, 'square aerial').

1988 Circulation of the BBC Radio Times reached 11.220m – the highest it would ever achieve. The use of teletext and EPGs (electronic programme quides) started to grow at a rapid pace.

ASTRA starts transmission

1989 SES ASTRA adds to the DTH (direct to home) satellite broadcasting industry and the dawn of a new broadcasting era from ASTRA 1A began transmitting on 5 February. Europeans could now receive DTH analogue TV and radio via a small fixed dish. United Cable of Denver merged with United Artists Cable International.

1989 The IBA relaxes rules on advertising sponsorship (of weather forecasts, arts and instructional programmes) and on advertising by charities.

1989 Sky starts transmission

 5 February at 6.00pm saw the start of domestic analogue satellite services by Sky Television – Sky News (Europe's first 24 h, news channel), Eurosport, and Sky Movies; action & thriller. Sky was to become the leading digital satellite TV broadcaster in the UK as well as the most popular pay-TV company.

The low-key ceremony was held on an industrial estate which the infant satellite broadcaster had set up in Isleworth, West London. Presenter Kay Burley (standing beside Rupert Murdoch) asked the Chairman, "Is this going to work?" Kay Burley is reported as saying, "He smiled his crooked smile, looked me in the eye, and confessed: "It's a wing and a prayer." Kay went on to say "This was the reality of the infant Sky – it was flung on air, as an experiment in progress. Those early days had a pioneering,

seat-of-the-pants feel. Everyone was frantically scrambling to meet a deadline, albeit in a hard-nosed manner, to defeat the rival. This was British Satellite Broadcasting, officially licensed by the Independent Broadcasting Authority in 1986, whose profligate failure would blow a huge hole in the finances of one shareholder, Granada Television, the leading ITV company."

Sky, in the event, got on air more than a year before the much-delayed BSB – which finally launched in April 1990 – and Murdoch was effectively able to force through his unregulated entry into British television. However, on that Sunday night launch in early 1989, Sky's Isleworth HQ was still a building site. Kay said "John Birt, then BBC deputy director general, was the only executive of any consequence from a rival UK broadcaster at a Sky dinner that night at nearby Syon House. Here was the old fashioned duopoly of ITV and the BBC being broken before our eyes in an experiment to sell TV channels direct to consumers. Yet most traditional broadcasters just wished it wasn't happening."

ASTRA satellites – Luxembourg ground station used by Sky

Sky chose to use the European Astra satellite system and broadcast in PAL with analogue sound; this system would require 60 cm (24 inch) dishes, although 80 cm versions were recommended for Scotland and the north of England.

BSB criticised Sky's proposals, claiming that the PAL pictures would be too degraded by satellite transmission, and that in any case, BSB would broadcast superior programming. SES Astra, the satellitte company, had no regulatory permission to broadcast, had plans (initially) for only one satellite with no backup, and the European satellite launch vehicle Ariane suffered repeated failures.

1988 House of Commons broadcast

The House of Commons was televised for the first time by the terrestrial channels. Senior Conservative Ian Gow, MP was the first to appear on screen.

BBC trials HDTV

This year, early HDTV digital recordings were made with the BBC's multiplex of D1 recorders at the Wimbledon Lawn Tennis Championships, the FA Cup Final and the Royal Albert Hall Promenade Concerts. The euroradio satellite system came on stream for Radio 1, extending its range.

Higher quality VHS tape

1989 This year, JVC introduced the S-VHS (Super-VHS) format for camcorders. This analog system separated the video signal into two separate channels, producing better colour and higher resolution (a brighter, sharper picture). The big attraction of this system was the copying and editing capabilities – no matter how many times it was copied, there was no deterioration in the quality of the image. At the same time, Sony introduced its first Hi8 camcorder – the digital camcorder market was now in full swing!

Windows 3.0 launched

1990 Since the early 1990s the BBC studios in West London have been home to fewer and fewer dramas – the last major drama series to be shot there being The House of Elliott, which ended in 1994, and the last single drama recorded was Henry IV, Part 1, in 1995. This was because drama production moved almost entirely on to film or single-camera video, and Television Centre is a video-based, multi-camera production environment.

Microsoft Windows scored a significant success with Windows 3.0, released this year. In addition to improved capabilities given to native applications, Windows also allowed users to better multitask older MS-DOS based software compared to Windows/386, thanks to the introduction of virtual memory.

First satellite UK subscription channel

In the UK 22.2m homes now had television. Sky Movies became Sky's first subscription channel. Sky offered the first ever live ball-by-ball coverage of an England cricket tour. The Simpsons made their UK debut on Sky One. Former deputy Prime Minister Viscount Whitelaw said to the House of Lords this year that Sky News had a very high reputation ..."I admire it, as do many other people, it will certainly waken up both the BBC and ITN and ensure that they compete with what is a very important news service."

1990 BSB on the air

When BSB finally went on air in March this year, with its squarial receiver, 13 months after Sky, the company's technical problems were resolved and its programming was critically acclaimed. But BSB's D-MAC receivers were incompatible and more expensive than Sky's PAL equivalents. Many potential customers compared the competition between the rival satellite. companies to the format war between the VHS and Betamax video systems Throughout the summer, many consumers chose to wait and see which company would win outright as opposed to buying potentially obsolete equipment.

WWW

Sir Tim Berners-Lee is the British engineer, computer scientist and MIT professor (Massachusetts Institute of Technology) credited with inventing the World Wide Web, making the first proposal for it in March 1989. On 25 December, with the help of Robert Cailliau and a young student staff at CERN – the European Organization for Nuclear Research – he implemented the first successful communication between an HTTP (hypertext transfer protocol) client and server via the Internet.

New Broadcasting Act

The Cable and Broadcasting Act 1984 and the Broadcasting Act 1981 were repealed and consolidated by the Broadcasting Act this year which implemented proposals in the Government's White Paper on Broadcasting in the 1990s. The act allowed regional companies, under specific conditions, to merge for the first time. It paved the way for the consolidation of ITV. The Broadcasting Act is often regarded by both its supporters and its critics as a quintessential example of Thatcherism. The aim of the Act was to reform the entire structure of British

Independent Television Commission

television. It led directly to the abolition of the IBA and its replacement with the ITC (Independent Television Commission), and the RA (Radio Authority which licenses and regulates Independent Radio services, otherwise known as commercial radio) was given the remit of regulating with a 'lighter touch' and did not have such strong powers as the IBA. Some referred to this as 'deregulation'. The ITC also began regulating non-terrestrial channels, whereas the IBA had only regulated ITV, Channel 4 and the ill-fated British Satellite Broadcasting. The ITC thus took over the responsibilities of the Cable Authority which had regulated the early non-terrestrial channels, that were only available to a very small audience in the 1980s. Under the new Broadcasting Act ITV's legal name became 'Channel 3', the number 3 having no real meaning other than to distinguish it from BBC I, BBC 2 and Channel 4. Prior to this, the network had no legal overall name. Channel 3 was assigned the third button on TV sets, the other stations being allocated to that of the number their name contained.

1990 DAB

First trials of Digital Audio Broadcasting (DAB) using the Eureka system were carried out in January from Crystal Palace with an active repeater at Kenley. In parallel, there was an evaluation of audio bit-rate reduction codecs.

BSB and SKY merge

By October this year, both BSB and Sky had begun to struggle with the burden of making huge losses and by November, the companies were merged 50:50 financially, operating as British Sky Broadcasting (BSkyB) but marketed as Sky. The Marco Polo House headquarters were vacated leading to redundancy for most BSB staff with only a few moving to work at Sky's HQ in Isleworth. The Marcopolo satellites were withdrawn and eventually sold in favour of the Astra system which was not subject to Ibq A regulation. (Marcopolo I was sold in December 1993 to NSAB of Sweden, and Marcopolo II in July 1992 to Telenor of Norway. Both companies had already one HS376 in orbit at the time). The merger may have saved Sky financially – Sky had very few major advertisers to begin with. Acquiring BSB's healthier advertising contracts and equipment helped to solve the company's problems. Sky News began broadcasting services to Scandinavia from the Thor satellites.

New BBC idents

1991 In the UK, there were now 22.9m homes. More new BBC idents appeared. Through Margaret Thatcher's influence, this year the cable companies were granted the right to offer telephony alongside their TV services. This would prove crucial in the battle against the satellite operator BSkyB, created as a result of

a merger between BSB and Sky television. Sky Sports launched the first of its dedicated sports channels. BSB and Sky's channels streamlined into a five channel network.

CNN now on the Sky platform

The American 24-hour rolling news channel CNN International launched on UK satellite and was placed on the Sky platform – Astra 1A, BBC World Service Television.

Digital camcorders

Camcorder research and development was pushing into high gear. The new digital technology had opened up a whole new world of possibilities for digital camcorders. The industry needed to develop cameras with sharper lenses, wider digital bandwidth, faster data rates, more storage space, and more pixels.

1992 ✜ General Election. Conservative Prime Minister, John Major.

Time Warner's 24-hour news channel

NY1 News, pronounced New York One, this year became Time Warner's 24-hour news channel in New York City, USA. Available on Time Warner Cable, the station covered the city's five boroughs. It started in the winter this year and offered news and weather forecasts as well as human interest features.

Oracle

(Optional Reception of Announcements by Coded Line Electronics) was a commercial teletext service first broadcast on ITV in 1974 and later on Channel 4 in the United Kingdom, finally ending on both channels at 11.59pm GMT on 31 December this year. Oracle is perhaps best remembered for its clever advertising slogan 'Page the Oracle'.

Sky pays £304m for FA coverage

1992 Sky Sports began exclusive live coverage of the new FA Premier League at a cost of £304m. BSkyB made an operating profit for the first time. Sky Sports introduced the clock and score line to live football in the UK. The gamble paid off as the lure of twice-weekly Premier League games helped dish sales soar.

Merger of ITV

A further merger of the ITV companies and the merger of some cable companies took place this year. TV-am closed – it was a breakfast television station that broadcast to the United Kingdom from 1 February 1983 to 31 December 1992. The BBC took a share in the satellite market, as its UK Gold channel – jointly owned with Thames – made its debut, joining the likes of MTV on the growing family of channels on the Astra satellites.

Launch of the third of the first-generation satellites, Arabsat-1C, on 26 February.

Sky in profit

1992 By March this year, Sky had turned from loss to profit which led Rupert Murdoch to say that, "Sky News, has quietly, if expensively, become the first building block of what we believe will become the premier worldwide electronic news-gathering network anywhere. Ask anyone in Europe, and particularly the BBC, and you will be told that Sky News has added a new and better dimension to television journalism."

Better camcorders

1992 This year, CCD technology was used in the development of camcorders. This is the use of electronic sensors to form an image, rather than chemicals on a film. It changed the camcorder market. Simply put, the CCD creates a superior video signal which, in turn, creates a sharper, brighter picture, with more radiant colours. And that's what people wanted. They were always looking for image quality that matched 35mm film, just like in the cinemas. This year, Sharp, in its quest to make filming easier, introduced the first colour LCD screen, so that videographers could see the display on a screen, without having to squint through a viewfinder. Today, this is a standard feature on all camcorders.

Radio Luxembourg closes

Radio Luxembourg closed on 30 December this year. It couldn't compete with the satellite commercial radio channels that were emerging across Europe, and lost its once huge listener groups and became commercially unviable.

Sky with 14 channels

1993 Sky launched its first multi-channel package, offering 14 basic channels, including Nickelodeon, UK Gold and the Discovery Channel. Sky News won its first of 21 RTS awards.

Birth of GMTV

After the closure of TV-am in 1992, the broadcast licence was awarded to GMTV (Good Morning Television)

which has remained No 1 at breakfast time in the UK since its inception on 1 January this year. GMTV won its broadcasting licence under the competitive tendering procedure laid down by the 1990 Broadcasting Act, to replace the previous licence holder TV-am. As a franchise holder, GMTV was managed independently, selling airtime through its own sales department in competition with all other ITV companies. GMTV's shareholders are ITV (75%) and Disney (25%). Transmitting daily from 6.00am to 9.25am, GMTV offered a lively mix of news, views and entertainment. The first hour with Penny Smith and John Stapleton (6.00am to 7.00am weekdays) provided a fast-paced mix of news, topical interviews, political debate and sport. The picture shows Michael Wilson and Fiona Armstrong.

Then from 7.00am to 8.30am weekdays Eamonn Holmes, Fiona Philips, Kate Garraway, Emma Crosby, Ben Shephard and Andrew Castle presented news and current affairs with celebrity interviews and special features. Lorraine Kelly's lifestyle show, GMTV with Lorraine, ran Monday to Thursday from 8.30am to 9.25am, while the Friday slot sees the focus shift to showbiz news and gossip.

Former LWT executive Greg Dyke was brought in as GMTV chairman in February 1993 after his success in turning around TV-am.

Eamonn Holmes replaced Michael Wilson on the sofa in 1993 after bosses deemed there was a lack of sexual chemistry between Wilson and co-presenter Armstrong.

1993 Other channels started this year; Sky Sports 2, QVC, and Challenge TV. More ITV franchises changes occurred: Thames, TSW, TVS, TVAM gave way to Carlton, Westcountry, Meridian and GMTV. A group of broadcasters were licensed as public broadcasters (PSB) the terms of which are set out in the Ofcom contracts. The designated PSB broadcasters were the BBC, Channel 3/ITV1, GMTV, Channel 4, Five, S4C and Teletext.

Cable mergers

The cable television company 'International CableTel (NTL's predecessor) was founded by Barclay Knapp, CEO, and George Blumenthal, Chairman. The company acquired the interests of Insight UK's cable systems, comprising about one million homes under franchise in cities such as Glasgow, Cardiff, Newport and Guildford.

1994 At GMTV further changes took place. Blue Peter's Anthea Turner (right) joined the show to replace Kelly, but famously had a difficult working relationship with Holmes. They are pictured with  entertainment correspondent Fiona Phillips, who became one of the main anchors from 1997 to 2008.

CBS changes hands

In America, the Westinghouse Electric Corporation acquired the CBS network this year and eventually adopted the name of the company it had bought to become the CBS Corporation

1994 Sky on the stock exchange

17% of BSkyB was floated on the UK and the US stock exchanges. MTV launched on Sky. Launch of Sky Sports 2. The X-Files made its UK debut on Sky One.

Agreement on videotape format

This year, Sony, Panasonic, and more than 50 other companies agreed on a DV tape format for camcorders.

1994 Broadband cable

This year saw the development of 'broadband' cable, capable of supporting a 750MHz+ bandwidth and served by a fibre-optic backbone that took cable TV forward in the mid-nineties. By then, consolidation was the key, with the first major acquisition being the American company International CableTel purchasing Insight Communications along with franchise-holders in South Wales and other regions. This year was a big build year for the cable television industry, as it sought to cover as many homes as possible in order to rival satellite provider Sky. CableTel started to contruct the company's high speed fibre optic network. By the end of the year, and following the acquisition of English Cable Enterprises, the company was providing TV and telephone services to customers in Hertfordshire and Bedfordshire as well as Glasgow, Cardiff, Newport and Guildford.

ITV merger

The first merger in ITV also took place this year with Granada buying LWT. By the new millennium, Granada owned 6 regional licences, Carlton owned 5, SMG owned 2 and Ulster and Channel remained independent.

Turksat 1A

Meanwhile, the Turksat 1A satellite system was the first launch of the Turkish project and was launched by Ariane 4 from Centre Spatial Guyanais in Kourou, French Guiana on January 24 this year.

TURKSAT

The first plasma screen

1995 This year saw the first plasma screen television (PDP – plasma display panel) replacing CRT (cathode ray tube) technology. Many tiny cells between just two panels of glass hold a mixture of noble gases. The gas in the cells is electrically turned into a plasma emitting ultraviolet light which then excites phosphors to emit visible light. Plasma displays should not be confused with LCDs, or LEDs which are different technologies.

Digital camcorders

This year, the next big breakthrough occurred in camcorder development. Panasonic and Sony introduced the first digital video cameras. Sharp and JVC followed soon after. Not to leave out the professional field, Sony gave them the DVCAM, an advanced video format good for high-end users.

1995 Sky in the FTSE 100

BSkyB entered the UK FTSE 100 index. The Ryder Cup was aired live on Sky Sports and shown live from beginning to end for the

first time ever on UK television. More channels open on satellite – Disney, God and Comedy.

Windows 95

After Windows
3.11, Microsoft began to develop a new consumer oriented version of the operating system code-named Chicago. Microsoft marketing adopted Windows 95 as the product name for Chicago when it was released on 24 August this year.

ASTRA digital

1996 The Société Européenne des Satellites (SES) pioneered the change from analogue to satellite digital transmission with the launch of ASTRA 1F in April this year. ASTRA 1G, 2A, 1H and 2C followed. With its constellation of Astra spacecraft, SES was delivering analogue as well as digital television and radio services across Europe.

Video disc formats

Video disc format war; MMCD vs SD. In the early 1990s, two high-density optical storage standards were being developed: one was the MultiMedia Compact Disc (MMCD), backed by Philips and Sony, and the other was the Super Density disc (SD), supported by Toshiba, Matsushita and many others. MMCD was optionally double-layer while SD was optionally double-sided. Movie studio support was split. This format war was settled before either went to market, by unifying the two formats. Following pressure from IBM, Philips and Sony abandoned their MMCD format and agreed upon the SD format with one modification based on MMCD technology – EFMPlus. The unified disc format, which included both dual-layer and double-sided options, was called DVD (igital ersatile isc) and was introduced in Japan in 1996 and in the rest of the world in 1997.

1995 First UK pay-per-view programme

The WBA Bruno vs Tyson world heavyweight title fight was the first nationwide domestic pay-per-view event on Sky in the UK. More channels opened on satellite – Sky 2 and Men & Motors.

1995 Cable merger

CableTel bought National Transcommunications Ltd (NTL) and decided to use the name NTL for all of its operations. The old names didn't disappear overnight however, living on in a hybrid arrangement – NTL CableTel, NTL Comcast and NTL Diamond Cable being examples. Meanwhile, Telewest was busily extending its coverage, purchasing franchises in Birmingham and Yorkshire among others. Slowly but surely, the small cable operators that had been licensed by the old Cable Authority – by now incorporated into the ITC – were swallowed up by the larger players, such as International CableTel, Cable & Wireless and Telewest Communications (later to merge as Virgin media).

Arabsat 2A

Launch of the first of the second-generation satellites, Arabsat-2A at 26°East, on 9 July, with a downlink footprint that included the UK.

1997 General Election. Labour Prime Minister, Tony Blair.

Early ONdigital

Heraldplace PLC was renamed British Digital Broadcasting PLC (later to become ONdigital PLC). Carlton Communications PLC, Granada Group PLC and British Sky Broadcasting Group PLC announced the formation of the new joint company. It was planned that each shareholder would own one third of the new company. British Digital Broadcasting (BDB) selected Castle Transmission International (CTI) to supply its transmission and distribution services.

BBC News 24

In November this year, BBC News launched a new 24 hour channel on the digital platforms.

More satellite channels

Launch of the world's first National Geographic Channel as part of a Sky joint venture. Sky Sports showed Rugby Union's Lions tour to South Africa – the first time an entire tour was shown live in the UK. Sky Box Office launched pay-per-view movies. More satellite channels introduced; Alibi and Home.

1997 Launch of Channel 5

Channel 5 was famously launched on 31 March by the Spice Girls. ITN won the contract to supply Channel 5's news programming. Five News adopted a studied presentational informality, including dispensing with that mainstay of news studios, the newscaster's desk. The channel saw it as a prop on which newscasters perched, rather than sat behind.

The development of DVD

1998 DVD launched in the UK in April this year. DVD is the work of many companies and many people and evolved from CD and related technologies. Some of the early proposals for 'high-density

CD' were made in 1993, and these efforts gradually divided into two competing proposed formats. The MMCD format was backed by Sony, Philips, and others. The SD format was backed by Toshiba, Matsushita, Time Warner, and others. A group of computer companies led by IBM insisted that the factions agree on a single standard.

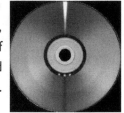

The combined DVD format was announced in September 1995, avoiding a confusing and costly repeat of the VHS vs Betamax videotape battle or the quadraphonic sound battle of the 1970s.

DVD, also known as Digital Versatile Disc or Digital Video Disc, is an optical disc storage media format. Its main uses are video and data storage. DVDs are of the same dimensions as compact discs (CDs), but store more than six times as much data. Variations of the term DVD often describe the way data is stored on the discs: DVD-ROM (read only memory) has data that can only be read and not written, DVD-R and DVD+R (recordable) can record data only once and then function as a DVD-ROM, DVD-RW (re-writable), DVD+RW, and DVD-RAM (random access memory) can all record and erase data multiple times. The wavelength used by standard DVD lasers is 650 nm; thus, the light has a red colour.

1998 ASTRA second satellite

SES ASTRA opened a second satellite orbital position at 28.2° East for UK digital services and went public on the Luxembourg and Frankfurt stock exchanges. This was ASTRA's prime orbital position for direct-to-home services in the UK and Ireland, providing capacity mainly for the transmission of broadcast and broadband multimedia services to consumer audiences.

1998 The footprint cast by the ASTRA satellite

The picture shows a receiving satellite dish with the LNB for 2 Sky decoder boxes to share the single dish. The abbreviation LNB stands for Low Noise Block – or the two feeds could drive a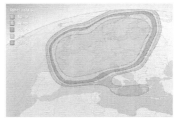

Sky+HD box. Four feeds can drive 2 Sky+HD
boxes. The LNB is the device on the front of
a satellite dish that receives the very low level
microwave signal from the satellite hub,
amplifies it, changes the signals to a lower

frequency band and sends them down the cable to the indoor
receiver.

1998 Size of dish required in the UK

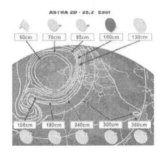

The size of the satellite dish required to receive transmissions
from ASTRA satellites depends on the beam as well as on the
location (distance from the hub of the satellite) of the dish.
ASTRA 2A uses two beams – a North beam and a South beam.

1998 Dish size across Europe

Astra has a reach far wider than the UK. Each broadcaster
operates to local regulations usually limited to international
borders. Each broadcaster has a carriage agreement with Astra to
use microwave spectrum capacity. The diagram below shows the
range of dish size – ranging from 60 cm to 350 cm. Again this is
related to the distance of the receiving dish to the satellite.

1998 Launch of Sky digital

This year, Sky Digital launched on 1 October with 140 channels; the UK's first digital TV satellite service. Sky Sports News launched as Europe's first dedicated sports news service .

1998 Cable mergers

The NTL network coverage was expanded to the midlands and to the south east of England following the acquisition of Comcast UK, ComTel and Diamond Cable, bringing the number of homes in the cable franchise to 5.2m.

DVR launch

The two early American consumer digital video recorders (DVRs), ReplayTV and TiVo, were launched at the Consumer Electronics Show in Las Vegas.

ITV 2

This year, ITV expanded its family of digital channels with the launch of ITV2.

1998 Wireless Telegraphy Act

Another Wireless Telegraphy Act was put onto the Statute book this year; an act to make provision for the grant of, and sums payable in respect of, licences under the Wireless Telegraphy Act 1949 other than television licences. It included the promotion of the efficient use and management of the electro-magnetic spectrum for wireless telegraphy, and for connected purposes.

More Sky channels

A large number of new channels on Sky started:

20 March: Prime TV

22 June: Sky Customer Channel
22 June: Sky Movies Family
22 June: Sky Movies Sci-Fi & Horror
22 June: Sky Movies Classics
22 June: Sky Movies Indie
22 June: Sky Movies Modern Greats
22 June: Sky Movies Drama
10 September: Sky Sports News
23 September: BBC Parliament
21 November: Film 4
07 December: ITV2

As stated above, BSkyB this year launched the UK's first digital satellite TV service and attracted 100,000 immediate extra customers in its first month. Sky Digital was the brand name for British Sky Broadcasting's television and radio service, transmitted from SES Astra satellites located at 28.2° East (Astra 2A/2B/2C/2D) and Eutelsat's Eurobird 1 satellite at 28.5° East.

1998 Launch of Ondigital

The new digital terrestrial television service ONdigital launched on 15 November including widescreen broadcasts. Some channels were free-to-air while others carried a subscription charge. ONdigital was the first terrestrial digital pay-tv service.

1998 Use of the spectrum

The spectrum required that the UK government license the broadcast channels in six groups, or multiplexes (abbreviated to 'mux') labelled 1, 2, A, B, C, and D. The ITC allocated each existing analogue terrestrial channel half the capacity of a multiplex each. The BBC made some use of its multiplex for three of its then four new television services; BBC Choice (which had started on 23 September 1998 with four national variations), BBC News 24 and BBC Parliament (albeit in sound only). ITV initially used their space to house ITV2 (from 7 December 1998) in England and Wales, You2 (later UTV2) in Northern Ireland and S2 in Scotland (now both ITV2), as well as GMTV2 during the early mornings. Channel 4 used their space for subscription channels Filmfour and E4 which, although not part of ONdigital, would be paid for and were only available through an ONdigital subscription. Channel 4's nationwide coverage on 'mux' 2 enabled it to be received terrestrially throughout much of Wales for the first time in its history, where previously only S4C had been available. Consequently, S4C's digital service, 'S4C Digidol' carries only Welsh-language programming, in contrast to S4C analogue which also carries English-language programmes commissioned and transmitted by Channel 4 in other parts of the UK.

Communal digital television aerial systems

In the UK, some 30% of the housing stock was flats having analogue television signals delivered to individual homes through old communal UHF aerial systems – rather than

individual aerials or dishes (although many households ignored planning rules and/or tenancy agreements and simply installed their own aerial and/or dish.

Sky Housing Team (L to R)

Jasmir Bains, Simon Jackson, Pascall Wharton, Sean McCartney, Lee Mercer, Peter Fox and Barry Shuter

Broadcasters addressed this issue by presenting landlords with a solution; manufacturers of digital components devised a method of distributing terrestrial and satellite signals together – to individual flats within a block.

In this way, residents in flats were given the choice of the same digital television services as those households who lived in houses (and could go to the High Street and choose for themselves). The new communal aerial system was called IRS (integrated reception systems) and became the solution for thousands of UK social landlords – especially during the switchover period 2008–2012.

1998 The objective which can be achieved with an IRS system is a block of flats dish free, but receiving the terrestrial and Sky television signals. The landlord can reasonably require individual dishes to be removed because a communal system will deliver the same and more in top quality. BSkyB put a housing team together in 1999 to present to nearly 3000 social landlords the implication of the switch-off of analogue broadcasting (the way it had been delivered since the 1920s). Digital UK also placed an advertisement aimed at social landlords. From this year to 2006 Sky advertised its IRS solution. Peter Fox, the then Sky National Account Manager for Local Authorities explained to social landlords up and down the country that, "There is

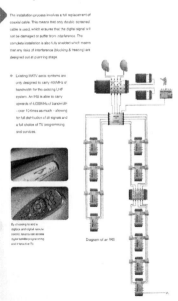

The installation process involves a full replacement of coaxial cable. This means that only double screened cable is used, which ensures that the digital signal will not be damaged or suffer from interference. The complete installation is also fully shielded which means that any risks of interference (blocking & freezing) are designed out at planning stage.

Existing MATV aerial systems are only designed to carry 400MHz of bandwidth for the existing UHF system. An IRS is able to carry upwards of 4,000MHz of bandwidth – over 10 times as much – allowing for full distribution of all signals and a full choice of TV programming and services.

By choosing to add a digibox and digital remote control, tenants can access digital satellite programming and interactive TV

Diagram of an IRS

an upcoming change in television that will affect the millions of social housing flats in the UK." Whilst TV is not a statutory LA service, Peter Fox explained that the option to do nothing was not viable. "Residents will blame the landlord when the screens go blank as switchover reaches their television region."

New BBC testcard

The BBC Testcards J and W were released, replacing F. Testcard J is a modified version of F, with improvements including an improved centre picture and a dot in the white area at the top.

W is similar but designed in 16:9 widescreen.

1998 First interactive football broadcast

Sky Sports broadcast the world's first interactive football match. Skysports.com offered the UK's first live football match streamed online. Launch of Sky News Radio.

1999 BSkyB reaches 1m subscribers. Tony Ball becomes the new chief executive of BSkyB.

1999 Caroline McDevitt succeeded John Fox as Chief Executive of BARB.

Free ONdigital and Sky boxes

As the competition between ONdigital and Sky increased this year ONdigital boxes became available from retailers free of charge in May. In June, Sky responded with Sky Digiboxes **becoming available free from retailers.**

2000 Start of digital cable

Digital cable started in July. Telewest purchased the remaining 50% stake in Cable London from NTL, adding 0.4 million franchise homes in north London. NTL and Telewest launched digital cable TV services. Sky introduced interactive services.

2000 Switchover announces ambition

The British Secretary of State announced ambition to complete digital switchover by 2012, and defined the switchover targets.

Tivo in the UK

TiVo (the American branded DVR) shipped their first units on 31 March. Hard disk-based DVRs make the 'time shifting' feature (previously achieved by a VCR) much more convenient, and also allow for 'trick modes' such as pausing live TV. Most DVRs use the MPEG format for compressing the digitized video signals. In the UK, DVRs were often referred to as 'plus boxes' (such as BSkyB's Sky+ and Virgin Media's V+ which integrates an HD capability.

2000 Cable merger

This was truly a monumental year in cable television, with NTL (as it was known then), buying Cable and Wireless' UK cable operations – which now contained digital TV capability in some franchises. There had been much speculation that either NTL or Telewest – by now the big players in the cable industry after most of the consolidation had been done. The general consensus was that there was room only

Is your TV HD ready? Perfect. Kick it into life with the V+HD box and watch in incredible HD.

for two big operators to rival Sky, and that it wouldn't be long before

NTL and Telewest merged. November of this year saw Telewest launch its 'Active Digital' service. Also this year, Telewest gained full control of Cable London after NTL sold its 50% stake in that operator.

CBS changes hands

2000 This year, the American CBS channel came under the control of Viacom, which coincidentally had  begun as a spin-off of CBS in 1971. In late 2005, Viacom split itself and reestablished CBS Corporation with the CBS television network at its core. The CBS Corporation and the new Viacom were controlled by Sumner Redstone through National Amusements, the parent of the two companies.

The BBC Radio Times reached its 4000th edition on 21 October. In the UK, 24.9m homes now had television.

WiFi vs Bluetooth

2000 This year saw another format war; wireless communication standards: Through the late 1990s, proponents of Bluetooth (such as Sony-Ericsson) vs WiFi competed to gain support for positioning one of these standards as the de facto computer-to-computer wireless communication protocol. This competition ended around 2000 with WiFi the undisputed winner (largely due to a very slow rollout of Bluetooth networking products). However, in the early 2000s, Bluetooth was repurposed as a device-to-computer wireless communication standard, and has succeeded well in this regard. Today's computers often feature separate equipment for both types of wireless communication, although Wireless USB is slowly gaining momentum to become a competitor of Bluetooth.

Interactive Sky News

Sky News launched the world's first interactive TV news service. Sky ran its first ever interactive advert.

2000 More cable mergers

In April, Telewest merged with Flextech (the content company). In November, Telewest extended its cable network with the acquisition of Eurobell, taking the total number of homes passed to 4.9m. It wasn't until May that NTL started rolling out 'digitalplus' in some of its franchises, and all cable operators took a substantial length of time to upgrade the old legacy cable systems to support digital service.

ITN 24 hr news

ITN's board agreed that the company should launch a digital rolling news channel to run on satellite, cable and subsequently on Freeview. With a modest operating budget the ITN News channel opened on 1 August. The company launched a news channel specially formulated for mobile telephones – ITN News for mobile.

2000 ONdigital reaches 1m

ONdigital was on course for 1 million customers this year. The Pay TV and interactive services platform announced on 11 April its latest quarterly figures. As at 31 March 2000 it had signed up 673,000 new customers, an increase of 22% since December 2000 and a fivefold increase in the year since 31 March 1999. This year saw television sets on sale with ONdigital installed as an integral feature – iDTV (integrated digital television). 'Onnet', Ondigital's new television Internet service, launched on 18 September with 47 brand names to be established on its portal.

Better camcorders

This year brought with it the introduction of a new video format for consumer digital camcorders – DV (digital video). The DV format produced increased luminance (brightness), with just over 500 lines of resolution. It also made productive use of an increased bandwidth, from 0.5MHz to 1.5MHz, which produced much brighter colours. Camcorders became smaller whilst producing increasingly better images. By now, digital camcorders, like the JVC digital video camera, were fairly small and very portable. Mini DV camcorders were the rage, joining DVD camcorders as a great way to record memories. Another aspect of digital video by this year was the camcorder industry looking at editing and copying. Sony's answer to this requirement was the DCM-M1 MiniDisc Camcorder. One of its best features was that it allowed in-camera non-linear editing. Images could now be copied to the computer for storing and editing. Software such as iMovie for Mac users, and Microsoft's Movie Maker, allowed users to do all kinds of professional-looking things with their movies.

2001 General Election. Labour Prime Minister, second term, Tony Blair.

DCMS guidelines

In December, the DCMS (Department for Culture, Media and Sport) published guidelines for social landlords on how to address the switchover to digital television. Dr Kim Howells MP, Minister at DCMS said – "around 20% of UK homes are flats served with a shared aerial system (MATV – master aerial television).

Digital TV
Information for
Landlords

We want to be sure that those households are included in the digital revolution to allow every home in a block of flats or an estate to have the same full choice as an individual home."

Windows XP

This year, Microsoft released Windows XP (code named 'Whistler').The merging of the Windows NT/2000 and Windows 95/98/Me lines was finally achieved with Windows XP. Windows XP uses the Windows NT 5.1  kernel, marking the entrance of the Windows NT core to the consumer market, to replace the aging 16/32-bit branch.

2001 Worldwide satellite fleet

SES Global was established following the acquisition of Ge  Americom, creating two new operating companies: Ses Astra for Europe, and Ses Americom for the Americas. Ses Global and its wholly owned operating companies and partners operate a worldwide fleet of 41 active satellites, the largest in the world.

In the UK, there were now 24.8m homes. Sky+ developed by Sky for launch in three years time. This year, Sky switched off its analogue satellite TV service.

ITV Digital

ONdigital reached 1m subscribers. On 11 July, ONdigital television was renamed/relaunched as ITV Digital.

More satellite channels

New satellite channels were launched; E4 and the Good Food Channel. BSkyB reached 5m digital subscribers.

Cable broadband services

NTL and Telewest launched broadband internet
services.

2001 Digital TV action plan

The British Government launched the Digital TV Action Plan for
the planned switch-off timetable for UK analogue television
broadcast by 2012. ITV Digital thought it could repeat Sky's
success of the 1990s by buying up the rights to the Nationwide
Football League for £315m, and showing them on its new ITV
Sport Channel. But the deal was a disaster – some matches were
seen by only a few thousand viewers. BskyB's
analogue broadcast service ended this year so
the service was now more commonly
marketed as just 'Sky' – all transmissions being
digital microwave signals.

2001 Sky+

September of this year saw the launch of Sky+ which is the DVR
and satellite receiver combined. This was the first box in the UK
to receive and record digital signals.

2002 NTL recapitalises

The American-listed NTL began a strategic recapitalisation
process in order to strengthen its balance sheet and reduce debt.
A plan was agreed with bondholders that £6.6bn ($10.9bn) in
debt would be converted into equity in two newly formed
companies: new NTL – which consisted of the UK and Ireland
assets; and Euroco – which consisted of certain continental
European and other assets. To implement the recapitalisation,
NTL and certain of its non-operating subsidiaries filed a pre-

agreed recapitalisation plan with the US Courts under the US Chapter 11 protective procedures.

2002 RTS award

The Royal Television Society awards Sky News 'News Channel of the Year'.

2002 Postal DVD rental

Love Films was founded this year by Paul Gardner and Graham Bosher. By 2009, the company expanded to  streaming movies on-line to internet television and computers.

ITV Digital goes off-air

ITV Digital was also in financial trouble this year – advertising revenue was down and the company realized that it had overpaid for the television rights for football. All ITV Digital subscription services except E4 and FilmFour went off-air on 1 May after the ITV digital consortium collapsed. Other  reasons for ITV Digital's failure included the facts that at least 40% of homes would need new UHF aerials to receive it, a high churn rate (percentage of subscribers leaving the pay TV service), poor point-of-sale marketing, no technical support for customers, a recently cracked hackable encryption system, the cost of having to provide free set-top boxes, and aggressive competition from BSkyB. ITV Digital was placed into liquidation, leaving behind debts of about £1.25bn. Nearly 1m former ITV Digital subscribers were asked to return their set-top boxes, or pay £39.99 to keep them. The liquidator then changed its mind and announced that ex-ITV Digital customers were to be given their set-top boxes free of charge.

2002 Creation of Freeview

The ITV multiplexes had to be returned to the ITC. A tender process ensued. The new contract was awarded to a new  consortium of the ITV broadcasters which resulted in the opening of Freeview – a completely free-to-air digital terrestrial service to replace pay ITV Digital.

More satellite channels

09 January: Living
09 February: BBC Three
01 March: Sky Travel
00 June: Tiny Pop
11 June: Price-Drop TV
01 September: Comedy Central Extra
31 October: 4 Music

Concorde's last commercial flight – 24 October 2003

Three flights landed at London Heathrow within five minutes of each other, watched by thousands of onlookers. The last transatlantic flight carried 100 celebrities from New York and touched down at 4.05pm BST.

2003 Digital Growth

By the end of the year, half of all UK households had digital TV of one type or another. The Royal Television Society awarded Sky News 'News Channel of the Year'.

2003 Creation of Sky Italia

Sky Italia is an Italian digital satellite television platform owned by News Corporation. It was launched on I August when the former platforms Tele+ (Canal+) and Stream TV (News Corporation and Telecom Italia) were merged. It is similar in many ways to BSkyB's Sky Digital in the United Kingdom and Ireland,

and like that network it is a major sports broadcaster.

2003 Formation of Skype – videophone

Skype is a software application that allows users to make voice calls and chats over the

Internet. Calls to other users within the Skype service are free, while calls to both traditional landline telephones and mobile phones can be made for a fee using a debit-based user account system. Skype has also become popular for its additional features which include instant messaging, file transfer, and video conferencing. The network is operated by Skype Limited, which has its headquarters in Luxembourg and is minority owned by eBay. Most of the development team of Skype is situated in Tallinn, Estonia for cost reasons and outsourced by the Luxembourg parent company.

2003 Creation of Ofcom

Regulation of commercial television now passed from the ITC to Ofcom following the merger of the ITC with other regulatory bodies. The new Communications Act this year provided the law to restructure telecommunications licensing and regulation.

Digital Television

TV IS CHANGING. IT'S GOING COMPLETELY DIGITAL.

Ofcom also sets and enforces the rules on fair competition between companies in these industries.

2004 Creation of Top Up TV

Top Up TV founded this year in Luxembourg as an optional add-on of pay TV to the free Freeview DTT platform. It is a  subscription video on-demand service broadcasting on the UK digital terrestrial platform, and first broadcast in 2006. The service offers an assortment of content from providers such as BBC, Warner, Cartoon Network and TCM. The content is accessed by a Top Up TV Freeview+ digital Television recorder. There are three viewing packs which customers are able to subscribe to; the standard pack being TV Favourites which costs £10.99 per month with no contract. The second viewing pack, called PictureBox, is a premium movies service providing 30 on-demand films a month from NBC Universal. The third viewing pack is ESPN on which for a monthly fee of £9.99 viewers can watch live premiership football amongst other sports such as UFC and MLS. ESPN is the permanent replacement for the now defunct Setanta Sports channel which went into administration, and ESPN America which was broadcast shortly after Setanta's collapse.

2004 RTS award

The Royal Television Society awards Sky News 'News Channel of the Year'.

End of ASTRA 1A

In December this year, the Astra 1A television satellite (launched in 1988) was moved into a graveyard orbit after some time at 5.2° East providing data services. SES ASTRA now spearheads the introduction of High Definition Television in Europe by transmitting the first European HDTV channel, Euro1080. Technical specifications for HDTV broadcasts were agreed by SES ASTRA and industry partners from all over Europe in the HDTV Forum.

Multiplexing

The broadcasting of radio and television was to develop in later years using multiplexing. In telecommunications, multiplexing (also known as muxing) is a process where multiple analog message signals or (much later) digital data streams are combined into one signal over a shared medium, for example, the UHF spectrum. The aim is to share an expensive resource. For instance, in telecommunications, several phone calls may be transferred using one wire. It originated in telegraphy, and is now widely applied in communications.

The multiplexed signal is transmitted over a communication channel, which may be a physical transmission medium. The multiplexing divides the capacity of the low-level communication channel into several higher-level logical channels, one for each message signal or data stream to be transferred. A reverse process, known as demultiplexing, can extract the original channels on the receiver side. A device that performs the multiplexing is called a multiplexer (MUX), and a device that performs the reverse process is called a demultiplexer (DEMUX). Inverse multiplexing (IMUX) has the opposite aim to multiplexing, namely to break one data stream into several streams, transfer them simultaneously over several communication channels, and recreate the original data stream. This is all happening within the electromagetic spectrum.

2004 Sale of the terrestrial network of transmitters

On 31 August, National Grid Transco bought Crown Castle International for £1.138bn to operate the entire network.

2004 Analog broadcasting

In FM broadcasting and other analog radio media, multiplexing is a term commonly given to the process of adding subcarriers to the audio signal before it enters the transmitter, where modulation occurs. Multiplexing in this sense is sometimes known as MPX, which in turn is also an old term for stereophonic FM, seen on stereo systems since the 1960s.

2004 Digital broadcasting

In digital television and digital radio systems, several variable bit-rate data streams are multiplexed together to a fixed bitrate transport stream by means of statistical multiplexing. This makes it possible to transfer several video and audio channels simultaneously over the same frequency channel, together with various services. In the digital television systems, this may involve several standard definition television (SDTV) programmes (particularly on DVB-T, DVB-S2, ISDB and ATSC-C), or one

HDTV, possibly with a single SDTV companion channel over one 6 to 8MHz-wide TV channel. The device that accomplishes this is called a statistical multiplexer. In several of these systems, the multiplexing results in an MPEG transport stream. The newer DVB standards, DVB-S2 and DVB-T2 have the capacity to carry several HDTV channels in one multiplex. Even the original DVB standards can carry more HDTV channels in a multiplex if the most advanced MPEG-4 compressions hardware is used. On communications satellites which carry broadcast television networks and radio networks, this is known as multiple channel per carrier or MCPC. Where multiplexing is not practical (such as where there are different sources using a single transponder), single channel per carrier mode is used. Signal multiplexing of satellite TV and radio channels is typically carried out in a central signal playout and uplink centre, such as ASTRA Platform Services in Germany, which provides playout, digital archiving, encryption, and satellite uplinks, as well as multiplexing, for hundreds of digital TV and radio channels. In digital radio, both the Eureka 147 system of digital audio broadcasting and the in-band on-channel HD Radio, FMeXtra, and Digital Radio Mondiale systems can multiplex channels. This is essentially required with DAB-type transmissions (where a multiplex is called an ensemble), but is entirely optional with IBOC systems.

Towards digital switchover

Two Government departments (the DTI with the DCMS) jointly published a report in March on the way forward for digital switchover. The Government's message to television retailers was: 'The Government is now firmly committed to digital switchover and is focusing on getting the conditions right for achieving it. Retailers have a key part to play as we begin to make some of the main decisions and implement actions that will take us there. There will be no switchover without consumers and you are one of the direct links with them and you  can help us to get the messages across. Providing consumers with information about switchover will give you the opportunity to promote your digital reception products now.

The Government booklet went on to say – 'digital television was launched in the UK only in 1998 and Sky said they were proud to say that the UK is the world leader. Digital TV is now already received in over 50% of UK households, providing the viewer with benefits such as additional channels, the most up-to-date technology and interactivity. Flat screen televisions started to appear in the market. Consumer demand for digital is fuelling growth in all industries associated with television – manufacturing, transmission, broadcast and, of course, retail. But we have to switch off analogue transmissions in order for all households to be able to enjoy the benefits of digital television'. The Government's vision for moving towards digital switchover was first outlined in 1999 by the then Secretary of State for Culture, Media and Sport, Chris Smith. He stated that, subject to key tests of availability and affordability of digital television being met, the switchover to digital could be completed by 2010.

2004 Freesat from Sky

21 October saw the relaunch of Freesat from Sky at a £150 one-off payment for the box. The advertising said – 'Join Freesat from Sky and enjoy more than 240 digital channels of free

entertainment – that's 4 times more channels than on Freeview – and they include all your BBC† and ITV favourites. Make a one-off single payment for the equipment and installation'.

Sky News was awarded the contract to supply news to Five. Sky Movies won the rights to screen the Oscars® to UK audiences.

This year saw the introduction of the first Sky+ decoder box. Its features were advertised as follows:

- Simple one touch recording.

- Record up to 40 hours of quality TV, without the need for tapes and timers.

- Series link – never miss an episode of your favourite shows. Record an entire series at the touch of a button.

- Sky Anytime offers a hand-picked collection of the week's unmissable TV, all ready to watch when you are.

- Rewind live TV – watch your favourite bits again and again.

- Pause live TV – never miss a second of the action.

2004 More satellite channels

More Sky channels opened:

19 January:	Information TV
08 March:	Eden
08 March:	Blighty

15 March:	The Fight Network
01 June:	Thomson TV
01 September:	Racing UK
18 October:	Real Estate TV
01 November:	ITV 3
01 November:	Your Destiny TV
01 December:	FX
01 December:	Your TV
13 December:	Living 2

The digital channel, ITN News relaunched this year but was never able to make a significant income and it finally closed on 23 December 2005, surrendering its channel to ITV 4. Since its closure the company has not ruled out the possibility that it could reappear at some point in the future.

2004 More ITV mergers

ITV, as it was known from 1955, has to be distinguished from ITV plc, the company that resulted from the merger of Granada plc and Carlton Communications, and which owns all of the Channel 3 broadcasting licences in England, Wales, the Scottish/English Borders channel and the Isle of Man channel. Similarly ITV1 remained the brand used by ITV plc for the Channel 3 service in these areas, with STV and UTV using their own brands in their own respective areas (North and Central Scotland and Northern Ireland). ITV3 was launched. The merger of Granada and Carlton was completed. The merged company, called ITV plc, held 15 regional licences. In late 2004, the Channel 5 news contract was re-tendered and was awarded to Sky News. ITN's involvement ceased at the end of that year.

2004 Launch of Facebook

Social networking on the internet grew to include users discussing television programmes – even while watching the programme live. Facebook was the first social network service and website that was operated and privately  owned by Facebook, Inc. (At the time of publishing Facebook had passed 1 billion active subscribers.) Facebook users can create a personal profile, add other users as friends and exchange messages, including automatic notifications when they update their profile. Additionally, users may join common interest user  groups, organized by workplace, school, or college, or other characteristics. The name of the service stems from the colloquial name for the book given to students at the start of the academic year by university administrations in the US with the intention of helping students to get to know each other better. Facebook allows anyone who declares themselves to be at least 13 years old to become a registered user of the website.

Facebook was founded by Mark Zuckerberg with his college room-mates and fellow computer science students Eduardo Saverin, Dustin Moskovitz and Chris Hughes. The website's membership was initially limited by the founders to Harvard students, but was expanded to other colleges in the Boston area, the Ivy League, and Stanford University. It gradually added support for students at various other universities before opening to high school students, and, finally, to anyone aged 13 and over.

2005 General Election. Labour Prime Minister, Tony Blair.

Switchover timetable announced

On 15 September, an announcement was made by Tessa Jowell, the then UK Secretary of State for Culture, Media and Sport in her keynote address to the Royal Television Society, setting out the Government's intention to switch off analogue transmission in the UK over a period from 2008 to 2012.

RTS award

The Royal Television Society awards Sky News 'News Channel of the Year'.

2005 Digital UK steps up advertising

The government statement regarding the switch off of analogue broadcasting became formal policy once it was announced on the

floor of the House of Commons. Digital UK immediately issued a national advert to announce the implications.

Sky News on mobile phones

Sky News and Sky Sports News were now streamed live to mobile phones for the first time as part of the Sky Mobile TV service. The 3G network was used to give sufficient bandwidth. Sky started to pioneer parental controls for television viewing.

The final cable merger announced

In October, Telewest announced a merger with NTL, which would create the UK's second largest communications company and leading triple-play service provider. Telewest Business was delivering a range of solutions, across the UK, including broadband and internet services, networking, voice and IP and multimedia services.

2005 ITV buys SDN (the future Freeview)

In April, ITV spent £134m buying SDN from United Business Media and S4C. Later that year ITV joined the Freeview consortium to own the Freeview multiplex. SDN not only gave it a new revenue stream but offered it capacity on Freeview for future channel launches.

BBC/ITV announce their own freesat product

In September this year, the BBC and ITV together announced that they would launch a free-to-air satellite service to work alongside the Freeview terrestrial service. At the end  of this year, ITV removed the encryption on their content which was being broadcast on the satellite Astra 2D – effectively allowing the BBC/ITV service Freesat to become a broad content service. The free-to-air 'Freesat' channels would be received using any generic digital satellite (DVB-S) receiver. However, the Freesat brand aimed to provide a richer service with an Electronic Programme Guide and interactive features similar to the Freeview service launched earlier. Unlike Freeview, however, these features would only be available to approved receivers manufactured under licence from Freesat. The initial BBC/ITV

Freesat project plan saw the launch of the service to take place in Q1 2006. This was postponed to Autumn 2007 when news that the BBC Trust would review the project was announced. The service was further delayed and eventually went live on 6 May 2008.

2005 Last cable merger takes place

On October 3, NTL and Telewest cable television companies announced a merger deal and became Virgin Media Inc. – the first 'quadruple-play' media company in the United Kingdom, bringing together a service consisting of television, Internet, mobile phone and fixed-line telephone services. Virgin Media represented a prime example of telecommunication convergence. Whilst US-headquartered, Virgin Media only operated in the United Kingdom, with its main office in Hook, Hampshire and its financial base in Bradford, West Yorkshire. As the only remaining (from 10) major cable company in the United Kingdom, Virgin Media now competed in the market with the other major pay-TV operator, satellite-based British Sky Broadcasting (Sky) which this year had more channels than any other provider in the UK and with Freeview, the free-to-air terrestrial service with a channel line-up attractive to those who wanted to retain free television.

More Sky channels

Digital ITV4 launched. On 23 December, the digital channel ITN News closed. Since its closure the company has not ruled out the possibility that it could reappear at some point in the future. More satellite channels opened:

10 January: Eurosport 2 UK

17 January: Max TV

17 January: One TV

24 January: Vectone World

31 January   Red Hot TV

08 February: Teachers TV

22 March: Channel S Television

31 March: Zee TV Gujarati

04 April: Inspiration Network (International)

05 April: Xtraview

18 April: Shop TV

18 April: JML Choice

25 April: Movies 4 Men

25 April: Movies 4 Men 2

29 April: True Movies

03 May: Loveworld TV

22 June: Super Casino

27 June: Speed Auction TV

15 July: SEE & TV

27 July: DM Digital TV

15 August: Choices UK TV

18 August: Aastha-Faith Channel

22 August: You TV 2 Extra

05 September: Star Bazaar

10 October: More 4

31 October: Sky 3

01 November: ITV 4

2005 The impact of digital television

The wonders of digital television have been heralded for more than two decades. Compared to the old analogue technology, digital compression allows more channels to be transmitted with better image quality and improved interactive applications. Roughly six times as many channels can be broadcast with the same amount of transmission capacity as is currently used for one analogue channel. The switch off of the analogue signal could result in a large increase in the supply of television channels available to viewers or in bandwidth being freed up for other uses.

Final cable merger complete

On 3 March this year, NTL completed a merger with Telewest Global, Inc., creating the UK's largest provider of residential broadband and the UK's leading provider of triple-play services. On 4 July, NTL completed its acquisition of Virgin Mobile, creating the first opportunity for customers in the UK to buy a quadruple-play of TV, Internet and fixed and mobile telephony services from a single operator.

2005 Telegrams stop in USA

On 27 January, The USA Western Union discontinued all telegram and commercial messaging services, though it still offered its money transfer service.

2005 E4 goes free-to-air

On 25 May, E4 relaunched free-to-air on Freeview.

2005 More4 airs

On 10 October, More4 launched free-to-air on Freeview.

2005 Freeview ownership

On 12 October, ITV and C4 joined Freeview founders BBC, Sky and National Grid Transco.

2005 Sky 3 airs

On 31 October, Sky launched its Sky Three
channel.

2005 ITV 4 starts

On 1 November, ITV 4 went on the air across the
platforms.

New BBC Royal Charter

BBC Royal Charter renewal – the charter gave continuance to the BBC. It was accepted by Her Majesty The Queen in Council on 19 July and took full effect on 1 January 2007.

2005 The Digital Dividend

On 17 December, Ofcom published the Digital
Dividend Review – how government can make
money by the selling of television frequencies C31-40 and C63-68. Ofcom, in the Digital Dividend Review ('DDR') examined the options arising from the release of UHF spectrum afforded by the digital switchover programme, and which could become available for new uses between 2008 and 2012. The potential future uses of this spectrum are wide ranging and include: broadband wireless access, cellular mobile (for example, 3G and systems beyond IMT-2000), further terrestrial digital television services (including standard definition television, high definition television and local digital TV), mobile digital multimedia (including mobile television), and Programme Making and Special Events ('PMSE').

2005 More satellite channels

06 February: Propeller TV
27 February: Red

01 March: York@54
11 March: CITV Channel
24 April: Nick Jr 2
24 April: Cartoon Network Too
15 May: BBC HD
26 June: Movies 24
01 September: Channel Punjab
04 September: Cartoon ITO
15 October: Fiver
16 October: Five USA
15 November: Al Jazeera English
20 November: The Business Channel
06 December: France 24

Astra 2D satellite

Above is an illustration of the Astra 2D satellite. The whole Astra television satellite fleet had grown by 2005 to become a worldwide delivery platform.

2005 ASTRA 2D, launched 19 December 2000, on Ariane 5 from the European space port in Kourou, French Guiana, features up to 16 Ku-band transponders in the frequency range of 10.70–10.95GHz and has a design life

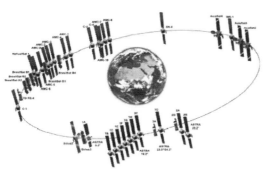

of 12 years. The spacecraft is used by UK broadcasters for digital services targeting the UK and Ireland. All of the BBC's television channels, ITV's regional variations, ITV2,

ITV3, ITV4, CITV, Men & Motors, Channel 4, E4, More4, Film 4, some Sky Digital services and Irish TV and radio broadcast on the Astra 2D satellite.

Co-positioned with ASTRA 2A and ASTRA 2B, the satellite allows SES to activate up to 56 transponders, spanning the frequency range 10.70–10.95 and 11.70–12.50GHZ, at the Company's second orbital position of 28.2° East. ASTRA 2D carries 16 active Ku-band transponders powered by 39-watt traveling wave tube amplifiers (TWTAs). The satellite's power is derived from two telescoping cylindrical solar panels manufactured in Sylmar, California, by Boeing's Spectrolab, Inc., subsidiary, the leading manufacturer of space and terrestrial solar power systems.

The panels feature gallium arsenide solar cells similar to those on many proven Boeing spacecraft. At launch the satellite weighed 3,186 pounds; in orbit, ASTRA 2D weighed 1,816 pounds. After its deployment, the cylindrical satellite became 26 feet 2 inches tall and 7 feet 1 inch in diameter with its solar panels deployed. Sky re-advertised its 'free' offer – Sky advertises its freesat offer.

SKY HD AT 'THE BEST OF STUFF SHOW 2005'

We know you are interested in Sky HD, so here's something that will excite you! Come along and see the Sky HD team at 'The Best Of Stuff Show 2005', where you'll be able to see our stunning Sky HD box and also witness just how amazing the HD experience is. Seeing HD truly is believing.

'The Best Of Stuff Show' runs from 4-6 November 2005 at the Novotel West London hotel and brings together all the hottest trends and latest products under one roof. It also offers 2 shows for the price of one as tickets will also give free entry to the prestigious What Hi-Fi? Sound and Vision Show.

Sky HD is the future and 'The Best Of Stuff Show' is a great opportunity to be the first to experience our Sky HD showreel.

Tickets can be purchased from www.bestofstuff.co.uk

All of us at Sky HD look forward to seeing you there!

Windows Vista

2006 Windows Vista (code-named Longhorn) was released on 30 November this year to business customers, with consumer versions following on 30 January.

Windows Vista

2006 CITV launches

On 11 March, CITV, ITV's children's channel, started broadcasting across the platforms.

2006 BBC HD

On 11 May, the BBC launched its HDTV service on cable, satellite and Freeview (London only). Broadcast HD is 1080i lines of resolution. Blue-ray is 1080p. This difference is explained later.

HDDVD vs Blue-ray

High-definition optical disc format war; Blu-ray Disc vs HD DVD. Several disc formats that were intended to improve on the performance of the DVD were developed, including Sony's Blu-ray and Toshiba's HD-DVD, as well as HVD, FVD and VMD. The first HD-DVD player was released in March this year, followed quickly by a Blu-ray player in June. Samsung's BD-

In addition to the home DVD standalone players for each format, Sony's PlayStation 3 video game console incorporates a Blu-ray Disc player and its games use that format as well. The format war went largely in Blu-ray's favour after the largest movie studio supporting HD DVD, Warner Brothers, decided to abandon releasing films on HD-DVD in January 2008. Shortly thereafter, several major North American rental services and retailers such as Netflix, Best Buy, and Wal-Mart, and disc manufacturers such as CMC Magnetics, Ritek, and Anwell, announced their exclusive support for Blu-ray products. Thus, Blu-ray won the HD war.

Blu-ray technical specification:
*   1080p High Definition Picture
*   24p True Cinema; Bravia® Theatre Sync™
*   x.v.Colour
*   1080p DVD Upscale
*   AVCHD Disc Playback
*   CD playback

*   BD-R/RE Playback
*   5.1 channel Dolby Digital/DTS
*   7.1ch LPCM output via HDMI •
*   Dolby True HD Decoding (7.1ch)
*   DTS-HD HA / Dolby TrueHD
*   HDMI Bit Stream output via HDMI ver1.3
*   5.1ch Gold Plated Analog Audio Out
*   Motorised Slide Door
*   Bitrate Display

2006 Sky HD launch

Sky became the world's first carbon neutral media company. On 22 May, Sky launched the UK's first nationwide HD TV service. Sky made movies, sport and entertainment available for download to PCs. The NTL and Telewest merger was completed in March, creating NTL:Telewest Business.

2006 Sky in your flat

Sky worked up a free shared dish (FSD) product to complement the IRS solution for landlords. FSD was created to cater for no more than 49 flats managed by private landlords or managing agents. A Shared Dish system uses a single satellite dish to which residents can be connected without having to put up their own minidishes. Cables are run into each flat, then directly into residents' Sky or Sky+HD set-top boxes. Residents who subscribed to Sky or chose Freesat would have access to all free-to-air channels, including BBC1, BBC2, ITV,  Channel 4 and Five. They would also have the option of signing up for other services such as Sky Broadband and Sky Talk. Sky offered a contribution to the cost of materials in most cases. In some cases, Sky needed four residents in each block to sign up for Sky before FSD was installed. (By 2010, advertising of FSD reached national television.)

2006 Launch of BT Vision

BT Group plc is a global telecommunications services company headquartered in London,  United Kingdom. It is one of the largest telecommunications services companies in the world and has operations in more than 170 countries. Its historic predecessor was the Electric Telegraph Company and then the Post Office,  founded in the City of London, United Kingdom in 1846. In December this year, BT Vision was launched. It is an IPTV pay-television service provided in the UK and owned by the BT Group. It requires access to a BT Broadband internet connection with BT's official router (BT Home Hub) to watch programmes, including on-demand services. Watching BT's on-demand service with the BT vision service uses none of the customer's broadband allowance.

2006 Film 4

On 23 July, Film 4 relaunched as a free channel and gained a 4.3% share of viewing.

2006 Launch of Twitter

Twitter is a website, owned and operated by Twitter Inc., which offers a social networking and microblogging service, enabling its users to send and read other users' messages called tweets. Tweets are text-based posts of up to 140 characters displayed on the user's profile page. Tweets are publicly visible by default, however, senders can restrict message delivery to their friends list. Users may subscribe to other users' tweets – this is known as following and subscribers are known as followers. Television watchers tweet each other about programmes they are watching – **twitter** exchanging views and opinions.

All users can send and receive tweets via the Twitter website, compatible external applications (such as for smartphones), or by Short Message Service (SMS) available in certain countries.[8] While the service is free, accessing it through SMS may incur phone service provider fees. The website is based in San Francisco, California. Twitter also has servers and offices in San Antonio, Texas, and Boston, Massachusetts.

Since its creation in 2006 by Jack Dorsey, Twitter has gained popularity worldwide and currently has more than 175 million users. Quantcast estimates Twitter has 54 million monthly unique US visitors. It is sometimes described as the 'SMS of the Internet'.

2007 Gordon Brown, Labour, appointed Prime Minister 27 June. Being mid-term, there was no general election.

2007 Freesat HD announced

On 27 April, the BBC and ITV announced the HD Freesat service to launch in the Spring of 2008.

Virgin Media loses Sky

On 1 March this year, the contract for Virgin Media to provide Sky's basic channels (including Sky News) on their cable TV service expired after a dispute between Virgin Media and BSkyB. At midnight, Sky News was removed, the Virgin electronic programming guide changed to 'SKY SNOOZE TRY BBC' until Sir Richard Branson demanded the message be removed saying, "I have asked them to take it down. We do not mean any disrespect to Sky News. I think it is a very good news channel." Sky News returned to Virgin Media Network along with all the other 'Sky Basics' channels that were removed in March. This deal between BSkyB and Virgin Media was confirmed on 4 November this year.

2006 Freeview reach improves

1 December saw 15 million total sales since Freeview's launch in 2002. It was estimated that Freeview was in 9m homes – some with multiple connections.

2007 News 24

On 8 May, NEWS 24 became the first BBC TV channel to go online.

2007 BBC iPlayer

On 27 June, the BBC put out a beta version of its iPlayer for testing. This marked another venture into Internet television. The iPlayer allowed users to access previously broadcast programmes and to watch them on their PC or laptop.

RTS Award

The Royal Television Society awarded Sky News 'News Channel of the Year'. Sky News continued as a free-to-air channel on the Astra 28.2° East satellite carrying Sky Digital. It was also available on DTT Freeview and analogue and digital cable. Freeview pending Ofcom approval (not yet implemented).

Sky Sports was given a new look – introduced at 7.00am on 5 August in time for the new football season.

2007 Switchover starts

On 17 October, Digital UK started work on the Whitehaven transmitter switchover.

2007 New Sky testcard

In the UK, there were now 25.9m homes. BSkyB created a 1080i line high definition test card for their recently launched HD service. The style similar to the 1967 BBC test card with Carole Hersee being replaced by Myleene Klasse.

2007 Freeview DVR playback starts

31 May saw the arrival of Freeview Playback digital TV recorders which make it easy to record digital TV. With Freeview playback users could:

- record programmes at the touch of a button

- pause and rewind live TV

- record one channel whilst watching another

- fit TV schedules around user preferences

Leading manufacturers Humax, Sony and TVonics were the first to offer Freeview Playback digital TV recorders, which became available from Argos, Comet, John Lewis and Tesco from May this year.

2007 More satellite channels

More sky channels opened:

20 February: Virgin Central

01 March: Sky Arts 1

01 March: Discovery Turbo

12 March: Current TV

19 March: Vinappris

26 March: MusFlash TV

16 May: Pulse

09 August: PopGirl

01 September: Overseas Property TV

03 September: Zone Romantica

13 September: Showcast TV

20 September: LFC TV

01 October: Virgin 1

01 October: Diva TV

15 October: Dave

15 November: My Channel

23 November: NME TV

2007 First time-shift channel

On 20 August, Channel 4 started the first time shift of a terrestrial channel with Channel 4+1 moving all programming one hour forward on its second channel.

2007 HD IPTV set-top box

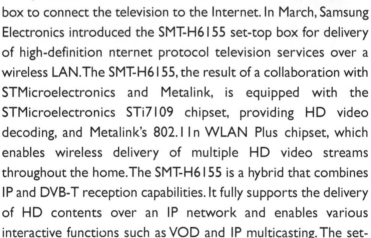

This year saw the launch of a television box to connect the television to the Internet. In March, Samsung Electronics introduced the SMT-H6155 set-top box for delivery of high-definition nternet protocol television services over a wireless LAN. The SMT-H6155, the result of a collaboration with STMicroelectronics and Metalink, is equipped with the STMicroelectronics STi7109 chipset, providing HD video decoding, and Metalink's 802.11n WLAN Plus chipset, which enables wireless delivery of multiple HD video streams throughout the home. The SMT-H6155 is a hybrid that combines IP and DVB-T reception capabilities. It fully supports the delivery of HD contents over an IP network and enables various interactive functions such as VOD and IP multicasting. The set-top box combines MPEG-4 AVC/H.264/CI capabilities on a single chipset produced using STMicroelectronics' SoC platform, and supports wireless digital video home networking using 802.11n.

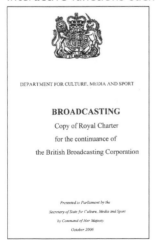

DEPARTMENT FOR CULTURE, MEDIA AND SPORT

BROADCASTING

Copy of Royal Charter

for the continuance of

the British Broadcasting Corporation

Presented to Parliament by the

Secretary of State for Culture, Media and Sport

by Command of Her Majesty

October 2006

2007 New BBC Charter

On 1 January, the new BBC Royal Charter took effect. On 18 January, Culture Secretary Tessa Jowell MP made an oral statement to Parliament detailing the BBC licence fee for the six year period, 2007 to 2013. The fee will be frozen.

First analogue switchover complete

On 14 November, the first analogue switch off was achieved at Whitehaven, Cumbria.

BBC largest Broadcaster

Sir Michael Lyons, Chairman BBC Trust said the BBC is still the world's largest broadcaster. The BBC Trust is the governing body of the BBC. It is operationally independent of BBC management and external bodies, and aims to act in the best interests of licence fee payers. The Trust was established by the Royal Charter for the BBC which came into effect on 1 January 2007. A Royal Charter is a legal instrument granted by a Sovereign to create institutions or other forms of incorporated bodies. In the British legal tradition, a royal charter is in the form of letters patent. Historically, royal charters were granted as an exercise of the Royal Prerogative, and were generally used to confer rights that would today be created by or under staute. The BBC Trust, and a formalised Executive Board, replaced the former Board of Governors. In summary, the main roles of the Trust are in setting the overall strategic direction of the BBC, including its priorities, and in exercising a general oversight of the work of the Executive Board. The Trust will perform these roles in the public interest, particularly the interest of licence fee payers.

2007 Ofcom announcements

On 3 December, Ofcom released the high frequency spectrum range for new broadband services. Ofcom announced details of its fourth auction of radio spectrum licences, which was part of a programme to release new spectrum for a wide range of uses. The high frequency spectrum was suitable for a number of different uses including, for example, high-capacity broadband for organisations seeking to share wireless internet connections across buildings in close proximity. The spectrum bands were between 10GHz and 40GHz. This meant that it could carry large amounts of data over distances of up to 12 kilometres. The provisional date for applications to take part in the auction was 16 January 2008, with confirmation to be made before Christmas.

2007 It was announced on 18 October that in order to meet a £2 billion shortfall in funding, the BBC intended to 'reduce the size of the property portfolio in West London by selling BBC Television Centre by the end the financial year 2012/13', with Director General Mark Thompson saying the plan will deliver 'a smaller, but fitter, BBC' in the digital age. A BBC spokeswoman has added that 'this is a full scale disposal of BBC Television Centre and we won't be leasing it back'.

2007 BBC iPlayer

On 25 December, the BBC took its iPlayer out of beta and was hard launched.

Sky back on cable and Internet Television

2008 On 4 November, BSkyB and Virgin Media signed new channel carriage agreements. It was a breakthrough for pay satellite and cable customers as carriage of 'basic' channels was secured until June 2011.

The media reported: 'Sky and Virgin Media today announced that, following successful negotiations, they have agreed two new channel carriage deals. The first agreement will see the return, on 13 November, of Sky's Basic channels – including Sky1, Sky2, Sky3, Sky News, Sky Sports News, Sky Arts 1, Sky Arts 2, Sky Real Lives and Sky Real Lives 2 – to Virgin Media's cable TV service. The second agreement provides for the continued carriage of Virgin Media TV's basic channels – Living, Living 2, Bravo, Bravo 2, Trouble, Challenge and Virgin 1 – as part of Sky's retailed channel line-up on satellite. Both deals will run concurrently until 12 June 2011. The agreements include fixed annual carriage fees for the channels with both channel suppliers able to secure additional capped payments if their channels meet certain performance-related targets. Commenting on the agreements, Virgin Media's CEO, Neil Berkett, said: "We are pleased to bring our carriage negotiations with Sky to a successful close. I believe this agreement represents a fair deal and is the right thing for our customers. We recognise the quality and popularity of Sky's channels and look forward to welcoming them back to Virgin Media's TV service. We are also pleased to secure Sky's continued carriage of the VMTV channels until June 2011." Jeremy Darroch, Sky's CEO, added: "This is great news for Sky and Virgin Media customers alike. We want our channels to be enjoyed by as many people as possible so we're delighted to secure their return to the Virgin Media platform." As part of the agreements, both Sky and Virgin Media have agreed to terminate all High Court proceedings against each other relating to the carriage of their respective basic channels.

2008 Many providers of internet television services now exist including conventional television stations that have taken advantage of the internet as a way to continue showing programmes after they have been broadcast, often advertised as 'On Demand' and 'Catch Up' services. Examples include the BBC, which introduced the BBC iPlayer on 25 June this year as an extension to its 'RadioPlayer' and already existing streamed video clip content, and Channel 4 that launched 4oD ('4 on Demand') in November 2006 allowing users to watch recently shown content. Most internet television services allow users to view content free of charge, however, some content is charged. Channel 4's internet television service employs a pay per-download system for some of its content. Other internet television providers include ITV player, Demand Five, Eurosport player and Sky Player.

In February this year (with a subsequent amendment in November), English Heritage requested listed status for the BBC Television Centre's scenery workshop, the canteen block adjoining the Blue Peter garden, and the central building. Previously, under a long standing deal between the BBC and English Heritage the building was not listed, to allow the BBC to make regular changes that are necessary in a broadcasting centre. In return, if the Corporation ever left TV Centre, it agreed that the fabric of the building would be restored to its mid-60s state, and English Heritage would then list notable features.

2008 RTS Award and Sky advances

The Royal Television Society awards Sky News 'News Channel of the Year'. Adam Boulton covered the US Presidential Elections in depth. Barak Obama became the first black US  President. Sky became the first ever principal partner of British Cycling. Sky reached nine million household customers – more than one in three homes in UK and Ireland. Sky Arts expanded output with a new channel portfolio. Sky demonstrated 3-D TV using a standard Sky+HD box. 3-D glasses are necessary. The upcoming 3-D screens will not require 3-D glasses. The initial BBC/ITV Freesat project plan saw the launch of the service to take place in Q1 2006. This was postponed to Autumn 2007 with the news that the new BBC Trust would review the project. The service was further delayed and went live on 6 May this year.

More satellite channels

08 January: DMAX
08 January: Arsenal TV
28 January: Clubland TV
06 May: ITV HD
19 May: Kix
09 June: The paranormal Channel
01 July: Challenge Jackpot
07 October: Watch
20 October: Sky Arts 2
20 October: Sky Arts HD

2008 Satellite freesat marketing starts

On the UK digital terrestrial platform, the channels have always been available free-to-air with the appropriate equipment in place. However, in 2008 Terrestrial Freeview is available to only 73% of the population because of transmitter limitations. After analogue TV services are replaced in the planned digital switchover (2012) the reach will increase to 98.5% for the public service channels and 90% for the full 'Freeview' service. In order to provide more widespread coverage and a larger number of channels, a digital satellite alternative was felt necessary. On 6 May, the BBC//ITV launched Freesat which is a free-to-air digital satellite television joint venture **freesat** between the BBC and ITV plc, serving the United Kingdom. The service was marketed from 6 May and offered a satellite alternative to the Freeview service on digital terrestrial television, with a selection of channels available without subscription for users purchasing a receiver. The service also makes use of the additional capacity available on the digital satellite (Astra 2D) broadcasting HD from the BBC and ITV. A subscription freesat service was also available from Sky but this proposition was not overly advertised.

2008 Children watching television – Freeview survey

18 November saw child psychologist Dr Tanya Byron, reporting on the effects of television viewing on young children. Nearly 2,000 parents took part in the research on parents' website

Mumsnet. Whilst the majority of parents clearly saw the benefits that can be gained through responsible TV viewing – 8 out of 10 parents believe television has a positive effect on their child's development, including helping them to expand their imagination and broaden their vocabulary. The research also highlighted some confusion around the different messages parents have read or heard on the potential impact of TV viewing on their children. In summary, the report concluded that a balanced television diet is something that many parents sensibly strive for by restricting time, monitoring programme content, quality and delivery (for example, via digital TV recorders) and maximising their interaction with their children about what they have watched.

2008 Towards switchover

Between 2008 and 2012, television services in the UK will go completely digital, TV region by TV region (the exception is Whitehaven in Cumbria which became the first place to switch in October 2007). The old analogue television signal will be switched off and viewers will need to convert or upgrade their TV equipment to receive digital signals, whether through their aerial, by satellite, cable or broadband. The Government is responsible for the policy of digital switchover, including the 2008–2012 switchover timetable and the establishment of a Help Scheme for those who may need practical assistance with switchover.

2008 The switchover Help Scheme

This UK scheme is designed to help older and disabled people who may find it difficult to switch to digital TV. The Switchover Help Scheme is run by the BBC and paid for from the licence fee. The scheme can help viewers to convert their television sets to digital. The qualifying categories are those viewers who:

- are aged 75 or over; or

- get or could get Disability Living Allowance, Attendance Allowance, Constant Attendance Allowance or mobility supplement; or

- have lived in a care home for six months or more; or

- are registered blind or partially sighted.

2008 The digital choice

With multichannel digital television the six service providers became:

Freeview broadcast through the UHF spectrum and accessible with a good quality roof-top (or loft) aerial and with either a Freeview decoder box or an IDTV (integrated digital television) television set. Freeview has a 72% reach of the UK – increasing to 98% after switchover is complete in 2012,

BBC/ITV Freesat Broadcast this year, 6 May 2008 from the three ASTRA satellites to individual dishes on each property. A decoder box is required. ASTRA has a reach of 98% of the UK.

Virgin Media Broadcast through either BT 'local loop' networks or through fibre optic cables. A decoder box is required. Cable has a reach of just over 50% of UK homes.

Sky Pay Television and Sky Freesat Broadcast from the three ASTRA satellites to individual dishes on each property. A decoder box is required. ASTRA has a reach of 98% of the UK.

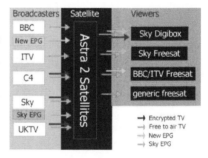

British Telecom Broadcast though BT's ADSL network. A decoder box is required. Potentially BT has a reach of 100% (see 'Digital Britian' report).

Tiscali (Broadband television in some areas of the UK – sometimes called IPTV internet protocol television.)

Türksat 3A

Türksat 3A is a Turkish communications satellite, to be operated by Turksat this year. It was constructed by Thales Alenia Space, based on the Spacebus 4000B2 satellite bus, and was launched by Arianespace atop an Ariane 5ECA carrier rocket, along with the British Skynet 5C satellite, in a dual-payload launch on 12 June, at 22:05:02 GMT, from ELA-3 at the Guiana Space Centre. It is part of the Turksat fleet of satellites, and is placed in geosynchronous orbit at 42° East to provide communications services to Turkey, Europe and the Middle East.

2008 Which? guide The independent consumer charity launched a guide for all UK households on switching to digital television. It successfully demystified the subject in a small and well written piece of advice.

2008 Statistics never made a home

- 23.3m homes now have digital television of one type or another (89.2% of all homes).

- Homes remaining on Analogue terrestrial, that is, still to make a digital television choice, has fallen to 2.6m.

- Of the total of 60.2m TV sets in UK homes 25.4m are main sets.

- 9.6m homes use satellite services – whether pay or free.

- The selection of cable is reducing as a TV choice; 3.3m in Q1 as opposed to 3.1m in Q2.

- BT Vision has 433,000 subscribers.

- Tiscali ADSL has 427,000 subscribers.

- Top-Up TV has 40,000 subscribers.

- Sky Freesat has 250,000 users.•

BBC/ITV Freesat has 450,000 users.

2008 NBC in the USA

The NBC network in the USA was part of the media company NBC Universal, a unit of General Electric, which, on 1 December this year purchased the remaining 20% stake of NBC Universal which it did not already own from Vivendi. On 3 December, Comcast announced that it planned to purchase a 51% stake of NBC Universal. NBC would then become available to an estimated 112 million USA households, 98.6% of those with televisions. NBC had 10 owned-and-operated stations and nearly 200 affiliates in the United States and its territories.

Offset Polarity

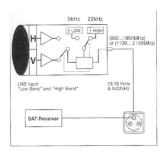

One fact that is critical to a good dish installation is how the dish is fixed to the wall. Because of the curvature of the earth the dish has to be squint to present as square to the hub of the ASTRA satellite. This is called offset polarity. The diagram on this page shows how the polarity is achieved Horizontal and Vertical. The two frequencies (high and low) achieved each carry a number of channels to effectively use the frequency available twice – so maximising the number of channels. At EPG level the join is seamless.

2008 Digital UK is the independent not-for-profit company leading the implementation of switchover.  Digital UK is owned by the UK's public service broadcasters (BBC, ITV, Channel 4, five, S4C and Teletext), and multiplex operators SDN and Arqiva. They provide impartial information on what households need to do to prepare for the switch to digital, and when they need to do it. The company was set up by public broadcasters at the request of the Government. Digital UK works closely with the Department for Culture, Media and Sport (DCMS) and the Department for Business, Innovation and Skills (BIS), as well as the regulator Ofcom, to prepare the UK for the biggest change in broadcasting since the introduction of colour.

2008 The UK government announced its intention of switching off all analogue television transmissions by 2012.

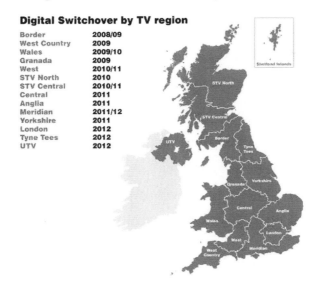

Digital Switchover by TV region

Border	2008/09
West Country	2009
Wales	2009/10
Granada	2009
West	2010/11
STV North	2010
STV Central	2010/11
Central	2011
Anglia	2011
Meridian	2011/12
Yorkshire	2011
London	2012
Tyne Tees	2012
UTV	2012

2008 ITV HD launches

On 7 June, ITV HD started Broadcasting.

SES ASTRA

SES, now SES ASTRA In Europe, pioneered direct-to-home (DTH) satellite broadcasting in Europe and rapidly established itself as Europe's leading DTH satellite system. It is used by a wide range of broadcast and multimedia companies to deliver broadcast

and broadband services to 122 million households. Space segment – satellites are located at five orbital positions:

19.2°East	28.2° East 2	3.5° East	5° East	31.5° East
ASTRA 1H	ASTRA 2A	ASTRA 3A	ASTRA 1C	ASTRA 2C
ASTRA KR	ASTRA 2B	ASTRA 1E	SIRIUS 3	ASTRA 1D
ASTRA 1L	ASTRA 2D	ASTRA 1G	SIRIUS 4	
ASTRA 1M				

2008 Satellite capabilities and coverage

The ASTRA fleet now consists of 15 satellites positioned at prime orbital positions 19.2° East, 28.2° East, 23.5° East, 5° East and 31.5° East. The satellites located at 19.2° East are mainly used for DTH

services to large audiences in markets like Germany, France and Spain. The satellites at 28.2° East provide DTH services to the UK and Ireland. 23.5° East is ASTRA's latest hot spot for DTH and broadband services, currently focusing on dynamic markets

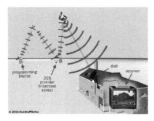

such as Italy, Benelux and Central and Eastern Europe. The innovative satellite broadband service ASTRA2 Connect is also transmitted from 23.5° East and is available in numerous markets across Europe. The satellites at 5° East provide DTH services in the Nordic countries and the Baltics, as well as in Eastern Europe. The satellites at 31.5° East primarily offer capacity suitable for cable contribution, DTT and other terrestrial feeds across Europe. YahLive, an ASTRA and YahSat partnership, uses the YahSat IA spacecraft at 52.5° East to offer DTH coverage in the MENA region and south-west Asia.

2008 Each ASTRA satellite weighs up to five tons and takes about three years to build. Extensive testing is carried out throughout the manufacturing process to ensure that the satellites perform perfectly in space. So far these three companies have built ASTRA

- Boeing Satellite Systems (formerly Hughes Space and Communications) built ASTRA IC–IH, ASTRA 2A, ASTRA 2C–2D, ASTRA 3A, SIRIUS 3 and SIRIUS I.

- EADS Astrium (formerly Matra Marconi Space) built ASTRA 2B and ASTRA IM, and is currently building ASTRA 3B.

- Lockheed Martin built ASTRA IA-B and ASTRA IKR, ASTRA IL and SIRIUS 4 / ASTRA 4A.

Thales Alenia Space (formerly Aerospatiale) built ASTRA 5A.

Two companies have launched ASTRA satellites – Arianespace and International Launch Services (ILS). Arianespace is a European consortium. It uses Ariane rockets, which are launched from the European Space

Centre in Kourou, French Guiana. ASTRA 1A to 1E and ASTRA 3A were launched using the Ariane 4 rocket; ASTRA 2B and 2D were launched on Ariane 5. ILS is a US-based joint venture owned by Lockheed Martin, Khrunichev Enterprises and RSC Energia. ILS uses the Russian Proton rocket, which is manufactured by Moscow-based Khrunichev Enterprise. The version used for ASTRA satellites is called Proton D1e. It uses a Block DM upper stage manufactured by RSC Energia of Moscow. Proton is launched from the Baikonur Cosmodrome in Kazakhstan.

In April 1996, ASTRA 1F was the first commercial western satellite to be launched on Proton. ASTRA 1G, 2A, 1H  and 2C followed. The Ariane and Proton launch vehicles are powerful enough to place payloads of up to five tons into orbit. After completion, the newly manufactured satellite is transferred to the launch site for final testing and fuelling, before being mated to the launch vehicle. The launch is a complex operation conducted in several stages, which differ according to the system used. An Ariane rocket launches the satellites into an elliptical temporary transfer orbit, typically as close as 200 km (with Ariane 4) or 560 km (with Ariane 5) to the Earth, but possibly as far as 36,000 km. Firing its on-board thrusters, the satellite then propels itself into its final circular geostationary orbit at 36,000 km. A Proton rocket fitted with a powerful and re-ignitable Block DM fourth stage takes the satellite higher (at least several thousand kilometres from the Earth, depending on the launch mass of the satellite). This reduces the amount of velocity (energy) required to reach geostationary orbit, which means satellites launched on Proton generally retain higher fuel reserves. ITV considers selling its Freeview terrestrial digital television business.

2008 BBC News 24

On 12 June, BBC News 24 became just BBC News.

2008 Freeview for sale?

This year, the BBC's executive chairman, Michael Grade, was finalising plans to raise cash as the group faced a slump in advertising revenues and further pressure from servicing its debt and pension fund. This was part of the preparation for ITV's

annual results on 4 March. It was realised that selling the Freeview multiplex that hosts Channel Five's channels, as well as the shopping channel QVC could raise about £200m. Although the business was profitable and brought in revenues of £36m in 2007, up 44% on the previous year, it was not seen as central to ITV's core identity as a producer-broadcaster. ITV Digital's attempt to create a terrestrial pay-TV rival to BSkyB, finally collapsed in 2002, having blown £1bn in the process. Having had its fingers burned so spectacularly, ITV was wary of ITV Digital's successor, Freeview, and stayed out of the consortium behind the venture. However, Freeview's remarkable success – and ITV's ability to benefit disproportionately from it – persuaded the company to become more closely involved.

2008 BBC Alba

On 19 September, Scottish Gaelic channel, Alba, started broadcasting on satellite and Virgin on demand.

2008 Digital Britain Report

In June this year, the UK Government published its report of the future of digital Britain. The report said –

1 The communications sector underpins everything we do as an economy and society, to a degree few could have imagined even a quarter of a century ago. Electronic systems and new technology have transformed core elements of UK industry, our media and our public services.

2 In the City, digital technologies are vital to the billions of transactions carried out each day by the stock exchange and financial institutions. For the designers, researchers and engineers in our advanced industries, computer generation and simulation and reliable large-scale file transfer are essential tools of the trade as they are now for any knowledge-based company. In the high street, stock ordering, inventory control and the cash tills are all completely dependent on electronic communications.

3 As consumers, some 90% of our high street purchases are transacted by plastic which depends on wired and wireless communications to work. That is in addition to the £50bn of consumer purchases and sales through e-commerce that takes place wholly online.

4 In transport, the phasing of street traffic lights, the operation of railway signals and points and the wireless systems that allow aircraft to take off and land safely all need communications; as does the national energy grid that heats, powers and lights our homes and businesses. In the public sector, our universities, schools

and libraries increasingly rely on electronic content and the richness of the Internet. Our National Health Service has one of the largest data and communications systems in Europe.

5 For individuals a quiet revolution has delivered seamless connectivity almost everywhere. That revolution ranges from personal pocket libraries of music, audiovisual content and increasingly electronic literature on a scale inconceivable ten years ago; inexpensive broadband which allows efficient and family-friendly working patterns in the knowledge sector of the economy – and broadband at increasing speeds – the next generation of which, already available to nearly half Britain's homes, allows us to send or receive 200 mp3 music files in five minutes, an entire Star Wars DVD in 3 minutes and the total digitised works of Charles Dickens in less than 10 minutes. It has given us access to a wide range of social networks, allowing us to share experiences and swap and create content. The digital revolution has also led to a huge expansion in the creation and availability of professional content. Today, the typical British consumer spends nearly half of their waking hours engaged in one form or another with the products and services of the communications sector.

6 The UK is already a digitally enabled and to a significant degree digitally dependent economy and society. The Digital Britain Report aims to be a guide path for how Britain can sustain its position as a leading digital economy and society.

7 A sector that underpins so much of our collective and individual lives is a

significant industry in its own right. Its precise scale is evolving continually. The pace of change, the blurring of boundaries between what national statisticians classified as separate activities and the creation of whole new areas of activity make measurement problematic. But on current definitions the Digital Britain sectors account for nearly £1 in every £10 that the whole economy produces each year.

8 Digital Britain is a leading exemplar of the new model of Industrial Activism set out in April's *'Building Britain's Future: New Industry, New Jobs'*. It is one of the major growth sectors on which our economy increasingly depends. It is a sector in which we have many relative strengths. Key themes from *Building Britain's Future* – modern infrastructure, upgraded skills capabilities, converting research and innovation into market-beating products and services, and smarter more joined-up Government – are all themes that feature through The Digital Britain Report.

9 Industrial Activism is at the centre of The Digital Britain Report. It is about the considered application of Government resources and policy-making across the areas where public policy and the market meet. There are many activities within the sector where public policy and the market do not impinge on one another: the market is working well and without any wider social policy consequences. Although the Digital Britain Report does not address them all, many are, nonetheless, significant creators of added value and consumer satisfaction. The simple position is that these sectors are working well and do not need commentary, intervention or unnecessary interference.

10 We published the Interim Digital Britain Report at the end

of January. That set out a view of the sector and an agenda for Industrial Activism in the large number of areas where the markets meet public policy. We identified five objectives:

i. Modernising and upgrading our wired, wireless and broadcasting infrastructure to sustain Britain's position as a leading digital economy;

ii. Providing a favourable climate for investment and innovation in digital content, applications and services;

iii. Securing a range of high quality public service content, particularly in news;

iv. Developing the nation's digital skills at all levels; and

v. Securing universal access to broadband, increasing its take-up and using broadband to deliver more public services more effectively and more efficiently.

11 The aim of publishing an Interim Report was to test whether the programme we had outlined was correct and sufficiently comprehensive, and to gauge the level of support for our focus on this sector. The Interim Report drew a substantial and substantive response from a very wide range of stakeholders, from the general public to global corporations. We received more than 250 formal written responses. Those responses have been supplemented by online engagement through the Digital Britain Forum and other social networking/blog sites, structured engagements in each of the Nations and the Digital Britain Summit at the British Library on 17 April. There have also been in total more than 500 bilateral engagements between stakeholders and Ministers or the core Digital Britain Team.

2008 Terrestrial Freeview + launch

23 October saw the launch of Freeview+ boxes – being able to record, pause and replay live television.

2008 Satellite Freesat HD launches

The BBC and ITV launched a satellite service, carrying limited HD programming in May this year. Astra 2D is used.

Freesat HD boxes and Freesat HD integrated television sets will soon follow with their own EPGs. Generic boxes looking at Astra 2D will also receive the microwave signals because they are not encrypted on the Sky EPG received from Astra 2D.

2008 More sky channels opened:

20 January: Investigation Discovery

20 March: Discovery Shed

19 May: Really

2008 Freeview+ through Sony Playstation

18 September saw Sony launch the PlayTV box enabling game players to watch and record Freeview through the PlayStation 3. PlayTV from Sony Computer Entertainment Europe, is a tiny black box

that gives the PLAYSTATION®3 the functionality of a state-of-the-art TV tuner and Personal Video Recorder (PVR). The viewer can watch, pause and record live TV chosen from up to48 Freeview digital TV channels.

2008 FIVE

On 20 November, Channel Five joined the Freeview platform.

2008 GMTV improvements

On 2 January, GMTV returned with a new set and new onscreen graphics. For the first time since the station's launch the logo was changed from the 'sun' logo.

Despite the changes, the same theme music and headline beds were still used throughout the programme. The previous programme names News Hour and GMTV Today were dropped in favour of just GMTV, with LK Today renamed GMTV with  Lorraine. Presenters continue to present in their previous slots and at the top of the hour refer to the show as GMTV with ... although this is not seen on screen. The channel has previously been criticised for its poor journalistic approach although from 2009 has taken on a more confident approach, with 7 minute bulletins at the top of the hour, a detailed bulletin at half-past the hour, and the Top Stories at 15 and 45 minutes past each hour. These replace the bulletins which were previously on the hour and half-hour. On 9 March, GMTV introduced new theme music and headline beds to its main programmes, replacing the previous music that had been in use since 2000.

2008 First transmitter to go digital – switchover progress in Border TV Region, Scotland

As already explained, digital terrestrial television in the United Kingdom encompasses over 100 television, radio and interactive services broadcast via the UK's terrestrial television network and receivable with a standard television aerial. The majority of services, including those from the existing five analogue broadcasters, are broadcast free-to-air, and a further selection of encrypted Pay-TV services (such as  ESPN) are also available. Digital Terrestrial services are often referred to with the Freeview name, however, this is only a brand name adopted by the broadcasters of free-to-air services. Freeview channels account for most, although not all, of the total available channels broadcast on digital terrestrial television, available at no extra cost and requiring no subscription other than payment of the annual TV licence fee. The digital broadcasting technology adopted in the UK is the DVB-T system (Digital Video Broadcasting – Terrestrial) carrying compressed digital audio, video and other data in a combined transport stream, using COFDM modulation. A total of six 'multiplexes' are broadcast in the UK, guaranteed to reach over 90% of the country when analogue signals are fully switched off. Three of the six multiplexes, carrying the free public service channels operated by the BBC, ITV, Channel 4 and Five, are guaranteed wider coverage still, reaching 98.5% of the country including areas dependent on low-power local relays.

Selkirk in Scotland (and its relays), became the first digital only main terrestrial transmitter for Freeview. No analogue service was then available. The Selkirk transmitter covers 24,000 homes.

On 6 November, 2008 Digital UK undertook the following work:

- The analogue BBC Two signal was switched off.

- BBC Two went digital, plus some new channels were added.

On 20 November 2008, the following occurred:

- The analogue BBC One, ITV, Channel 4 and Five signals were switched off.

- The digital versions of these channels, and many more, became available to everyone.

Switchover was then complete for this terrestrial television region.

2008 Using the UHF spectrum

The use of the freed up UHF spectrum: Indepen (a research company) undertook research for Ofcom on the potential use and value of the UHF spectrum not used after switchover is complete in 2012. The capital receipt is called the DD – the digital dividend. The report sets out how the impact assessment of options for assigning the DDR dividend in respect of high definition (HD) public service broadcasting (PSB) services should be structured and, where possible, quantifies impacts. Ofcom has concluded that the dividend from digital switchover should be assigned on a technology and service neutral basis through an auction – termed a market-based approach. Ofcom's analysis compares assignment by auction with options for intervention in respect of a number of services, including HD PSB services.

Barbarians

Attitudes to television and its affect on society were still debated in the press this year. The Sunday Times reported that BBC news presenter, Jeremy Paxman (reputed £1m p.a. salary) dismissed the British public as a 'bunch of barbarians' for watching television rather than reading books or visiting art galleries. His outburst resonated with middle-class Britons who worry that television is somehow a malign influence. Contrary views existed – such as some academics arguing that television is a powerful agent of change in the world – for the better.

The rate of growth of digital television in British Homes showed further growth compared to previous quarters – but reached its highest percentage point of 92% of all homes by 2 July 2010. This is 25.8m homes.

Web television

2009 Television manufacturer, Cello launched the first 'Web TV' – an integrated internet television set, becoming the first television able to connect to the internet and stream video content without the need for a computer or set-top box. The iViewer taps into the home broadband connection via a cable or optional wi-fi dongle. At launch, the sites it could access were limited. The device did include the BBC iPlayer, YouTube and some of the best internet television content – for example, Jamie's Ministry of Food. The iViewer can also display videos and photos from a PC or laptop on the same network.

2009 CNN launches on Freeview platform

On 15 January, CNN International was
available on Freeview channel 84 everyday
from 9.00pm to 1.00am. A retune of boxes
was required to see this new service.

2009 Windows 7

Windows 7 became the latest public
release version of Microsoft Windows, a
series of operating systems produced by
Microsoft for use on personal computers,

including home and business desktops, laptops, netbooks, tablet
PCs, and media center PCs. Windows 7 was released to
manufacturing on 22 July and reached general retail availability on
22 October less than three years after the release of its
predecessor, Windows Vista.

2009 / 2010 Size of the digital television platforms

The breakdown between the different platforms at 2 July 2010,
was as follows:

Free-to-View Sat 1.3m homes)
(Sky Freesat + BBC/ITV Freesat)
DDT Freeview   10.2m "   ) 'Free-to air' digital TV = 11.5m)
Sky digital   9.7m "   )   ) **25.8m**
Virgin Cable   3.7m "   ) 'Pay' digital TV = 14.3m   ) total
Other pay platforms 0.9m ")
(Top-Up TV, BT Vision, Talk Talk (Tiscali)   source q1 Ofcom 2 July 2010

Freeview (the successor to broadcasters ONdigital and ITVdigital
as the terrestrial suppliers of digital television) was now the
biggest supplier of digital television in the United Kingdom with
over 10m homes buying a Freeview box or an iDTV with

Freeview built in. Many households chose Freeview to compliment Sky or Virgin on the main television set. Sky maintained its position as the largest supplier of pay digital television services in the United Kingdom. Sky's market penetration was as follows:

- Churn (the proportion of subscribers ending contracts)  increased in the latest quarter from 9.6% to 9.9%.

- Number of customers having multiroom (more than one Sky box) was 2.06m.

- Number of customers with Sky+ (box includes a PVR) was 6.5m.

- Number of customers with Sky+HD (High Definition) was 2.5m.

2009 Analogue broadcast

80% of all TV sets had converted to digital television by the end of Q1 2010 (up 7.0 percentage points in a year). The remaining 20% of sets continued to receive analogue terrestrial broadcasts.

2009 Film rental on-line and through IPTV

LoveFilm is a British company which provides online video rental (rental-by-mail) and resale of DVD-Video,  Blu-ray, and video game console Disc, as well as on-demand video streaming over the internet of movies in the UK, Germany and Scandinavia. It operates the LoveFilm website, as well as providing the actual website and delivery infrastructure for an array of branded services in partnership with other British companies. In January this year, LoveFilm claimed to have over 1,000,000 members, over 67,000 titles, and over 4 million rentals per month across five countries. Through a series of mergers and acquisitions, the latest being the Amazon DVD rental activities, LoveFilm has, in a few years, become the dominant online DVD rental outlet in the UK. The company used to offer a download service alongside postal delivery, but this ceased (at least temporarily) on 23 February 2009. Instead, the company has started a 'watch online' service which offers over 3,500 films available to watch as part of subscription. This online viewing is available free for subscribers who have opted for one of their unlimited monthly rental plans; there is also some pay-per-view content available to all.

2009 BBC brings live TV to mobile phones

The BBC has unveiled a new service that will enable people to watch live television on their mobile phones. On 6 April, the BBC announced that the programming will be simulcast on handsets at the same time as they are broadcast on air through the terrestrial platform. The service, dubbed Live TV, is still in the

'beta' testing stage, but will enable viewers to watch channels such as BBC One, BBC Four, CBeebies and BBC News over a Wi-Fi connection using a compatible mobile phone. Radio shows can also be streamed live to handsets. Users don't need to install any additional software in order to watch the shows, but they do need to hold a colour TV licence in order to enjoy the live programmes, which have been optimised for the small screens of mobile phones. Some programmes, such as sports events and imported shows, will be absent from the line-up due to broadcast rights restrictions. The BBC said it hoped to add further channels and stations to the service 'in due course', as well as the ability to watch live television over the 3G mobile phone network wherever people are.

Pop Vox 2009

By this year, 'Pop Vox' (see 1954) had taken on a new lease of life with the public using their mobile technology to express opinions to broadcasters and to supply imagery from their camera phones. The social network websites, using myriads of people with camera mobile phones are capturing sound and pictures of events from around the world which find their way onto the Internet and then occasionally are broadcast on mainstream television. Examples include scenes from Iraq, Iran, Afghanistan, the bombs on the London Tube system and elsewhere.

2009 BNP on the BBC

On 22 October, the BBC allowed the first appearance of the British National Party (BNP – Leader Nick Griffin) on to British television. The flagship programme 'Question Time' was aired with a panel comprising Jack Straw, the  Labour Government Justice Secretary, the Liberal Democrat Home Affairs Spokesman Chris Hulme, the Conservative shadow cabinet member, Baroness Sayeeda Wasi (a Muslim) and American author Bonnie Greer. This was the first time a so-called racist party had appeared on a chat show with other mainstream political parties. The BNP is a non-white party generally derided by the majority of the public who were aghast at the decision to allow the appearance. The BBC said that Griffin was an elected politician would had a voice and an opinion to be heard. The BBC Director General Mark Thompson said that 'censorship cannot be outsourced to the BBC'. The event caused huge opposition despite the BNP having been elected to Local Authority seats and to two MEP (Member of the European Parliament) seats. There was a crowd protest at the BBC television centre in West London and huge media coverage of the event.

Growth of DTH (Direct to Home)

2009 Sky celebrated its 20th anniversary on 5 February. Sky has unveiled its eagerly awaited new HD electronic programme guide – bringing a major overhaul to the look of its flagship HD service. The new television guide was announced back in 2008, but the company insisted that they would not rush it out until they were happy with the look and feel of the EPG. That moment, it appears, has finally arrived, with the first group of HD customers to receive the new look EPG on 10 March.

On 17 June this year, the Department for Culture, Media and Sport decided to list at Grade II the Central Ring of the West London BBC Television Centre building and Studio 1, noting in particular the John Piper mosaic, central drum with its mosaic tiles, the Huxley-Jones gilded statue of Helios, full-height glazing of the stair and the original clock in the Central Ring. The 'atomic dots' and name of Studio 1, along with the cantilevered porch on

its exterior were noted as important architectural features of that building. The Department did not consider the other buildings, including all other studios, scenery block and canteen, of sufficient special interest to warrant listing them, and specifically excluded them.

In March this year, over 10 million households in the UK and Ireland were receiving television broadcasts directly via ASTRA satellites.

26 November 2009

ITV took full control of the breakfast TV broadcaster GMTV, buying the 25% share it did not already own from Disney for £22.25m. The deal was structured as a one-off cash payment of £18m to Disney for its 25% stake, plus a further sum of £4.25m, which represents its share of the forecast cash balance in the GMTV business as at the year end. It is likely that ITV will seek to cut costs as it integrates the GMTV team with the rest of its broadcasting and production business.

Product placement

Based on the early USA television model, ITV looked at product placement because of the downturn in ad revenue.

2009 Launch of Freeview HD

2 December saw the launch of  Freeview HD with BBC HD, ITV1 HD, and Channel 4 HD.

The low-key launch of Freeview high-definition (HD) transmissions, from the Winter Hill and Crystal Palace transmitters, came and went largely unnoticed by most of the 18 million Freeview viewers in the UK. Terrestrial HD is set to change as Freeview – the company owned and run by the BBC, BSkyB, Channel 4, ITV and Arqiva – starts to promote its new HD service in advance of this summer's football World Cup – 2010.

High-definition television is not new. BSkyB launched an HD service in early 2006, as did Telewest (now Virgin Media) on cable. Freesat, jointly funded by the BBC and ITV, launched a satellite service, carrying limited HD programming in May 2008. Freeview, last to the HD table, but with the most viewers, was only recently able to add HD channels to its standard-definition line-up. It has done this by reorganising the multiplexes that carry its channels, and adopting new more efficient DVB-T2 technology (Digital Video Broadcast, T2 – signifying it's a terrestrial second generation standard), which enables more channels to be carried.

LED screens

2009 This year saw a relatively new application for LEDs, or light emitting diodes, that caused something of a stir in the consumer electronics industry. LEDs have existed for some time, and have been used in a wide variety of applications, but the new LED TVs are something that has not been seen before. They have a good number of advantages over standard televisions, and are even edging ahead of standard LCD televisions and plasma TVs in terms of image quality and performance. Let's take a look at how they work, and some of their advantages.

LED TVs work by having a large screen of diodes that actually emit light rather than

 reflecting it, making them much brighter than other technologies. They are one-way electronic semiconductors, making them respond very quickly to being turned on and off – one of the major pitfalls of technologies like plasma and LCD is that they do not respond quickly enough to being turned on and off, resulting in motion blur with moving images. LED televisions do not experience this problem. They also do not lose their colour when there is a drop in electrical current.

LED TVs also have a number of advantages available to them that other types of televisions do not. For example, the application of 'eyelids', which are short veneers that shade each LED, allow them to retain their image and colour even in bright sunlight, reducing glare and allowing viewers to maintain the image even when viewed from the side or from below. The colours are much truer to life, due to the large amount of diodes used in conjunction with each other. They can even compensate for over saturation with colour space conversion.

There were by now two great examples of the advantages of LED TVs available on the market worldwide; the Samsung UE40B6000 and the Samsung UE46B6000, which have 40 inch and 46 inch screens, respectively. These televisions both offer exceptional image quality, with contrast ratios in the thousands, and full HD capabilities. They are also equipped to play Blu-ray technology and run using 40% less power than a standard LCD television. The blacks are darker and the colours are more vibrant than with other modern televisions, and they are capable of 100Hz motion as well as having 1080p resolution and Ultra Clear Panel capabilities. These televisions are for the true viewer who wants the highest level of performance from their TV.

2010 HD 3D from Virgin Media

The latest package offer arrived from
Virgin this year – starting at £18 per
month.

What has Digital Broadcasting become?

Broadcasting is the distribution of sound and picture signals which
transmit programmes to an audience. The audience may be the
general public or a relatively large sub-audience, such as children
or young adults. The sequencing of content in a broadcast is called
a schedule. In the 21st century, television can be broadcast
through different platforms:

• Terrestrial UHF aerials (Freeview available to 75% of the UK).

• ADSL telephone lines (BT Home Vision and others), (available
to homes in London from some suppliers and nationally from
BT).

• Underground cables (50% of homes passed by Virgin Media)

• Satellites (Sky and others), (available to 98% of homes).

• Internet television channels viewable through broadband
connectivity.

By coding some of the signals and by having decoding equipment
in homes, the latter also enables some
subscription-based channels and pay-per-view
services. In 1927, of course, only the VHF
spectrum was available for radio signal
broadcasts. The term 'broadcast' originally
referred to the sowing of seeds by scattering them over a wide
field. It was adopted by early radio engineers from the
Midwestern United States to refer to the analogous

dissemination of radio signals. Broadcasting forms a very large segment of the mass media. Broadcasting to a very narrow range of audience is called narrowcasting.

Quattron LED televisions

In June this year, Sharp had  developed a fourth colour gun to the traditional RGB (red, green, blue) spectrum. A yellow gun introduces an RGBY colour spectrum.

The 811 Series LCD TVs include the standard Quattron features:

*   HD ready 1080p
*   Quattron Technology
*   Freeview HD
*   Co•ntemporary Slim Design
*   100Hz
*   Mega contrast
*   2.1Ch Sound system (10w x 2 + 15W Subwoofer Audio Output)
*   Media player for video (DivX HD supported), pictures and music playback via USB

There are currently 2 sizes available in the 811 Series:

*   40 inch screen on the LC-40LE811E
*   46 inch screen on the LC-46LE811E

The 821 Series adds on the specification of the 811 Series with:

- Full Flat and Seamless Front Design

- Timeshift function is 120 mins for SD and 50 mins for HD

- Home Network (DLNA)

The Quattron television sets also deliver Freeview HD giving BBC HD, 4 HD and ITV HD

The visual brain creates every colour of the rainbow by comparing the amounts of red light in relation to green, and the strength of blue light in relation to yellow at every point across the fovea – the colour-sensitive region right at the centre of the retina – which collects detailed information from the surfaces of objects. The red/green and blue/yellow comparisons are then combined, and then readings from adjacent patches of space are compared in a specialized part of the visual brain to create our perception of colour. Sharp's new Quattron technology provides all four of these channels of light so that the eye has exactly what it requires to produce a complete and convincing spectrum of colours in our mind's eye.

Growth of SKY HD

In March of this year, ITV HD joined the newly improved SKY EPG. On 30 March, following an investigation into the pay TV market, Ofcom, the communications regulator, confirmed that Sky will be required to make its premium sports channels available to other pay TV retailers (for example, Freeview, BT Telecom and Virgin Media) at regulated prices. Sky fundamentally disagreed with Ofcom's conclusions and intended to launch a legal appeal against the ruling.

The latest comparison of the five UK digital broadcasters is as follows:

	Satellite	Cable	Broadband	Aerial	Satellite
Monthly Cost	From £18	From £5.50	From £7.50	FREE	FREE
Setup Cost	£30	£75	£30	FREE	£80
Channels	Over 400	Over 150	Up to 50	Up to 50	Over 140
HD	Yes – 37 channels	Yes – 7 channels	No	Beginning – 3	Yes – 3 channels
Sky Sports	Yes	Yes (partial)	No	No	No
Sky Movies	Yes	Yes (partial)	No	No	No
Multi-Room	Yes	Yes	No	No	No
Gifts	£25 M&S voucher	No	No	No	No

Aril 2010   Sky launched 3DTV as a single demonstration station with a further 3D channel expected in October 2010 – although some football broadcasts took place at launch of the demo channel. 3D blu-ray machines and 1080p 3D CDs were also now available. The DVD player must match the technology of the television set. This is because there are two types of 3D television broadcast:

- Active shutter 3D display and

- Passive shutter 3D display

Most big brand television makers have selected the active shutter method. 3D glasses synchronise with the television set via an infrared signal and rapidly blink on and off playing back 1080p resolution images to each eye at 50 frames per second. The disadvantage of the active display is that the glasses are more expensive and require a power source to operate which makes them heavy. They also only work with their own brand of television set.

The alternative is the passive shutter, sometimes called the polarising display. This method uses a polarising film over the screen that separates the image into left and right types. The glasses require no power source, are lighter for the viewer and are cheaper to buy. They just filter out the unwanted image and let only the correct image through the left and right eye to fool the brain into believing that the image has three dimensions

Costs of 3D television sets at launch varied from £1,800 to over £3,000 excluding the 3D glasses. The viewer must also pay a provider to supply the 3D broadcasts through the set top box to the 3D television set.

2010 Sky + boxes discontinued

Sky discontinued the sale of the standard definition Sky+ box as of 28 January this year. This did not affect Sky's existing customers. If a Sky subscriber already had a Sky TV subscription package with Sky+ they would still be able to receive channels as normal – the only difference is that new customers would not be able to choose the Sky+ box at sign up. The standard box is now Sky+HD.

Associated Newspapers announced it would end the Teletext news and information services on digital and analogue television in January this year – two years earlier than previously proposed and ahead of the date for the UK's digital TV switchover.

On 6 March, Eutelsat W2 at 16° East expired with a major technical fault on 27 January .All traffic was moved over to the co-located Eurobird 16A, Eutelsat W2M (moved to 16° East in early January) and Eutelsat Sesat I (moved from 36° East when W7 went into service and on station at 36° East by the end of January.

Sky announced that the number of customers choosing Sky+HD, the UK's only satellite high definition service currently capable of broadcasting 3D services, had increased to 2m following record growth.

Customers have responded in record numbers to Sky's high quality and great value HD service. Sky has more than doubled the number of HD customers in the last year alone with over 90 customers an hour joining Sky+HD.

In the next step in the Sky+HD journey, Sky announced in July 2009 that it will launch the UK's first 3D channel this year. The channel will offer a broad selection of the best available 3D programming, which is expected to include movies, entertainment and sport. The service will be broadcast across Sky's existing HD infrastructure and be available via the current generation of Sky+HD set-top boxes. To watch 3D, customers will also require one of the new '3D Ready' TVs, which are expected to be on sale in the UK next year.

This commitment follows extensive research and development activity into 3D, which included Sky becoming the first TV company in Europe to broadcast a live event in 3D TV. On 2 April 2009, Sky successfully broadcast a performance by Keane live from Abbey Road Studios via the company's satellite network to a Sky+HD set-top box and domestic 3D Ready TV.

Sky has also confirmed the launch of a comprehensive 'pull' video-on-demand (VOD) service next year, to provide Sky+HD customers with additional choice and control to complement Sky+ and the current Sky Anytime 'push' VOD service. This new service will use the broadband capability of existing Sky+HD boxes.

2010 Averting another format war, this time in 3D TV

With virtually every major TV manufacturer now eyeing the release of 3-D HDTVs, almost 200 companies in the global entertainment and consumer electronics industries are now working on uniting behind a common set of technology standards for consumer viewing of movies and other 3-D content on home TVs. Their hope is to avoid a repeat of the ugly HD video disc format war, which left Toshiba badly bruised and HD DVD a distant memory. However, it can already be seen that two types of 3D technology have been produced so the consumer still has a choice – until one starts to dominate the market – probably the passive shutter method. Despite the far greater complexities of 3D technology over something as simple as 1080p video, industry players from a variety of camps are bent on preventing similar divisiveness this time around.

Fractionalization among 3D technologies in the areas of content distribution, video compression, and decoding "Just wouldn't be good for any of us," said George Palmer, a Mitsubishi senior product manager, in a meeting with Betanews. Instead, many HDTV makers are gearing up to adhere to a set of 3D standards about to be formulated by a task force formed in May by the Blu-ray Disc Association (BDA); an organization consisting of about 175 companies, including several major motion picture houses. Toshiba, however, is not a BDA member. "Whatever the task force decides, then that's what we'll do," said Mitsubishi's Palmer. He added, that he hopes the resulting standards will be backward-compatible with any 3D products released before the standards are finalized. Attendees also spoke to the issue of whether and when 3D glasses will no longer be needed. Steve Schklair, CEO of 3ality Digital Systems, predicted that consumers won't be able to toss the goggles aside for about another five or six years. But Palmer forecast that 3D glasses will never really go away, since they'll keep being needed for "displaying a wide enough viewing angle."

Also at the show, Mitsubishi rolled out plans to release a total of eight new 3D-capable HDTVs, including a massive 82 inch product called the DLP Model WD-82737. Beginning this week, Naranjo said, Mitsubishi will send a 53 foot trailer to its 700 retail sites in the US, to give demos to consumers of 3D and its other digital TV technologies and products, such as a set of Unisen LCD TVs with newly enhanced Integrated Sound Projector technology. "Once you see [3-D], you won't want to see anything else," Naranjo contended. So far, however, home 3-D screens are rather few and far between, with much of the available 3D content consisting of games. A couple of years ago, Samsung introduced 3-D-ready DLP TVs, later extending the 3D capabilities to flat-panel plasma TVs. Mitsubishi already sells rear projection 3-D TVs. Hyundai offers a 3-D-capable 46 inch LCD TV, but only in Japan. In April of this year, Panasonic unveiled plans for a professional HD production system with a camera recorder and HD plasma display for filming 3-D movies and TV shows. The following month, LG announced a forthcoming 23 inch 3D screen.

2010 At the CES show in Las Vegas in January, Sony demonstrated a 3-D TV prototype, while also telling reporters that the specific technology shown won't necessarily be incorporated into specific consumer products. Viewing of 3-D content on today's 3-D TVs means consumers must purchase a separate accessory kit, which typically includes PC software, an emitter for hooking up the PC to the TV, and a pair of 3D goggles. Yet 3-D TV will "be driven by guys like the Mitsubishis," according to Steve Schklair, who pointed to sports and other events as additional catalysts. "Over time, costs associated with 3-D TVs will come down," Schklair maintained. "3-D TV will also save money on TV production," he said. "Only about half as many cameras will be required for broadcasting football games, for example."

A recent survey by analyst firm the NPD Group showed that 17% of consumers already want to be able to watch 3-D theatrical films in 'advanced 3-D' on their home TVs. Studios have fared well this year with 3-D flicks in movie theatres. Many consumers have shown themselves willing to spring for prices around 50% higher than those of regular movie tickets to view 3-D feature films ranging from Disney/Pixar's Up to Lionsgate's My Bloody Valentine.

Growth of digital TV

This year saw more growth in the number of UK homes with digital television of one form or another – up to 92%.

Talk Talk Digital Television

Talk Talk bought the television service from Tiscali. All packages come with TV Variety Pack, superfast broadband, phone line rental and UK weekend and international calls. Subscribers can choose to tailor the package by adding any of their channel mixes.

2010 Internet television

This year saw television first equipped with internet broadband connectivity and telephone software – allowing free calls from the television set to other similar users – and those on videophone or PC with similar software. Switchover towards switching off analogue broadcast continued on target.

3-D television

Sony chief executive Howard Stringer hit the nail on the head when, during his news conference before the Consumer Electronics Show in Las Vegas this year, he said, "This whole thing is turning into the CES 3-D show."

Indeed, Sony and its competitors – major electronics makers including LG, Toshiba, Samsung, Sharp and Panasonic – took turns during the pre-CES media day trying to outdo each other in the burgeoning market of 3-D television. Stringer, for his part, promised Sony would have three-dimension-enabled televisions, providing the same sort of immersive high-definition depth found in movies such as the box-office blockbuster Avatar, in stores by the summer. He also confirmed that a downloadable software update for Sony's PlayStation 3 later this year would enable the video game console to play 3-D Blu-ray movies. Panasonic is barrelling full-throttle into 3-D with plans to launch enabled Viera televisions and Blu-ray players in the spring, as well as the first 3-D camcorder – which looks like the sort of coin-operated binoculars found at tourist attractions. The company also announced a partnership to promote 3-D with US satellite provider DirecTV, which itself unveiled plans to have two channels showing three-dimensional sports, music and other content by June.

2010 Sky first to air with 3-D

Sky became the first broadcaster in the world to air a 3-D programme – the Manchester United vs Arsenal Premier football on 31 January. It was displayed in pubs with 3-D screens. 3-D Television sets are to be on sale by April at £2,000+.

This year, there will be an exciting new way to watch television – Sky 3D. And the great news is, you'll be able to watch it through your existing Sky+HD box with a 3D ready TV. We're starting by showcasing 3D in pubs from the beginning of April. Later in the year you'll be able to watch some of the best of Sky Sports, Sky Movies and Sky Entertainment in 3D from the comfort of your living room.

SUPERTELLY from Sky

Sky now describing Sky HD as SUPERTELLY

2010 New ITV Chief Executive

Adam Crozier, previously CE of the Post Office, became Chief Executive of ITV – appointed on 28 January.

2010 Television on demand

Every night in the UK the use of On Demand TV peaks at around 10.00pm. Most providers of the service provide several different formats and quality controls so that the service can be viewed on many different devices. Some services now offer a high definition service alongside their standard definition; streaming is the same but offers the quality of HD to the device being used, as long as it is using a HD screen. During Peak times the BBC's iPlayer transmits 12GB (gigabytes) of information per second. Over the course of a month the iPlayer sends 7PB (petabytes) of information.

Before 2006, most Catch-up services used peer-to-peer (P2P) networking, in which users downloaded an application and data

would be shared between the users rather than
the service provider giving the now more
commonly used streaming method. Now most
service providers have moved away from the P2P
systems and are using the streaming media. This is
good for the service provider as in the old P2P
system the distribution costs were high and the servers normally
couldn't handle the large amount of downloading and data
transfer.

2010 Freeview and Sky on iPhones

 On 24 August, Freeview launched on iphones
– the latest version of the Freeview HD TV
Guide APP (software application). Other
broadcasters launched live and catch-up
television on the 'phones – as well as EPGs.
The carrier was 3G mobile or wi-fi
broadband.
Further
channel and
programmes updates for the
iPhone iOS 4 onto the iphone
4s and iphone 5 (2012) followed.

2010 Watching internet television – IPTV

Internet Protocol television has become more popular. Internet
television (otherwise known as Internet TV, Catch-up TV, or
Online TV or IPTV) are television services distributed via the
Internet. It has become very popular during the 21st century with
services such as the Hulu in the United States and BBC iPlayer in
the United Kingdom.

IPTV Features

- Over 80+ channels more & more being added daily
- Exclusive movie channels and movies On Demand
- 7 Day 'catch up' for programme's you missed (Go back and watch TV from the past 7 days).
- Video On Demand
- Store unlimited hours of TV on our secure server
- Record Live TV, programme's you missed & plan ahead
- The very latest Internet TV technology.
- Easily portable to wherever you want to watch UKTV
- Includes local community TV channels
- Easy to manage parental control
- Plug and play... Easy to set up.
- All you need is a 2MB broadband connection.

By this year, UK broadcasters BBC, Sky, Channel 4, Five and ITV had developed online television services that enable viewers to watch or download television programmes over the internet. There are two types of on-line television – streamed or downloaded content. To view television programmes in real time, content is streamed to the home computer over the internet as it is watched. If the broadband connection can't stream the programme (for lack of speed) the result will be patchy viewing quality with frequent screen freezes while the computer waits for the next packet of data to arrive. Downloading television content doesn't have the slow streaming problem. The computer receives the entire programme before it can be viewed. The downloaded files can be very large so there are the issues of sufficient storage capacity and time taken to download. The television content is found on the website of the broadcaster. The home computer must have media player software which is also available on-line.

Computer software media player is also now available which will give access to television services from around the world on the home computer. This can be downloaded at a price. There are no annual subscription payments with selected software. Currently over 3500 channels are available on-line:

Controlling television content on the internet presents a challenge for most providers. To try and ensure that a user is allowed to view content such as programmes with age certificates, providers use methods such as parental controls that allow restrictions to be placed upon the use and access of certificated material. The BBC iPlayer makes use of a parental control system giving parents the option to 'lock' content, meaning that a password would have to be used to access it. Flagging systems can be used to warn a user that content may be certified or that it may be post watershed for a programme. Honour systems are also used where users are asked for their date of birth or age to verify if they are able to view certain content. Wireless IPTV appeared on the market this year.

2010 Broadcasting rights change from country to country and even within provinces of countries. These rights govern the distribution of copyrighted content and media and allow the sole distribution of that content at any one time. An example of programmes only being aired in certain countries is BBC iPlayer. Users can only stream content from iPlayer from Britain because the BBC only allows free use of their product for users within Britain. This is because those users pay a TV licence to fund part of the BBC. Broadcasting rights can also be restricted to allowing a broadcaster rights to distribute that content for a limited time. Channel 4's online service 4OD can only stream shows created in the US by companies such as 'HBO' for 30 days after they are aired on one of the Channel 4 group channels. This is to boost

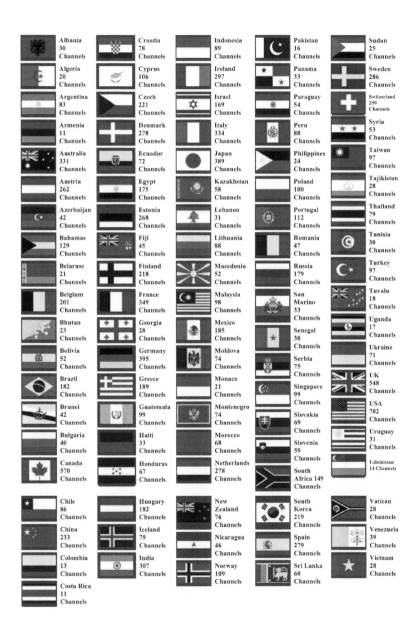

Albania 30 Channels	Croatia 78 Channels	Indonesia 89 Channels	Pakistan 16 Channels	Sudan 25 Channels
Algeria 20 Channels	Cyprus 106 Channels	Ireland 297 Channels	Panama 33 Channels	Sweden 286 Channels
Argentina 83 Channels	Czech 221 Channels	Israel 169 Channels	Paraguay 54 Channels	Switzerland 259 Channels
Armenia 11 Channels	Denmark 278 Channels	Italy 334 Channels	Peru 88 Channels	Syria 53 Channels
Australia 331 Channels	Ecuador 72 Channels	Japan 389 Channels	Philippines 24 Channels	Taiwan 97 Channels
Austria 262 Channels	Egypt 175 Channels	Kazakhstan 58 Channels	Poland 100 Channels	Tajikistan 28 Channels
Azerbaijan 42 Channels	Estonia 268 Channels	Lebanon 31 Channels	Portugal 112 Channels	Thailand 79 Channels
Bahamas 129 Channels	Fiji 45 Channels	Lithuania 88 Channels	Romania 47 Channels	Tunisia 30 Channels
Belaruse 21 Channels	Finland 218 Channels	Macedonia 52 Channels	Russia 179 Channels	Turkey 97 Channels
Belgium 201 Channels	France 349 Channels	Malaysia 98 Channels	San Marino 33 Channels	Tuvalu 18 Channels
Bhutan 23 Channels	Georgia 28 Channels	Mexico 185 Channels	Senegal 30 Channels	Uganda 17 Channels
Bolivia 52 Channels	Germany 395 Channels	Moldova 74 Channels	Serbia 75 Channels	Ukraine 71 Channels
Brazil 182 Channels	Greece 189 Channels	Monaco 21 Channels	Singapore 99 Channels	UK 548 Channels
Brunei 42 Channels	Guatemala 99 Channels	Montenegro 74 Channels	Slovakia 69 Channels	USA 702 Channels
Bulgaria 40 Channels	Haiti 33 Channels	Morocco 68 Channels	Slovenia 59 Channels	Uruguay 31 Channels
Canada 570 Channels	Honduras 67 Channels	Netherlands 278 Channels	South Africa 149 Channels	Uzbekistan 14 Channels
Chile 86 Channels	Hungary 182 Channels	New Zealand 76 Channels	South Korea 219 Channels	Vatican 28 Channels
China 233 Channels	Iceland 79 Channels	Nicaragua 46 Channels	Spain 279 Channels	Venezuela 39 Channels
Colombia 13 Channels	India 307 Channels	Norway 109 Channels	Sri Lanka 60 Channels	Vietnam 28 Channels
Costa Rica 11 Channels				

DVD sales for the companies who produce that media. Some companies pay very large amounts for broadcasting rights, with sports and US sitcoms usually fetching the highest price from UK based broadcasters.

Radio digital switchover

In this year, the UK government announced a scrappage scheme to encourage the sale of digital radios (DAB) for the planned switchover of 2015 – although this is a target rather than a policy. Those in the industry say that 2015 is over optimistic – some commentators are saying 2020+.

Freeview HD roll-out timetable

Key locations where Freeview HD would be available before the World Cup in June 2010:

London (Crystal Palace) December 2009, Newcastle and Tyneside (Pontop Pike) February 2010. Leeds/Bradford (Emley Moor) March 2010. Birmingham (Lichfield) March 2010. Glasgow, central (Scotland Black Hill) February 2010.

The following locations will be upgraded as part of the digital switchover programme or after switchover has taken place:

England

Manchester (Winter Hill) December 2009. Liverpool, central Lancashire, Cheshire, north Staffordshire (Winter Hill relays) March 2010. Exeter, parts of Devon, Somerset, Dorset (Stockland Hill) April 2010. Bristol, Somerset, Dorset, Wiltshire, Gloucestershire (Mendip) April 2010.

Wales

Cardiff, Newport (Wenvoe) March 2010. Swansea (Kilvey Hill) March 2010. West and central Wales (Blaenplwyf) March 2010. Carmarthenshire (Carmel) April 2010. Rest of Wales, Long Mountain, (Moel y Parc, Presely) June 2010.

Scotland

Shetland (Bressay) May 2010. Orkney (Keelylang Hill) May 2010. Caithness, North Sutherland (Rumster Forest) June 2010.

Freeview HD roll-out after the World Cup

England

Devon, Cornwall, and the Isles of Scilly (Beacon Hill, Caradon Hill, Huntshaw Cross, Redruth) August 2010. Cumbria and the Lake District (Caldbeck) October 2010.

and into the future:

2011

Bedfordshire, Berkshire (parts), Buckinghamshire, Cambridgeshire, East Anglia, East Midlands, East Yorkshire, Gloucestershire, Herefordshire, Humberside, Lincolnshire, Northamptonshire, Oxfordshire, Shropshire, South Yorkshire, Staffordshire (parts), Stoke-on-Trent, West Midlands (remainder), and West Yorkshire (remainder).

2012

Berkshire (remainder), County Durham, Greater London (remainder), Hampshire, Isle of Wight, Kent, Northumberland, North Yorkshire, Surrey, Sussex, Teesside, Tyneside.

Wales

Wales will have switched over to digital and the roll-out of Freeview HD will be complete by the end of July 2010. Anglesey (Llanddona) July 2010.

Scotland

Lewis, Wester Ross, North West Sutherland, Western Isles (Eitshal Skriaig) July 2010. Angus, Dundee, Perth, and parts of Fife (Angus) August 2010. Aberdeenshire (Durris) September 2010. Morayshire, Strathspey, and parts of Easter Ross (Knockmore) October 2010. South West Scotland (Caldbeck Scotland) October 2010. Inverness and the Great Glen (Rosemarkie) October 2010. South West Highlands and Islands (Torosay) October 2010. Scottish Borders (Selkirk) November 2010.

Northern Ireland

Freeview HD rolls out with the rest of the switchover programme so that the whole of Northern Ireland is switched over to digital and will be able to receive Freeview HD by the end of 2012.

Other areas

Isle of Man (Douglas) October 2010. Channel Islands (Fremont Point) end of 2010.

One thing that may disappoint viewers is the limited number of channels available. Freeview doesn't have the luxury of the bandwidth available to competing digital services, such as Sky and Virgin Media, so currently there are only three HD slots. These carry the BBC HD service and ITV1 HD. BBC HD by May this year was still just broadcasting demonstration programmes and ITV HD by May still had a low proportion of programme content filmed and broadcast in HD. Channel 4's HD service, already available on Sky and Virgin, is due to launch soon on FREEVIEW with a higher proportion of content in HD, and (see later) viewers in Wales are to receive their own Welsh FREEVIEW HD channel (the HD version of S4C) in April. Channel Five has been given permission to launch HD by the media regulator Ofcom, but it looks now as if it will not be launching an HD service on Freeview until 2012, after failing to give a launch date or programming schedule to Ofcom.

2009 National Freeview retune day – 30 September

   The issue of Freeview equipment obsolescence, raised its head again. During 2008 changes to the Freeview system rendered many older set-top boxes obsolete. From lunchtime onwards on 30 September 2009 (National Freeview retune day), a retune of Freeview frequencies, needed to make space for new HD channels, left many viewers unable to pick up ITV3 and ITV4. All viewers with a Freeview digital TV or box (including homes with Top Up TV and BT Vision) needed to retune their equipment after Wednesday 30 September 2009, to continue receiving their available digital channels. Furthermore, an estimated 20,000 older set-top boxes, and some early Freeview integrated television sets stopped working all together.

One of the main attractions of Freeview HD is that once a viewer has paid for the equipment, whether it be a set-top box, or a  television with an integrated Freeview HD tuner, there are no ongoing monthly subscription charges for HD. Sky and Virgin

Media both offer a much better range of HD channels, but viewers have to pay a subscription. Viewers pay even if they don't subscribe to any premium content. Sky, for example, charges £10 per month just to access HD, plus additional fees if you want to use the Sky+ recording features of your set-top box.

If you'd rather not pay a monthly subscription and you don't have Freeview HD coverage, Freesat, the satellite service from the BBC and ITV, is an option. Although it currently only carries the BBC HD and ITV HD channels, Freesat has the advantage that it already provides almost complete UK coverage and potentially has the capacity to carry far more HD channels than Freeview. Set-top boxes and Freesat integrated television sets are also cheaper than the currently available Freeview HD products. That said, the price of Freeview HD equipment will fall as more products are launched this year.

Following the launch of Freeview HD from the Winter Hill and Crystal Palace transmitters, additional transmitters have been brought into service ahead of their digital switchover dates to provide HD coverage for key metropolitan areas. Freeview estimates that 50% of homes will be covered by the time of the World Cup in South Africa this June.

This will bring HD services to key areas including Glasgow, Newcastle, Birmingham and Leeds/Bradford earlier than was previously planned. In most other areas Freeview HD will roll-out with the switchover programme.

Change of Sky viewing card

 Sky wanted to change the blue viewing cards of 9.2m subscription customers with a further 1.7m viewing cards being issued by

multi room customers. This process took several months to complete. Sky had

FOR YOUR INFORMATION

Please insert your new Sky viewing card or visit skyviewinghelp.com

previously changed cards, altering the function of the embedded chip. Customers were sent new white cards by post and had to do the changeover themselves. The viewing card is used by the Sky box to give access to a range of encrypted channels. Not replacing the card would mean that the Sky viewing card would lose access to those channels. When the customer tries to access an affected channel a blue screen would be presented with a message that states the program is unavailable.

The Sky channels affected were:

- ITV1 (if the customer lives in one of the following ITV1 regions: ITV Anglia West, ITV Central South West, ITV Meridian North, ITV Meridian South East, ITV Tyne Tees South or ITV Yorkshire East)

- FIVE (if you live in London, the North of England or Scotland)

- FIVE USA, FIVE USA+1, FIVER, FIVER+1

- Channel 4 HD

- Sky3

The card replaced earlier by Sky looked like this:

2010 The launch of Freeview HD and the associated consumer marketing campaign, followed the launch of Freeview HD-compatible television sets and set-top boxes. Humax was first to market, with the HD-FOX T2 in February. It is currently available for around £160 – fairly expensive for a basic set-top box that doesn't record. Sony and Panasonic have been the first manufacturers to launch television sets with integrated Freeview

HD tuners – with an increasing number
of companies, including Samsung, LG
and Bush, developing products too. Set-
top boxes that record, designated by a
Freeview+ HD logo, will be available in
time for the World Cup.

Residents who want FREEVIEW HD have two routes to follow
if they want to pick up Freeview HD. Viewers must have an HD
Ready television and a FREEVIEW
HD set-top box, such as the Humax
mentioned above. As time passes,

the range of set-top boxes will increase, and Freeview+HD boxes
that record will become available. Television sets with a built-in
Freeview HD tuner will soon start to appear in the shops.

2010 Product Placement on ITV

In February, the government, through Ofcom, announced the
relaxation of advertising rules within a year. Imbedded advertising
(product placement) will be allowed on ITV but NOT the advert
free BBC channels. Programme sponsorship is now well in place
in UK commercial television.

RTS award

In February, The Royal Television Society
yet again awarded Sky News 'News
Channel of the Year". In March, the BBC
announced the closure of two radio

stations – Asian Network and 6 Radio. It also plans to half the
size of its website to reduce costs. First UK live broadcast of the
three political leaders together in a public debate. The 15 April
saw the run-up to the General Election (6 May) where the three

political leaders debate live questions from the audience. This was the first of three debates over the subsequent three weeks – ITV-HD, SkyNews HD and the BBC.

2010 First UK broadcasts in HD and 3D

22 April saw the launch of the SkyNews HD channel with the second broadcast of the three political leaders at 8.30pm. At 9.00pm on Thursday 6 May SkyNews HD, channel 517, broadcast the UK General Election results. This was the first full evening of programmes broadcast in High Definition.

The General Election of 6 May 2010 produced the first hung parliament in 36 years. 326 MPs of one party were required to win. The result was:

Conservative	307
Labour	258
Liberal Democrat	57

New Coalition UK Government

The Conservatives formed a coalition government with the Liberal Democrats. Gordon Brown left 10 Downing Street to return to the back benches. Conservative David Cameron became Prime Minister appointing Liberal Democrat, Nick Clegg as Deputy Prime Minister.

Digital terrestrial FREEVIEW HD goes Welsh with S4C Clirlun

On 30 April, FREEVIEW HD channel 53 marked the launch of S4C Clirlun –

the new high definition channel on Freeview HD in Wales. S4C asked its viewers to help choose a name for the new HD channel that would convey the exciting and innovative nature of the service. The name Clirlun – translated as 'clear picture' – was suggested by Mrs Ann Evans of Crwbin in the Gwendraeth Valley.

2010 Full HD 3D TV

With Full High Definition 3D, Wi-Fi and an impressive Monolithic Design, the Signature range of BRAVIA® TVs from Sony are the next generation of home entertainment. Launch cost at June 2010 was £3000 with Sky being the only broadcaster with a single 3D channel (channel 217).

3D Full High Definition TV from Sony is a totally new dimension in entertainment. Forget about the old days of cardboard glasses and blurry images: Full HD 3D offers an incredibly life-like, completely immersive experience, unlike anything you've ever seen before.

Blu-ray HD recorder

June this year saw the launch in the UK of the first Blu-ray HD recorder with two Freeview HD tuners on board. The new Panasonic Blu-ray recorders allow the viewer to watch, store and manage their High Definition content in one place. Viewers can pause, rewind and record HD programmes subscription free, and

keep favourite HD content safe on Blu-ray disc. The Panasonic box is available with either Freeview+HD or Freesat+HD built in.

BSkyB and Virgin Media reach agreement on sale of Virgin Media Television

2010 4 June this year, saw British Sky Broadcasting and Virgin Media announce that they have reached agreement for the acquisition by Sky of Virgin Media Television. The companies have,

in parallel, agreed to enter into a number of agreements providing for the carriage of certain of the Virgin and Sky standard and high-definition (HD) channels on both the Virgin cable platform and the Sky satellite platform.

The agreements cover the following:

Sky acquires Virgin Media Television for £160 million in cash, with £105 million paid on completion and the remainder paid following the regulatory process. The acquisition will expand Sky's portfolio of basic pay TV channels and eliminate the carriage fees it currently pays for distributing Virgin Media Television channels on its TV services.

Sky will assume responsibility for selling advertising for the newly acquired Virgin Media Television channels from January 2011.

- New carriage agreements will secure wholesale distribution of Sky's basic channel line-up, including Sky1 and Sky Arts, and the newly acquired Virgin Media Television channels, on Virgin •

- For an incremental wholesale fee, Virgin Media will, for the first time, have the option of carrying any of Sky's basic HD channels, Sky Sports HD 1 and Sky Sports HD 2, and all Sky Movies HD channels.

- Virgin Media will make available through its on-demand TV service a range of content from Sky's basic and premium channels, including the newly acquired Virgin Media Television channels. Virgin Media will also have access to red button interactive sports coverage and the opportunity to deliver selected standard definition programming over the internet.

Completion of the agreements is conditional on obtaining merger control clearance in the Republic of Ireland.

Jeremy Darroch, CEO, BSkyB, said: "Virgin Media Television is an attractive investment opportunity which complements our existing content business and delivers strategic and financial benefits. We are pleased that, through commercial negotiation, we have been able to ensure wide distribution of our channels to a growing pay TV universe."

Neil Berkett, CEO, Virgin Media, said: "The sale of our channels business has generated substantial value. Together with the new commercial agreements we've announced today, it will allow us to focus more closely on our strategy of exploiting Virgin Media's super-fast connectivity to offer our customers a range of the very best content through a highly versatile next generation entertainment application."

July 2010 The UK Five television channel sold by RTL to Richard Desmond, proprietor of the Daily Express. Desmond paid £104m. Dawn Airey, Five" chief executive, said she was 'looking forward' to working with the new owners. Richard Desmond is different from previous owners of public service TV channels in that he controls his company – Northern and Shell – personally.

August 2010 On 23 August, Sky Sports News went HD on the Sky platform and left the Freeview platform on standard definition.

2010 GMTV closed on Friday 3 September

Good Morning Television closed as a brand
– after 17 years on British Television.
GMTV could only muster 912k (22.6% of
the breakfast audience) for its final ever
edition on 3 September, according to overnight data. Between
6.00am and 9.25am, 892k (22.1%) were tuned in to ITV1 for the
GMTV slot, and a further 20k (0.5%) watched the network's HD
channel. BBC One's Breakfast programme, however, appealed to
1.23m (31.1%) between 6.00am and 9.15am. The BBC morning
programme consistently eclipsed ITV in the early morning ratings
battle for two years. Before its revamp last year, GMTV topped
1.5m on a regular basis.

6 September 2010 After
acquiring the majority
shareholding of GMTV, the
early morning weekday slot
was replaced by ITV with the
magazine programme –
'Daybreak' - hosted by Adrian
Chiles and Christine Bleakley imported from the BBC with a 3-
year contract for each presenter – Adrian £6m and Christine
£4m. The lead presenters are:

Adrian Chiles

Christine Bleakley

Kate Garraway

On 15 September the press reported that Daybreak had lost one fifth of the previous GMTV audience.

2010 BBC Chairman resigns

On 15 September, the UK press covered the resignation of 60 year old, Sir Michael Lyons, Chairman of the BBC Trust when his term of office comes to an end next May. Sir Michael announced that he was standing down because his relationship with the new coalition government had deteriorated rapidly. Government (the National Audit Office) wants to subject the BBC to greater scrutiny – especially of salaries for staff and stars. The Prime Minister will recommend a new Chairman to the Her Majesty the Queen. The selection process will start in earnest in about a month's time with DCMS appointing a selection panel, which will advertise the vacancy. They will then assess candidates in accordance with the code of practice of the Office of the Commissioner for Public Appointments – the so-called 'Nolan rules'. At least two candidates will be recommended to ministers, who will then advise the Queen, who in turn will make the new appointment by order in Council under the royal prerogative. The salary is reported to be £142,000 p.a. Pretty much the first job for the new chairman will be to negotiate a new licence fee settlement with Jeremy Hunt, Secretary of State for Culture, Media and Sport, to take effect in 2012 or 2013.

Here is the letter of resignation:

14 September 2010

Dear Jeremy

As my four-year term as Chair of the BBC Trust enters its last eight months, I have taken time over the summer to reflect on whether I would want to be considered for reappointment.

It has been a privilege to lead the BBC Trust and to make a reality of the model established in the 2007 Charter. For all the continuing debate, I am clear that this model is robust, workable and effective. I am  *proud of what we have achieved in safeguarding the BBC's independence against significant challenge, and bringing the interests of audiences in all their diversity to the centre of the BBC's thinking. We have worked to shape BBC services in a way which maximises public value and secures the highest editorial standards, at the same time seeking to ensure that the BBC operates within clear boundaries and cooperates effectively with others. We have taken openness and transparency to a new level. Most important of all, under the Trust's guardianship – and with the leadership of the Director General and his team – the quality and public service focus of the BBC's output has improved and the public's affection for the BBC has strengthened. Much of course remains to be done, but I think that this represents good progress and a strong foundation on which to build. all the positives associated with this agenda, I have to acknowledge that the role of Chairman has been far more demanding than the nominal three to four days a week in the job specification. It is of course a compelling aspect of working at the BBC that it can become an all-consuming part of one's life – and this applies equally to the staff across the BBC whose great commitment helps underpin its position as the world's leading public broadcaster. But this workload has now reached a point where I am increasingly concerned that it is crowding out other appointments to which I remain committed and other activity that I wish to undertake. So balancing all the factors I have on reflection concluded that my preference would be to limit my appointment to a single term and not seek reappointment from next*

May. I raise this now both to set a clear context for our forthcoming discussions on policy issues and to leave you enough time to find a successor.

In the meantime, you can be assured that I will give my full energy to the Trust's important agenda in the months ahead. This includes both the continuing public debate about funding and other issues, and our work to conclude the Strategy Review, not least its strand on value for money, which will shape the BBC for the years ahead.

While it is not normal practice to make correspondence between the BBC Chairman and the Secretary of State public, given the public interest in this matter and in the interests of openness and transparency the BBC Trust will shortly be publishing this letter.

Yours,

*Michael
Sir Michael Lyons
Chairman, BBC Trust"*

One option government may consider is to transfer the regulator role of the BBC Trust to Ofcom and to appoint a part time non-executive Chairman. A second BBC person also resigned yesterday – Jay Hunt, Controller of BBC 1 who is joining Channel 4 as Chief Creative Officer on a salary reputed to be £400,000.

2010 Multi-Channel Development 1992–2010

BARB summaries the growth of multi-channel television. This includes mostly digital channels provided by the different service providers – including analogue cable which is falling very fast. The figures are the number of homes in 000s –

Date	Satellite	Cable	DTT/Freeview	Total
1992	1,893	409	-	2,302
1993	2,387	625	-	3,012
1994	2,754	735	-	3,489
1995	3,060	973	-	4,033
1996	3,542	1,399	-	4,941
1997	3,804	1,845	-	5,649
1998	4,117	2,471	-	6,588
1999	4,184	2,942	-	7,126
2000	3,963	3,352	303	7,618
2001	4,991	3,490	529	9,010
2002	5,732	3,794	794	10,320
2003	6,409	3,440	873	10,600
2004	6,946	3,277	2,075	12,036
2005	7,277	3,363	4,216	14,327
2006	7,932	3,297	6,363	16,815
2007	8,437	3,301	8,831	18,637
2008	8,860	3,405	12,017	21,276
2009	9,332	3,442	14,008	22,294
2010	10,262	3,664	16,882	23,831

Source: BARB (The Broadcasters' Audience Research Board is the organisation responsible for providing the official measurement of UK television audiences.) Viewing estimates are obtained from a panel of television owning private homes representing the viewing behaviour of the 26 million TV households within the UK. The panel is selected to be representative of each ITV and BBC region, with pre-determined sample sizes. Each home represents, on average, about 5,000 of the UK population.

2010 The BARB and Ofcom figures are the same. BARB says that 91.65% of homes have multi-channel television – which is the same as the rounded Ofcom figure of 92%.

More Sky HD channels

Sky plan to have 50 HD channels by Christmas 2010.

DCMS announced on 19 October that the BBC licence fee will remain at £145.50 p.a. for another six years (March 2016).

Audience share

2010 saw one television programme pulling in huge audiences. The X Factor talent show was pulling in 10.9m viewers (Saturday 13 September). This was an enormous achievement by ITV – although the TV rights are owned my Simon Cowell the originator of the format. ITV benefits from the increased advertising income.

2010 22 September this year saw the 50th birthday of ITV.

2010 25 September saw the launch of The Spenglers Sky Monster TV Advert. Sky+ released a new fully-integrated national campaign which includes TV, outdoor, radio, and online, and brings to life a monster family enjoying the benefits of Sky+, with the campaign line 'More Family Time'.

September 2010 Virgin 3D

On 28 September, Virgin Media launched what it claimed is the first commercially available 3D TV service for domestic viewers. The cable TV company unveiled the service, called 3D Movies on Demand, which will give customers access to 3D  versions of films including StreetDance, Garfield's Pet Force, Disney's A Christmas Carol and Despicable Me. BSkyB said it is gearing up to launch Europe's first 3D HD TV channel using the technology, from 1 October. The Sky channel has to date run a loop of preview programming since April 2010. In contrast, Sky has been broadcasting Premier League football matches to viewers in pubs since early April 2010.

2010 Sky 3D channel

Sky 3D – Europe's first three dimensional entertainment TV channel on 217, was launched on 1 October. The channel is available for no extra charge to Sky+HD subscribers – providing they have a 3D TV set capable of displaying the images and a Sky World HD bundle. Sky 3D will mainly carry movies and sport upon its initial unveiling, with the launch weekend taking in the Ryder Cup complete with 3D bunkers, and two 3D feature film animations, Disney's Bolt and Dreamworks' Monsters vs Aliens. Sky has also just filmed a new SkyArts 3D production in partnership with the English National

Ballet, which features a 'spectacular' Bollywood dance routine. 3D movies will run up to Christmas include Alice in Wonderland, Ice Age: Dawn of the Dinosaurs, Coraline, Fly

Me To The Moon, Harry Potter and the Half-Blood Prince and My Bloody Valentine.

Jeremy Darroch, Sky's Chief Executive, commented, "As with High Definition, 3D is set to transform the way TV is enjoyed in homes nationwide. Following hot on the heels of the success of 3D cinema, Sky customers will now be the first anywhere in Europe to experience 3D TV from the comfort of their living rooms.  They can look forward to a fantastic mix of live sport, blockbuster movies, and innovative entertainment and arts shows. Sky 3D will be compatible with all 3D sets being introduced by Sony, Samsung, Panasonic and LG, functioning with both active and passive three dimensional formats. When we saw Jaws 3D back in the eighties, never in a million years did we imagine there'd come a time when 3D films were shown in the living room."

October – digital growth

The breakdown between the different platforms at 7 October 2010, was as follows:

Free-to-View Sat 1.62m homes)
(Sky Freesat + BBC/ITV Freesat)

DDT Freeview	10.1m	) 'Free-to air' digital TV = 11.72m)		
Sky digital	9.86m	)	)	**26.2m**
Virgin Cable	3.72m	) 'pay' digital TV = 14.48m)		**total**
Other pay platforms 0.9m		)		

(Top-Up TV, BT Vision, Talk Talk (Tiscali)   Source q2 Ofcom 7 October 2010

Sky multiroom reaches 2.12m homes. Sky HD reaches 2.9m homes. Virgin V+ reaches 1.9m homes. So, by October 2010 (some two years before switchover is complete) 26.2m UK homes have digital television of one form or another – 92.7%.

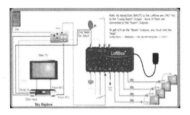 

October 2010 TV world-wide audience for the Chilean mine rescue exceeded 1 billion – most of it live broadcast of the rescue.

28 October 2010 After 6 weeks on air, the ratings for ITV Daybreak fell to only 530,000 – a third of the audience of BBC breakfast time. Launch week saw the viewing figure to be above 900,000. The Daybreak audience fell further to 200,000 below its predecessor GMTV. This major drop adversely affects the value of advertising time.

November 2010 On its latest television advert, Sky announced its first choice as the LG LED 3D television set. Rupert Murdoch of News Corporation made a £12billion bid for the 61% of BSkyB shares not yet owned by the parent company. The UK Government Business Secretary referred the bid to regulator Ofcom on 'media plurality' grounds. Sky reached 50 HD channels this month. Panasonic launched 3D Blu-Ray Players. 3D camcorders now on sale.

November 2010 The final of the X Factor attracted an ITV audience in excess of 20m. The cost of advertising reached £300,000 for a 30 second slot during the final show.

November 2010 On 14 November, the BBC Trust published its strategy review arising from the earlier Government decision to 'freeze' the licence fee for 6

years at £145.50. The press reported this to be a cut, in real terms, of 16%. There was speculation that some of the BBC television and radio digital channels may close.

November 2010 The satellite platform 'BBC/ITV Freesat' commissioned a survey of attitudes to television which was published this  month. The sample frame was 2000 people and the report was called 'The Joy of Sets' on 23 November. The Managing Director of Freesat said that, "We are watching more television than ever – and we are using it to shape our lives." The survey was undertaken by the University of Exeter, Department of Psychology of Media. Author Dr Brian Young, said that, "the unassuming box in the corner of the living room is no longer a piece of furniture the family gather around at key times of the year. (Dr Brian Young is a leading media psychologist at the University of Exeter and an expert in the field of TV and media.) Now, thanks to the digital age of greater channel choice, it is increasingly influential in changing lives, helping people to meet new people and learn new skills. Television in 2010 is about fuelling friendships, inspiring careers and whetting appetites for new adventures."

He reported as follows –

- 1/3rd of the UK population admits to watching 50% more television than 5 years ago.

- Increased audiences are influenced by Saturday night programming by the BBC and ITV. 'Strictly Come Dancing' and 'Dr Who' each drawing an audience share of more than 12m. 'The X Factor' draws 17m viewers.

- Sky+ which can DVR 2 programmes at once and the proliferation of channel choice has created niche audiences ranging from gardening to history. 'Catch-up' services such as sky+ and ITV and BBC i-player and others has allowed television to fit better into modern lifestyles – with audiences increasingly watching when it suited them best.

- Where once watching television was viewed as anti-social, many feel that it actually helps them forge friendships and be more sociable. Almost 40% of those interviewed said they spend up to 5 hours a week talking with others about their favourite programmes, while nearly half of those polled said that television shows have helped them make new friends.

- Hundreds of thousands of X Factor and Strictly Come Dancing viewers take to websites such as Facebook and Twitter to debate and rage with the weekly results.

- The report suggests that far from creating a generation of 'couch potatoes' modern programming was encouraging viewers to take up new hobbies and visit new places. Four in five viewers have taken up a pastime because of a television show, while 85% say travel programming has encouraged them to holiday somewhere else. Buying a new home is influenced by television programmes.

- Women have charge of the remote control in more than half of households.

- Parents are no longer as strict about what children can watch – on average between 1 and 3 hours of television a day. 76% of parents feel that the 9.00pm watershed is still relevant.

- Almost two thirds of parents said that they did not feel that television was a bad influence and actually felt shows inspired their children and taught them new things.

- 80% of those interviewed said they now cook more and increasingly entertain at home – guided by television chefs and 'Come Dine With Me'.

- More than half said that they were inspired to change career because of something they had seen on television.

- 81% want all television to be high definition within 20 years.

- 1 in 6 households owns 5 television sets and two thirds have 3 or more. The popularity of features such as flat screens, high definition and 3D has seen sales soar in recent years. Analogue switchover is also influencing the purchase of integrated television sets.

- Interestingly, more than half of consumers said that emerging TV technologies such as IPTV, mobile and tablet computers would be  unlikely to change their physical television viewing habits, while 73% claimed that watching TV on the living room screen would always beat the handheld viewing experience.

2010 Ofcom announces plans for 'white space technology'

On 9 November, Ofcom announced plans for a new wireless technology. This followed an earlier consultation period, exploring the potential of the technology, which could be used for a wide range of innovative applications. For example, technology manufacturers have suggested that it might wirelessly link up

different devices and offer
enhanced broadband access in
rural areas.

The technology works by searching for unused radio waves called 'white spaces' between TV channels to transmit and receive wireless signals. Compared with other forms of wireless technology, such as Bluetooth and WiFi, white-space devices are being designed to use lower frequencies that have traditionally been reserved for TV. Signals at these frequencies travel further and more easily through walls.

How white space will work

Spectrum is typically managed in one of two ways. Most spectrum is licensed to a particular user, such as a mobile network operator, who has exclusive rights to make use of the spectrum. The remainder, around 6% or so, is exempt from licensing. Unlicensed spectrum is used by a wide range of devices, most notably devices based on the WiFi and BlueTooth standards.

Following the switch-off of analogue television in 2012, the freed up spectrum (called the digital dividend), has many potential uses – all being considered by Ofcom's Digital Dividend Review group. While it is not clear what applications will emerge in the white spaces, suggestions have included rural broadband, WiFi routers with increased range, city-wide broadband data networks, increased wireless device interconnectivity, hospital data networks and much more.

White space technology will work in a similar way to WiFi, which uses a wireless router to send and receive information to other wireless devices. A key difference is that the white space router will first need to consult a list of geolocation databases hosted online. It will describe its location and device characteristics to one of these databases on a regular basis. The database will then return details of the frequencies and power levels it is allowed to use.

Professor William Webb, Director of Technology Resources at Ofcom, said, "The airwaves that wireless devices depend on are becoming increasingly congested. We need to think about more efficient ways of using this limited resource. Using the white spaces between TV channels is a good example of how we can both use spectrum more efficiently and provide opportunities for innovative new applications and services.

"Our role is to encourage innovation rather than decide on what technology and applications should succeed. To that end, we hope that these frequencies, which offer improved signal reliability, capacity, and range over existing wireless technologies, will bring clear benefits for consumers."

2010 Latest Arabsat

Successful launch of Arabsat BADR-5 at 26° East and Arabsat-5A at 30.5° East

December 2010 News Corporation, BSkyB and Government

British Business Secretary Vince Cable will remain Business Secretary but will not take decisions on News Corporation after telling undercover reporters he had 'declared war' on Rupert Murdoch's media empire. A Downing Street spokesman said the Prime Minister was clear that Mr Cable's comments were 'totally unacceptable and inappropriate'. The statement said: 'Following comments made by Vince Cable to the Daily Telegraph, the Prime Minister has decided that he will play no further part in the decision over News Corporation's proposed takeover of BSkyB.

In addition, all responsibility for competition and policy issues relating to media, broadcasting, digital and telecoms sectors will be transferred immediately to the Secretary of State for Culture, Media and Sport. This includes full responsibility for OFCOM's activities in these areas'.

The decision puts Culture Secretary Jeremy Hunt in charge of ruling on the News Corporation bid. Mr Cable said he fully accepted the decision. "I deeply regret the comments I made and apologise for the embarrassment that I have caused the Government," he said in a statement. His remarks about Mr Murdoch were not included in the paper's coverage of Mr Cable's comments last night. The BBC claims a whistleblower passed on a copy of the transcript. Mr Cable appears to have told undercover reporters, "I don't know if you have been following what has been happening with the Murdoch press, where I have declared war on Mr Murdoch and I think we are going to win." He continued, "I have blocked it using the powers that I have got and they are legal powers that I have got. I can't politicise it but from the people that know what is happening this is a big, big thing. His whole empire is now under attack ... So there are things like that we do in government, that we can't do ... all we can do in opposition is protest." The comments relate to News Corporporation's bid to take full ownership of BSkyB, the parent company of Sky News. As Business Secretary, Mr Cable referred the bid to Ofcom and may decide to ask the Competition Commission to examine it.

A News Corporation spokesman said, "News Corporation is shocked and dismayed by reports of Mr Cable's comments. They raise serious questions about fairness and due process." Before

Downing Street released a statement, Sky's political editor Adam Boulton said the latest development could mean Mr Cable was not seen as impartial enough to rule on the bid. "There would have to be questions over his future," Mr Boulton said, before adding he did not want to predict the outcome as it would be very difficult for the Government to lose such a senior figure. The Telegraph may also have to answer why it did not publish the quotes in its original article, as they are 'clearly the most salient thing' Mr Cable said in the secretly-recorded interview said Adam Boulton.

2010 BBC Eastenders in HD

On Christmas Day, EastEnders was broadcast for the first time in high definition on BBC One HD. To make the Queen Victoria ready for her appearance in HD,

beer labels on bottles and the pumps on the bar were redesigned with sharper graphics alongside the beer mats on the pub's tables. The ambience and background music of the pub now plays in surround sound thanks to the HD audio and the chitter-chatter of the bar will be clearer than ever before, ensuring no gossip goes unheard.

DAILY◉NEWS

"New Times demands new journalism" – first touchscreen, internet-only daily newspaper

2011 17 January saw the launch of the first issue of 'The Daily' newspaper on the Apple iPad. Rupert Murdoch publishers said "The Daily has the depth and quality of a magazine, but is delivered daily like a newspaper and updated in real-time like the web." The website said – "The Daily launched with the mission to provide the best news experience by combining world-class storytelling with the unique interactive capabilities of the iPad. Led by Editor-in-Chief Jesse Angelo and Publisher  Greg Clayman, The Daily is a category first: a tablet-native national news brand built from the ground up to publish original content exclusively for the iPad. The Daily is incisive, optimistic, and independent. It's not just an app – it's a new voice. The Daily is offered in the USA as an exclusive in Apple's iPad App Store and is available free for two weeks after launch. It costs just 99 cents a week, or US $39.99 a year."

2011 EU courts to consider Sky's monopoly on Premier Football

In February, a UK pub landlord challenged Sky by displaying football television in her pub – not supplied by Sky Sports – but by a supplier from Greece. On 3 February, the EU courts considered this test case involving landlady Karen Murphy of Portsmouth who had switched supplier because of the cost of football from Sky. Mrs Murphy switched to an imported decoder box paying just £800 per year instead of £600 per month with Sky. Mrs Murphy argued that the EU single market should let her use any European satellite provider. One of the eight advocate generals of the European Courts of Justice agreed with her. The matter will be considered further in the European Courts. The issue will surround the way in which football television rights are distributed. Sky and ESPN have the exclusive broadcast rights to live Premier League football in the UK. The Premier League sold three years of live television rights to Sky and ESPN for £1.782billion with Sky paying £1.6billion of that sum.

2011 Product placement

Product Placement allowed in UK television programmes from 28 February 2011. Product placement is when a company pays a TV channel or a programme-maker to include its products or brands in a programme, for example, a fashion company might pay for a  presenter to wear its clothes during a programme, or a car manufacturer might pay for a character to mention one of its cars in a scene in a drama. Product placement in films and international programmes (such as US drama series) has been allowed on UK television for many years. Does this mean that all products I see in a programme made after this date have been paid for? No, programme-makers also use 'props' (for example, to 'dress' a set in a TV soap). The difference between product placement and the use of props is that the TV channel and the programme-maker don't receive any payment for including props. They pay to use them or get them free, rather than being paid to include them, so they're not product placement. It's also possible that a product could appear in a programme by chance, not because the company has paid for it to be included – for instance, a member of the public interviewed in the street might be wearing clothing that shows a company's logo.

What are the rules for product placement? Ofcom's Broadcasting Code contains rules about what type of products can be placed in programmes, where product placement is allowed, and how placed products can be featured. These rules are required by both European and UK law. Which programmes can contain product placement? Product placement is allowed in films (including dramas and documentaries), TV series (including soaps), entertainment shows and sports programmes. Where can't products be placed? Products cannot be placed in news or children's programmes. They also  cannot be placed in religious, current affairs and consumer advice programmes made for UK audiences.

Will there be product placement on the BBC? Under the terms of the BBC Agreement product placement is not allowed in programmes made for BBC licence fee funded services. However, Ofcom's rules apply to any product placement in programmes which the BBC acquires from elsewhere and those made by the BBC's commercial TV services. What products can't be placed? Cigarettes and other tobacco products, along with medicines that are available only on prescription, can't be product placed in any programmes. Alcoholic drinks, gambling products, all other types of medicines, food and drink that is high in fat, salt, or sugar and baby milk can't be product placed in UK programmes. Also, products that can't be advertised (such as guns and other weapons) can't be product placed in UK programmes either.

How can products be placed? There must be 'editorial justification' for a product to be placed in a programme. That means the product must be relevant to what the programme is about. The content of programmes shouldn't seem to be created or distorted, just to feature the placed products. How will I know if a programme contains product placement? If a UK programme contains product placement, the TV channel has to show a special logo. This will let viewers know that the TV channel or the programme-maker has been paid to include products in that programme. The logo is pictured below – there are two versions so that it can be used on a light or dark background. Programmes also can't promote placed products or give them too much prominence. So there shouldn't be any claims made about how good a placed product is, or so many references to a product that it feels like it is being promoted. The logo has to be shown at the beginning of the programme, and repeated after any advertising break during the programme. It also has to be shown again at the end of the programme. TV channels don't have to show the logo on programmes that were originally broadcast outside the UK (for example, a US drama series that is then shown in the UK). Any programme that is made to be shown on an Ofcom licensed channel, including those that broadcast outside the UK, must include the product placement logo where necessary.

2011 New BBC Trust Chairman

On 18 February, there was speculation in the press that Lord Patten (The Right Honourable, Christopher Francis Patten, Baron Patten of Barnes, CH, PC) had been recommended by the Secretary of State for Culture, Media and Sport, Jeremy Hunt to Prime Minister, David Cameron as the next Chairman of the BBC Trust from May 2011.

2011 First Product Placement

On 28 February, ITV (12.10am) became the first UK commercial television channel to broadcast product placement. Nestle and ITV placed a Dolce Gusto branded coffee machine into the 'This Morning' programme. ITV said – "We are currently talking to clients about a number of product placement opportunities spanning a range of programmes and channels." It was reported in the press that the deal was brokered by WPP media agency Mindshare and was valued at £100,000.

2011 Changes at Freeview

On 28 February, Sky3 became Pick TV.

2011 Freeview+ USB tuner

1 March saw the introduction of the USB Freeview+ tuner – turning the computer into a digital television set. The Freeview USB TV Tuner is a small USB device that allows a PC or Mac to receive Freeview TV signals from an aerial source in a part of the UK receiving the Freeview terrestrial service. Windows 7 or Windows Vista computers already have Windows Media Centre on them. When used with a USB TV Tuner, Windows Media Centre allows the computer to watch, record and store TV shows to the computer's hard drive and  provide the features of Freeview+ including a TV guide, programme search, series link and the ability to pause and rewind live TV. Windows 7 also has the benefits of Red Button interactive services, the very same way a Freeview box or TV with Freeview built in would. Using the HDMI output of the computer can connect the Freeview service to a large HD screen. USB Digital TV Sticks start from around £20.

2011 July q1 – latest digital television take-up and platform share

Free-to-View Sat 2.04m homes)   digital services

(Sky Freesat + BBC/ITV Freesat)

DTT Freeview   19.0m   )'Free-to air' digital TV = 21.04m)

Sky digital   11.14m)   ) **36.85m**

Virgin Cable   3.77m   ) 'pay' digital TV = 15.81m)   **total**

Other pay platforms 0.9m)

(Top-Up TV, BT Vision, Talk Talk (Tiscali) Source q1 Ofcom July 2011

There are 25m homes in the UK – 70% owner occupied. Some homes have both Sky and Freeview or Virgin and Freeview. 'Churn' is the measure of customers leaving the service per annum. At this point Sky reports 9.9% and Virgin reports 15.9%.

2012 October – Jimmy Savile

Jimmy Savile died on 29 October 2011. In October 2012, an ITV documentary examining claims of alleged sexual abuse against Savile led to broad media coverage and a substantial and rapidly growing body of witness statements and sexual abuse claims, including accusations against public bodies for covering up or failure of duty. Scotland Yard launched a criminal investigation into allegations of child sex abuse by Savile over six decades, describing him as a 'predatory sex offender', and later stated that they were pursuing over 400 lines of inquiry based on the testimony of 300 potential victims via fourteen police forces across the UK. By late October 2012, the scandal had resulted in inquiries or reviews at the BBC, within the National Health Service, the Crown Prosecution Service, and the Department of Health

23 October 2012 Switchover complete

The digital switchover (DSO) was completed on this date as the analogue signal is finally switched off in Northern Ireland. The switch-off also brought an end to the 38-year-old Ceefax service launched in 1974.

2012 Autostereoscopic television – Toshiba 55ZL2

The industry finally launched a 3D television which can be viewed WITHOUT wearing 3D glasses. The cost of around £7,000 is very high – but as other manufacturer's gather pace costs should reduce to more realistic levels.

2012 On-Demand television

The television gets more intelligent (sometimes called "smart"), with the ability to go backwards in the electronic programme guide and watch previously broadcast programmes 'on-demand'. YouView is an example of a  new box which can turn a non-intelligent television set into one equal to the new sets with integrated intelligence on board. YouView, launched in July, combines Freeview with internet catch-up television from all four main broadcasters – BBC iplayer, ITV iplayer, 4oD and Demand 5. It's a free service – no contract and no subscription. In addition, it provides some pay-television services – NowTV from Sky and Freetime from Freeview and rental film services such as LOVEfilms (now owned by Amazon).

Connection to internet radio and social networking sites is also available.

2012 q1 – latest take-up of digital television

Digital Television is almost universal as DSO comes to an end in October 2012

Proportion of UK adults

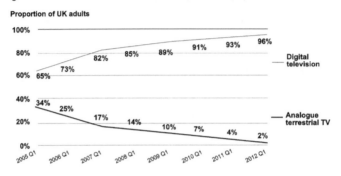

TV screens are getting bigger

Percentage of TV sets sold larger than 26" - Q1 2012

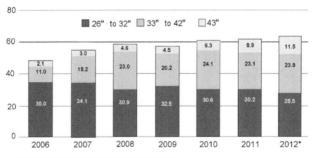

Source: GfK sales data estimates   *2012 data represents Q1 only

Ofcom reports that 96.2% of homes in the UK now have digital television. There are now 60m television sets in the UK compared to 25m homes.

2012 First newscaster in vision dies

The death of the first BBC news reader to be seen in vision on 14 September 1955 (Kenneth Kendal aged 88) occurred on 14 December this year.

2012 Latest mobile network

The emergence of 4G mobile networks allowing 5x faster (than 3G) broadband downloads and greater access to portable telephone-delivered television from the growing number of wfi hotspots. The press start to report possible interference problems between the 4G and digital terrestrial television (Freeview) signals. It is thought that around 950,000 homes, living close to base stations, will suffer interference ranging from image distortion to the total loss of some channels as superfast broadband is rolled out. A solution is said to being worked up "using filters".

2013 Listen with mother presenter dies

On 5 January, Daphne Oxenford, former BBC presenter for Listen With Mother, died at the age of 93. The presenter and actress became the voice behind 15 minutes of magic for a generation of children during the 1950s and 60s. They sat eagerly around the wireless to hear her familiar opening words: 'Are you sitting comfortably? Then I'll begin.'

14 January 2013 ITV introduces new idents –

23 January 2013 The NTA

The biggest stars from the world of television were out in force for the 2013 National Television Awards. Strictly Come Dancing beat The X Factor to win the best talent show prize, ending the singing competitions three year run. Ant and Dec won the best presenter award for the 12th year in a row. All the prizes handed out at the ceremony at London's O2 Arena were voted for by the public.

National TV Awards 2013: Winners

Comedy panel show – QI

Best daytime show – This Morning

Best drama – Downton Abbey

Drama performance female – Miranda Hart (Call The Midwife)

Drama performance male – Melin Morgan (Merlin)

Documentary series – Frozen Planet

Entertainment programme – I'm A Celebrity... Get Me Out Of Here!

Entertainment presenter – Ant and Dec

Factual entertainment – Paul O'Grady: For The Love Of Dogs

Newcomer – David Witts (EastEnders)

Serial drama – Coronation Street

Serial drama performance – Alan Halsall (Coronation Street)

Situation comedy – Mrs Brown's Boys

Talent Show – Strictly Come Dancing

Television has arrived – after many years of hard work and the dedication of so many around the world. Arguably the UK still leads the way.

The future of television

We are likely to see further television developments:

1 Ultra Hi-Def television with digital resolution well above 1080 lines. The latest in a line of broadcast and media resolutions, 4K/UHD will replace 1080i/p (1,920x1,080 pixels) as the highest-resolution signal available for movies and, perhaps, television. Though there are several different standards, "4K" in general refers to a resolution of roughly 4,000 pixels wide and about 2,000  pixels high. That makes it the equivalent of four 1080p screens in height and length. 4K is a catch-all term for a number of standards that are reasonably close to that resolution, and the TVs we'll soon see and labeled "4K" will actually be Ultra HD.

2 Interactive commercial advertising becomes regular.

3 The gradual end of CRT, Plasma, RPTV and DLP television.

4 More advertising slots between programme segments.

5 More and more HD channels until HD becomes the de-facto format.

6 Introduction of 'white space' technology for more mobile television and mobile devices and peripherals – for example, home cinema sound speakers.

7 Bigger DVR and DVB hard discs. DVRs with multiple hard discs and tuners.

8 A splitter for digital signals to drive more than one digital tuner from one dish.

9 Cheaper 3D television sets requiring no 3D glasses. More 3D channels on all delivery platforms – especially after switchover in 2012.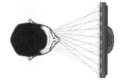

10 Greater scrutiny of the BBC finances. Media salary reductions.

11 BBC decentralisation of some BBC services out of London to Salford and other regional centres.

12 More ITV sponsored programme advertising.

13 Local TV will probably be delivered via Internet Protocol Television (IPTV) rather than 'traditional' broadcast in the long term, according to an independent report by Nicholas Shott, Head of UK Investment Banking at Lazard.

14 More advertising time between programme segments on commercial channels.

15 More tablet television.

16 More product placement in television programmes.

17 More television sets with integrated internet access.

18 More television sets with integrated DVD and Blu-ray functionality.

19 Cheaper Blu-ray DVDs.

20 More interactivity on digital television. Television shopping using an interactive card. Greater expansion of E-Government on television.

21 DVR triple tuner boxes and larger memory hard discs..

22 After 2012 Freeview reach grows from 73% to 100% of the

UK. Signal strength improves. Takeup will be greater than Sky or Virgin Media.

23 A policy projected date for the switch off of analogue radio will be established.

24 98% rising to 99.5% of homes will have digital TV from one platform or another.

25 Refusenics will gradually make it 100% of homes who want digital television.

26 Improved mobile 'phone television – even faster 4G and further speeds allowing live portable television anywhere in the UK.

27 Delivery of television on satellite navigation systems.

28 The end of plasma television because of 'burn-in'.

29 Improved LCD and LED television.

30 Improved IPTV services.

31 OLED (organic light emitting diode) television sets.

32 LCOS (liquids crystal on Silicon) television sets.

33 FED (field emission display) television sets.

34 Holographic television sets.

35 Voice activated television sets.

36 Laser television sets increasing the screen colour spectrum the eye can see.

37 Interactive TV EPGs.

38 Eye contact lenses that transmit television.

39 Television screens on public transport. Pay TV/ internet on aeroplanes.

40 Huge growth of worldwide Internet TV content providers – Web-enabled TV.

41 More explicit adult pay-television channels allowed by Ofcom.

42 Integration of television with on-line games consoles, music player, iphones, etc.

43 Number of satellite channels will pass 1000.

44 Expansion of ITV iplayer, BBC iplayer and Sky iplayer.

45 Sky HD channels will reach 100+ and grow further.

Television presenters and live television programmes develop greater use of social networking and blogging sites to encourage greater interactivity with the television audience. Live television programmes will encourage viewers to call in from their laptops (webcam), from iphones, tablets and so on – for an interview or to express their opinion.

.... and much, much more !

END

Note to readers

Every attempt has been made on accuracy of content. However, I don't pretend that I have it absolutely right first time. I would welcome feedback – criticism, pointing out errors and better ways of describing details. If you wish, I will acknowledge your contribution in the next edition.

Also, every attempt has been made to use materials from the public domain, but if any permissions have not been  identified, please contact the author via the publishers, so that this can be rectified for the next edition.